Improving Software Practice
Case Experiences

Edited by

Colin Tully

Colin Tully Associates, UK

JOHN WILEY & SONS

Chichester • New York • Weinheim • Brisbane • Singapore • Toronto

Other Wiley Editorial Offices

John Wiley & Sons, Inc., 605 Third Avenue,
New York, NY 10158-0012, USA

WILEY-VCH Verlag GmbH
Pappelallee 3, D-69469 Weinheim, Germany

Jacaranda Wiley Ltd, 33 Park Road, Milton,
Queensland 4064, Australia

John Wiley & Sons (Canada) Ltd, 22 Worcester Road
Rexdale, Ontario, M9W 1L1, Canada

John Wiley & Sons (Asia) Pte Ltd, 2 Clementi Loop #02-01,
Jin Xing Distripark, Singapore 129809

British Library Cataloguing in Publication Data

A catalogue record for this book is available from the British Library

ISBN 0 471 98254 7

Typeset in 10/12pt Times by Keyword Typesetting Services
Printed and bound in Great Britain by Bookcraft (Bath) Ltd.
This book is printed on acid-free paper responsibly manufactured from sustainable forestation, for which at least two trees are planted for each one used for paper production.

Contents

Editor's Preface

THE SETTING FOR THE ESSI PROGRAMME

Oil and software are the two principal obstacles to economic progress.

That was the *Wall Street Journal* in the 1980s putting a memorable spin on the notion of the *software crisis*, by suggesting that we are as dependent on the immaterial gold of software as on the black gold of oil. Both sources of power are indispensable to modern civilization. Oil turned against us in the 1970s; software is turning against us as we approach year 2000. Can we treat those as isolated problems, or are they early warnings of worse to come?

Throughout the second half of our century, getting the right software for products and business processes, and getting value for money from it, has consistently defeated management. Organizations of all kinds have suffered from an abdication of control to the technical high priesthood – the alchemists who claim to turn the base metal of corporate requirements into the gold of fit-for-purpose software. If the priests are left uncontrolled, it should be no surprise if there is a software crisis, and very often business crises in consequence.

Business process improvement is in vogue. For many organizations, the software process (the set of practices by which software is acquired and developed) is the most complex, unpredictable and ill-managed of all business processes. It can also be critical. Take just one city: the recent failures of the London Stock Exchange and the London Ambulance Service provide vivid evidence of the importance and precariousness of the software process, and the financial and human costs suffered when it breaks down.

In such circumstances, it might be expected that ways of improving the software process, if they were available, and tried and tested, would be eagerly adopted. That is indeed the case in the USA, where there has been widespread take-up of the so-called Capability Maturity Model (CMM). The CMM was pioneered by the Software Engineering Institute (SEI), which is funded by the Department of Defense and located in Pittsburgh at Carnegie Mellon University.

The CMM for Software offers a descriptive model of the software process, together with a scale for measuring an organization's maturity in performing it. The scale identifies five levels, ranging from level 1 (ad hoc, chaotic, haphazard) to level 5 (continuously improving, fully instrumented, fit for purpose). Those levels provide an easily understood roadmap for improvement. It is supported by CBA (CMM-Based Appraisal), a set of methods for determining the level an organization has reached on the maturity scale. Appraisal results allow an organization to track its broad improvement progress.

The first serious application of CMM, at the end of the 1980s, was to assess DoD software contractors. Almost all were found to be at level 1 (chaotic) – a result which had a shock impact on the US software industry. Those level 1 companies were supposedly the cream of the US software industry, and on their software capability rested US military capability.

The shock had two major effects. First, the DoD mandated maturity level 3 as a prerequisite to being invited to tender, so that DoD software suppliers put improvement programmes in place aimed at reaching level 3. Level 3 is characterized by a standardized and documented process, with a special *process group* in charge of its development and maintenance.

Then, more strikingly, the process movement spread from the defence industry to the software-producing community at large. Thousands of organizations are driving to reach level 3, and have set up process groups to power the drive. Thus a significant proportion of American software developers now have a clear mission to improve.

Taken overall, nothing short of a management revolution is sweeping the US software industry. The belief is growing that software product quality, predictability of costs and schedules, return on investment in methods and tools, and control of technical staff, are at last achievable. The philosophy and details of CMM and CBA might not always be fully understood, and success in applying them might be less than total; but happiness is to be able to claim that yours is a level 3 organization.

If we turn to Japan, the situation is less easy to characterize with confidence. Japan is not subject to revolutionary and fashion-driven change. It seeks to apply to software the culture which it has fine-tuned in the postwar years, largely in its major consumer-based mass-market industries such as motor manufacture and electronics. That is the culture of quality, extensive detailed metrication of both product and process, and continuous improvement of both product and process by small increments based on those accumulated measurements.

That culture does not transplant straightforwardly to the software process. It is harder to determine what measurements are appropriate, and how to interpret them. The software process is not a manufacturing process, and is far more dependent on human creative skills. Nevertheless, nearly 30 years' practical experience of the software factory concept has made many Japanese companies adept at applying their traditional approaches at least to those software practices that are more easily defined and measured.

The important point is that Japan has an ingrained quality culture. If reliable methods for achieving quality in software are developed by competitor nations, the Japanese will have no difficulty in adopting them and fitting them into that culture. Barriers of management attitude, resistance to change, anti-metrics bias, and others that impede progress elsewhere, will not impede them.

What, in this global context, of Europe? Some leading-edge European companies match the best anywhere. What is missing, however, is the mass movement of the USA or the ingrained improvement culture of Japan. The average European software-producing organization is unaware of the need or the methods for process improvement, or regards it as another cost with no corresponding return, or does not see how it differs from ISO 9001 quality audits.

Faced with this situation, the European Commission has put in place a bold and imaginative programme to stimulate a widespread European improvement culture in software process. The programme is called ESSI (European Systems and Software Initiative). ESSI's primary role is to fund process improvement projects. It also funds supporting activities, such as dissemination, training and networking.

The success of the Commission's investment will not be measured in the aggregate success of the ESSI projects, however: the number of organizations which it is possible to support with limited funds is an order of magnitude fewer than the thousands in the States. Real success will lie in leveraging off those pioneer projects, achieving a multiplier effect, setting a bandwagon rolling, capturing management attention and turning it into vision and commitment.

This approach accords well with the economist Will Hutton's recipe for action appropriate to the contemporary state: 'to find points of maximum leverage on the private sector which will set in train the dynamics it wants to see, while protecting and advancing the interests of those institutions that embody the public interest. . . . The individual moves may be small, even cautious, as they are tested by their results, but they should be designed to produce large effects from small changes. And the effects should make sense as part of a larger strategic whole.' [Will Hutton. *The State to Come.* Vintage 1997.]

Europe may be a minor player in the global market for commodity software; but European companies have traditionally been strong in the strategically important game of using software for competitive advantage in products and business processes. As the millennium turns, retaining and building on that strength will be crucial for Europe's survival and success in the global marketplace, and that means that software processes which are fit and continuously improving are essential. That is the strategic case for ESSI.

This book tells, and reflects on, a small selection of stories from ESSI.

Colin Tully
Colin Tully Associates, UK

Contributors

Editor:

Colin Tully   Colin Tully Associates, 8 Manchester Close, Stevenage, Hertfordshire
                           SG1 4TQ, UK

Authors:

M. Basso   TXT Ingegneria Informatica, Milano, Italy

D. Bell   Philips Research Laboratories, Cross Oak Lane, Redhill, Surrey RH1 5HA,
                           UK

Janet Byrne   The Voluntary Health Insurance Board, 20 Lower Abbey Street, Dublin 1,
                           Ireland

E. Ciapessoni   CISE Tecnologie Innovative, Segrate, Italy

E. Crivelli   ENEL/CRA, Cologno Monzese, Italy

Anne Downey   Q-SET, Campus Technology Park, Upper Newcastle, Galway, Ireland

Mikel Emaldi   Departamentos de Tecnologias de la Informacion y Calidad/
                           Competitividad: Parque Tecnológico Edificio, 101, 48170 Zamudio,
                           Aptdo.: 1234-48080 Bilbao, Spain

A. Gupta   Philips Research Laboratories, Cross Oak Lane, Redhill, Surry RH1 5HA,
                           UK

Fran Keating   Q-SET, Campus Technology Park, Upper Newcastle, Galway, Ireland

Carlo Leonardi   Digital Equipment Corporation, Viale F. Testi 280/6, 20126 Milano, Italy

D. Mandrioli   Dipartimento di Elettronica e Informazione, Politecnico di Milano, Milano,
                           Italy

Geoff Marlow   Cambridge Consultants Ltd., Science Park, Milton Road,
                           Cambridge CB4 4DW, UK

Giuseppe Menga   Dipartimento di Automatica e Informatica, Politecnico di Torino,
                           Corso Duca degli Abruzzi 24, 10129 Torino, Italy

Nicola Morfuni   ENGINEERING – Ingegneria Informatica S.p.A., Via dei Mille 56,
                           00185 Roma, Italy

Maurizio Morisio   Dipartimento di Automatica e Informatica, Politecnico di Torino,
                           Corso Duca degli Abruzzi 24, 10129 Torino, Italy

A. Morzenti   CISE Tecnologie Innovative, Segrate, Italy

Fergal O'Sullivan   CSK Financial Software, Lisle House, Molesworth Street, Dublin 2, Ireland

Stefano de Panfilis   ENGINEERING – Ingegneria Informatica S.p.A., Via dei Mille 56, 00185 Roma, Italy

Theoni Pitoura   First Informatics SA, 73–75 Kanakari Street, 26221 Patras, Greece

Jose Manuel Villalba Quesada   ELIOP, SA, Avda. de Manoteras 30, 28050 Madrid, Spain

P. San Pietro   Dipartimento di Elettronica e Informazione, Politecnico di Milano, Milano, Italy

E. Spencer   EDS, 1–3 Bartley Heath Business Park, Hook, Hampshire RG27 9XA, UK

Colin Tully   Colin Tully Associates, 8 Manchester Close, Stevenage SG1 4TQ, UK

1

Introduction and Overview

Colin Tully

Colin Tully Associates, Stevenage UK

1.1 ESSI – A BRIEF SUMMARY

The European Commission defines the goal and aim of ESSI as follows.

> The goal of ESSI is to promote improvements in the software development process so as to achieve greater efficiency, higher quality and greater economy. This is to be accomplished by applying the state of the art in software engineering in a wide range of industries. The full impact of ESSI will be driven by a multiplier effect which is achieved through dissemination across national borders and across industrial sectors.
>
> The aim of the initiative is to ensure that European software developers in both user and vendor organisations continue to have the world class skills, the associated technology and the improved practices necessary to build the increasingly complex and varied systems demanded by the marketplace.

ESSI operates by paying eligible costs of competitively selected projects. At the time of writing, there have been three overlapping phases of ESSI projects.

The first, or pilot, phase was launched with a call for proposals in March 1993. The 109 projects spanned a period from December 1993 (earliest start date) to October 1996 (latest planned completion date).

During the pilot phase, it was judged that the ESSI concept was sufficiently successful to justify further phases. Accordingly a second call for proposals was issued in March 1995, and the 135 selected projects span a period from January 1996 (earliest start date) to March 1998 (latest planned completion date). A third call for proposals was issued in March 1996,

and the resulting projects began to come on stream around the end of that year.

An individual ESSI project may be undertaken by a single enterprise or by a consortium. A consortium may comprise partners from one or more countries, one of which has the role of *prime partner*; the Commission contracts with the prime partner for the whole project, and the prime partner is then responsible for separate contracts with other consortium partners.

In each phase, most support has been devoted to *process improvement projects*, called *application experiments (AEs)* in the pilot phase and *process improvement experiments (PIEs)* in subsequent phases. There were 97 AEs out of the 109 projects from the 1993 call, and 98 PIEs out of the 135 projects from the 1995 call.

Other projects may be classified as *support projects* and *assessment projects*. Support projects cover *dissemination*, *training* and *networking*: there were 12 from the 1993 call and 13 from the 1995 call. Assessment projects support assessments only, with the intention that they will be used as the basis of subsequent improvement: they were not included in the 1993 call, and there were 24 from the 1995 call.

Information on the first two phases of ESSI is summarized in Table 1.1.

This book presents case histories of eight of the pilot phase application experiments. Further general information on AEs is given in Section 1.2 below.

ESSI is part of a broad programme of Research and Technology Development (RTD) in Information Technologies, conducted by Directorate–General III (Industry) of the European Commission. This programme is generally known under the acronym ESPRIT (European Strategic Programme of

Table 1.1 First and second ESSI calls

	Timespan (earliest start to latest planned completion	Improvement projects	Support projects	Assessment projects
1st call 03/1993 (Pilot Phase)	12/1993 –10/1996	97 application experiments (AEs)	12 dissemination and training actions	None
2nd call 03/1995	01/1996 –03/1998	98 process improvement experiments (PIEs)	13 dissemination, training and networking actions	24

Research and Development in Information Technology). ESPRIT has been a major part of successive EC R&D Framework Programmes since 1984.

While being formally a part of ESPRIT, ESSI takes it into new territory. Normal ESPRIT projects have been (and are) of a research nature: they address technological experiment and innovation, and the generation of new knowledge. ESSI, by contrast, addresses organizational experiment and innovation, the take-up of knowledge into business practice, and sharing the experience of that practice.

ESSI is an ambitious and important initiative. It is the largest single concerted process improvement effort yet undertaken anywhere. It offers the opportunity to build an experience base which can power and motivate improvement on a Europe-wide basis, to create an effective community of interest, and to develop a culture of openness and collaboration.

The ESSI community may be viewed as a virtual learning organization. ESSI participants are together attempting an innovative and challenging experiment in collaborative learning. What is meant by that is that the players are not only learning within their own individual enterprises, but ESSI as a whole is learning how to operate as a collaborative partnership, to serve the individual players and Europe as a whole.

Europe needs to think in these terms, and to embrace such an ambitious vision, if it is to match the speed of change achieved in the USA, the results of continuous and incremental improvement in Japan, and indeed the spectacular achievements of young software industries springing up, unencumbered by the outdated practices of past decades, in other regions.

A key factor in the US scene is the pivotal role played by the SEI. It serves as the development and maintenance authority for existing CMMs, creates and supports collaborations among leading industrial players for the development of new CMMs, supports SEPGs (Software Engineering Process Groups within individual enterprises), supports SPINs (Software Process Improvement Networks for information exchange among SEPGs), runs a huge annual process improvement conference, maintains a register of qualified process assessors, and runs courses and workshops. It is directly funded by the federal government, and occupies a prime site at one of the nation's most prestigious universities. At least in the software process field, it has thrown off the shackles of seeming to be predominantly academic and the creature of the Department of Defense. It has a secure and dominant position of leadership in the US software industry. It is hard to over-emphasize its importance and achievement, and hard to see how that rôle can be replicated in Europe.

A second key factor underpinning American progress is the existence of a substantial number (more than 50) of leading-edge industrial companies and arms of government, who have a high-profile commitment to software process improvement. They make available results and experience. They support and collaborate with the SEI, and collaborate among themselves, with the purpose of advancing the state of the art and of practice. Such behaviour is far from the stereotype of American capitalism, red in tooth and claw; it is the sign of a mature industrial economy which, while remaining strongly competitive, recognizes the need for openness and collaboration to solve difficult and critical problems. That is a challenge to large European companies to which (with a few honourable exceptions) they seem loath to respond.

The preface and the opening section of this chapter have sought to show that software process improvement is being adopted at a different speed and in a different setting in Europe, by comparison with other parts of the world. Interest in the case histories should not be confined, however, to Europe. The lessons they offer are of general value; but those lessons may be better appreciated if the context from which they spring is understood.

1.2 APPLICATION EXPERIMENTS IN DETAIL

Understanding the case histories will be made easier if more detail about pilot phase application experiments (AEs) is sketched in.

To qualify for support as an AE, improvement plans must be tested in use, in the context of a practical application project (hence the term 'application experiment'). A practical application project on which improvement plans are tested is called, in ESSI jargon, a *baseline project*. Baseline projects may be in any application domain. ESSI funding is not applicable to the baseline projects themselves, only to the additional costs of improvement.

It has been estimated that baseline projects are divided in approximately equal numbers between the following three main categories.

- *Business:* sales/marketing, personnel, financial, reservations, material requirements planning, office automation
- *Technical:* CAD/CAM, CASE, simulation, document image processing
- *Embedded/control:* communication/command/ control, consumer products, process control, industrial automation, signal processing, telecoms

Improvement may be undertaken by changing some combination of factors such as organization, management, process, methods, tools, metrics, procedures or skills. Within that range, the scope of improvement may be broad or narrow.

Over half of the AEs had planned durations of the maximum permitted length (18 months). The shortest planned duration was 10 months, and the average was 16.

Over half of the AEs were single-enterprise projects. The remainder comprised consortia, of between two and five partners (average 2.6). Fourteen of the consortia contained partners from more than one country.

About three-quarters of AE participants came from industrial sectors that are users of IT rather than suppliers – in other words, they were enterprises that develop software for their own in-house use. That proportion is closely representative of the pattern for Europe as a whole. About half of the prime partners were SMEs (small and medium-sized enterprises), and SMEs were represented in almost all the consortia.

The intention of ESSI was that AEs should have a strong multiplier effect in terms of spreading improvements. That multiplier effect should be achieved by dissemination at two levels:

- *internal dissemination* (inside the individual enterprise), by spreading improvements from the baseline project to other projects, and by adopting them into the established practice of the enterprise;
- *external dissemination* (outside the individual enterprise), by spreading information about improvements to other enterprises (including vendors) operating in the same application domain, the same industry, the same country, or more generally.

AEs were contractually bound, in return for receiving EC funding, to undertake at least a minimum of external dissemination. ESSI dissemination actions played a key role in such dissemination.

1.3 IMPROVEMENT GOALS

Common topics of concern to AEs may be roughly grouped into three levels – major concern, medium concern and minor concern – as follows.

- *Major:* object-oriented design, reuse, process development models, requirements management, standards
- *Medium:* testing, project management, maintenance, CSCW, architecture/design, reverse engineering, systems integration, metrics
- *Minor:* procurement and customer relationships, cost estimating, configuration management, project planning, risk management

The predominant focus was technical. There was less interest in quality and management topics such as configuration management, cost estimating, risk management and project planning. Note that, where AEs aimed to introduce new methods and/or tools, in over 80% of cases they were to support 'life-cycle' (technical development) processes as opposed to support processes in the management and organizational domains. To do justice to them, most AEs that introduced new tools considered the underlying method carefully first and did not attempt to use tools as instant problem solvers. The message 'first the method, then the tool' appears to have been followed.

The following form an illustrative cross-section of objectives as stated by AEs.

Assess thoroughly our performance with our current toolset, introduce a new set of modern high-productivity tools into our workflow and measure the effects of adopting the new tools.

[Investigate] the potential benefits attributable to second generation object-oriented methods ... and ... identify the impact on development team structure and approach.

Reuse of software components and ... reuse of architectural components with the exploitation of a new concept ... during the design. ... Address the robustness of applications which are made of well-used components.

Apply [the approach] to a range of different software engineering methods to enhance their design of end-user interfaces.

Experiment on the development and establishment of a decision support system.

The software system for the administration of software errors will be implemented, together with the appropriate procedures to improve the contact between end-users and support centres.

Improve methodological and process maturity issues that impact critically [on] business competitiveness in EDI.

Experiment with and evaluate the PRINCE project management methodology to improve overall software engineering productivity, quality and time-to-market.

Assess the impact that the use of emerging software process modelling and support techniques can have ... with respect to software quality, productivity and overall acceptance in ... software development teams and management.

AEs varied as to whether their goals were expressed in such a way that success could be subsequently verified. Such statements of success criteria can be divided into four categories: *qualitative, operational, assessment-based* and *quantitative*.

Most AEs used *qualitative* success criteria, such as 'more involvement of users throughout development', 'better understanding of customer requirements by developers', or 'better software specifications'. Where objectives are stated in this way, it is possible to observe subjectively whether they have been met, and many AEs claim to have done so. They could often in principle have been expressed quantitatively.

A few AEs used *operational* success criteria, such as 'perform training of method X for developers' or 'introduce phase Y in the life-cycle model of the company'. These can be verified in terms of whether or not they have been achieved, but they say little about the quality or extent of the improvement.

Over half the AEs referred in some way or other to *assessment-based* models such as ISO 9001 (predominantly), CMM or Bootstrap. That is to say, they selected improvement objectives from among the process attributes described in such models. Too rarely, however, projects actually incorporated assessments that would enable them to derive measured improvements against the models.

Few AEs gave *quantitative* success criteria such as deviation from schedule or defect levels. This is despite such measures being relatively well established in industrial software practice. There were even fewer quantitative criteria in business terms.

The above observations indicate the degree of immaturity of the European software industry in terms of software metrics and, more generally, in terms of measurement-driven business performance improvement.

1.4 FACTORS INFLUENCING SUCCESS OR FAILURE

This section summarizes some of the lessons learned during the pilot phase about software process improvement (SPI). They are based on information derived via a variety of channels from AEs.

Despite the strong tendency for AEs to focus on technical problems and solutions in defining their projects, there was a wide subsequent consensus, based on the experience gained during the projects, that the key issues in SPI centre round organizational and human factors. That consensus was not weakened by the wide variety of technical background and type of business represented among the AEs. If you understand these issues well, and deal with them, they are critical success factors. If you get them wrong, they are major barriers to success.

1.4.1 Senior Management

- *Authority*. The impact and implications of a serious programme of SPI are such that only senior management can authorize it. Software practitioners often are (and should be) aware of the need and potential, but do not (and should not) have the authority to commit the company.

- *Awareness*. Often senior executives are unaware of the need and potential for SPI. Software practitioners need to transfer their awareness to senior management (see below).

- *Leadership*. 'The leader's primary role is to act as visionary and motivator. By fashioning and articulating a vision of the kind of organization that he or she wants to create, the leader invests everyone in the company with a purpose and a sense of mission ... We define a leader not as someone who makes other people *do* what he or she wants, but as someone who makes them *want* what he or she wants. A leader doesn't coerce people into change that they resist.' [Michael Hammer and James Champy. *Reengineering the Corporation: a Manifesto for Business Revolution.* Nicholas Brealey Publishing, 1993.]

- *Commitment, involvement, support, sponsorship.* These must be visible by means of specific management actions, in a way which is understandable to practitioners. They should be demonstrated not only by the individual executive who fills the leadership role (above), but he or she should ensure they are shared by the whole senior management team and transmitted to all software practitioners.

- *Link to business objectives.* There should be a clear link between the expected benefits of SPI and broader business objectives. It is the responsibility of senior management to have defined those business objectives, to understand the link, and to communicate that definition and understanding to software practitioners. All too often, even if strategic plans, mission statements etc. exist, they are not known about by all employees.

- *Long-term view.* SPI is not a short-term effort, and it cannot be achieved by a one-off project. Senior management must therefore commit for the long haul, and accept (for instance) that the implications for SPI of business objectives changing over time must be carefully handled.

1.4.2 Making the Case to Senior Management

- *Practitioner responsibility.* It is rare that senior management will discover the need for SPI, or fully understand the nature of the role, on their own. Software practitioners typically grumble about the deficiencies of management; but often it is largely their own fault. They need to do a better job of selling SPI to key executives.

- *Enter their culture.* Practitioners should try to speak the language of management, to explain the characteristics and issues relating to SPI in a way which is understandable. They should also realize the suspicion that often exists of IT motives and capability. Management is accustomed to IT

not delivering, and making overinflated claims. This leads to a reluctance to consider fundamental change in what they see as the unstable and uncontrolled environment of software development.

- *Quantify potential benefits.* Management often requires a quantified business case, rather than being asked to make an act of faith. Unfortunately there is a catch-22 situation here: organizations starting from a low maturity level (which is of course normally the case) by definition do not have a valid baseline in relation to which the benefits of SPI can be forecast. The ability to predict benefits correlates with the maturity of the organization. At least a limited reliance on an act of faith may therefore be unavoidable.

  Assuming, however, that some attempt must be made to quantify benefits, then one or two sound principles apply. Make sure the benefits offered are not just technical benefits, but are understandable in business terms. (For instance, translate reduced defects into lower maintenance costs and increased customer satisfaction; translate a higher maturity level into remaining on approved supplier lists.) Make your prediction credible by showing that other companies have achieved comparable benefits. Seek at least some benefits that can be achieved quickly and with minimum risk, and will be high-profile, so as to maximize the chance that you can build on success. Keep it simple.

- *Benchmark.* An intermediate strategy, between the quantified business case and the act of faith, is to show that the company is not reaching levels of good practice achieved elsewhere. A benchmark is a means of doing that. For the purposes of persuading senior management, an appropriate benchmark should have at least three key characteristics: (a) it should describe good practice in terms that are meaningful to management; (b) it should be easy and cheap, both to use and to verify, in self-assessment mode; (c) a database of results from many other companies should be available in the public domain, against which the company's profile can be compared. A good candidate for such a benchmark is the Software Development Benchmark developed by IBM Europe.

1.4.3 Skills and Training – Teams and Individuals

- *Skill base and balance.* The software process is dependent throughout on teams. There will be teams for achieving process improvement, as well as the conventional development teams who enact the processes. Typically individuals will be called upon to be active in more than one team simultaneously. Teams' performance depends on the levels and balance of individuals' skills, and these are especially critical during periods of change. This requires careful attention to staff recruitment, development and training.

- *Multi-skilled individuals.* A team can benefit greatly from having individuals with a range of skills and knowledge. For instance, a person who understands both technical and management issues helps to bridge the divide between these two sides.

- *Team training.* Train complete development teams, not just seeded individuals. Give the training when it is needed, so that it can be related to the team's immediate objectives, and can be put into practice at once.

- *Job rotation.* This can be a useful means to improve the flexibility of a team and to help with the personal development of staff.

- *Mentoring.* Access to sources of expertise, to help individuals cope with unexpected problems, is an important complement to training, and is especially valuable during periods of change and challenge.

- *Continuous team building.* If such policies are implemented they can provide a process of continuous team building, and a corporate capability for teamworking, which will contribute to the long-term success of the company.

1.4.4 Motivation, and Overcoming Resistance to Change

- *Motivation.* Process change is hard, creative and often risky work, which for most people makes demands beyond their normal job descriptions. Some personality types are naturally motivated to work like that; most are not, and need psychological, financial or other forms of motivation to persuade them to take the plunge. Training in itself is not adequate to meet the requirements for successful implementation of change, to provide positive motivation and reduce resistance. It needs to be amplified, not only through management's dealings with individuals but also through the culture that management creates company-wide. The role of the process champion can be important here.

- *Conservatism.* A frequent barrier to change lies in a dogged adherence to traditional ways of doing things. Despite their commitment to achieving change for other people, technical staff often display unexpected conservatism with respect to their own work. They are dedicated to practices which embody their pride in their job or which they imagine make them indispensable.

- *Fear.* It is important to remove the fear which exists in less adventurous employees when it comes to taking on new practices. Fear produces a resistance to change and generates low morale and motivation. It may relate to lack of capability to respond to change, reduction in status or income or job satisfaction, or even loss of job.

- *Not invented here.* Even within a single organization, there can be difficulties in changes pioneered in one group gaining acceptance by others. One project may come up with wonderful results, but if they lie gathering dust on a shelf, instead of influencing the whole organization to change, then that project will in a very important way have failed. Demonstrations of successful improvement can be a good way of overcoming this form of resistance – and these should show not just technical success but also the benefits of change to those who have taken part in it.

- *Disseminate evidence of success.* One of the characteristics of companies that succeed with SPI is that company notice-boards, newsletters etc. are commandeered to communicate evidence of continuous and measured improvement. This is done by charting progress on a small number of carefully selected and understandable key performance indicators. Of course there may from time to time be negative progress: provided that doesn't happen too often, it should also contribute to positive motivation.

- *Dealing with failure.* Not all improvement initiatives will succeed. Some will fail, and how those failures are handled can have a big effect on motivation and resistance. A culture which regards failure as a learning opportunity – and, as such, essentially an asset – will improve far more consistently than a blame culture in which failures, and those 'responsible', are invariably punished.

- *Improvement involves everyone.* There is a lot of evidence that success in SPI is correlated with getting everyone involved. SPI should not be the preserve of a clique or élite, who dream up changes that are then 'imposed' on the less privileged practitioners.

- *Empowering and encouraging everyone to contribute.* If everyone should be involved then it is good practice (a) to allow everyone to charge a proportion of their time to SPI, (b) to include SPI goals and achievements in personal appraisals, (c) to encourage and reward suggestions from individuals.

- *Awareness groups.* These can be a good motivational technique, helping to confront and reduce fear and conservatism, and contributing to team building and better communication.

1.4.5 Managing Improvement

- *Organize for SPI.* Embarking seriously on SPI is a major undertaking. It is a way of life which, once adopted, will not end. An important determinant of success is having an appropriate organization which is charged with strategy, planning and implementation of SPI, at a level above the individual software projects in which the software process is enacted. What that organization is like will vary according to the different characteristics of different companies, in terms of size, reporting, full-time or part-time etc. The key thing is to establish ownership and responsibility; without them, nothing is likely to happen. That need is one of the many reasons why senior management backing is essential.

- *Define improvement steps as projects.* We now move from the overall management of SPI to the management of individual improvement initiatives (for instance, the introduction of formal inspections). Each such initiative should be defined, organized and managed as a project, using normal project management disciplines. Note that it would be normal for the members of an improvement project team concurrently to be members of other project teams.

- *Manage the impact of SPI on development projects.* When specific improvements are being first prototyped in, and then rolled out across, development projects, they will inevitably have an impact on those projects, effectively in the form of increased risk. Project managers must be willing to accept those risks, and able to manage them.

1.4.6 Communication

- *Communication is key.* Good communication is implicit in many of the points made above, and it is a common factor of all success stories. Poor communication, on the other hand, was found to be a frequent complaint among AEs, and is a major contributor to failure – particularly the failure to exploit widely a local success.

- *Communication doesn't happen by chance.* Good communication is not accidental. It is only achieved by effort and at a cost. Part of that cost is the measurable economic cost of making sure that effective channels of communication exist and are used. Part is the intangible cost of creating and maintaining a culture within which people communicate willingly and easily.

- *Communication needs to overcome 'language' barriers.* A company is a federation of many specialisms, each with their own sub-culture and ways of thinking and talking. It is a mistake to think that SPI only affects software people, and need only be discussed in their language. All kinds of other people need to understand why change is being sought. We have noted above that talking effectively to senior management is important, but that is not the only language barrier that may need to be crossed. Effective communication may be particularly important, for instance, with marketing, end-users, personnel and training departments, production, and customers and suppliers. Software process changes may affect these groups, or may depend on their collaboration.

1.4.7 Measurement

- *Measurement is key.* If good communication is a pervasive success factor, so is appropriate measurement. We have already discussed the importance of quantified forecasts of benefits. They need to be followed up by quantified evidence of achievement. Achievement needs to be compared to forecast, and any variance analysed to extract lessons for the future. That is the normal Shewhart (plan – do – check – act) cycle. We have also seen the motivational importance of communicating measured improvements widely among staff; it may have an even wider importance among customers, and in persuading senior management to continue and strengthen its support.

- *Design appropriate measures.* Measurements should be designed to be fit for purpose. The measures that are widely used, as above, to show proof of improvement, should be relatively few; those few measures, however, will typically be derived from an infrastructure of more basic measures. Questions to ask about the 'shop window' measures include: Do they convey information that is understandable and relevant to those who will see them and whom they are intended to influence? What is the appropriate frequency for calculating and displaying them? Does the benefit gained from them justify the cost of deriving them? What confidence can we have that they will normally show an improving trend?

- *Assign responsibility*. Regular calculation and dissemination of measurements is a nontrivial task. If it is not specifically assigned, there is a risk it will not be done, or not be done properly. Responsibility for major performance indicators should be assigned to specific individuals.

1.4.8 Tools

- *Not sufficient, but normally necessary*. With respect to tools, we have already noted two things about the pilot phase AEs: (a) the majority involved the introduction of new technology (methods and/or tools), in contrast to an approach driven by maturity models; (b) the majority claimed (at least) to understand that tools should be subordinated to methods, and should not be regarded as ends in themselves. Point (b) indicates that the lessons of the CASE fiasco have been learned, although it would have been preferable if there had been a more general recognition of the need to subordinate both methods and tools to process. Even if tools are subordinate, however, they are usually necessary to support process improvement.

Table 1.2   AEs included as case histories

Chapter	Project number, acronym and full title	Countries and organizations participating	Start and duration	Improvement objective
2	10070: AEFTA Application Enabler Technology for Factor Automation	Italy Digital Equipment Corporation, Politecnico di Torino, SYCO	06/1994 15 months	Reuse and object orientation
3	10146: ALCAST Implementation of an Automated Lifecycle Approach to Softwave Testing in the Finance and Insurance Sector	Ireland Voluntary Health Insurance Board, Quay Financial Software Limited, Q–SET Limited	01/1994 18 months	Testing and formal reviews
4	10290: BIUSEM Benefits of Integrating Usability and Software Engineering Methods	UK Philips Research Laboratories, Electrowatt Engineering Services, EDS Scicon, University College London The Netherlands Philips Analytical X-Ray	02/1994 18 months	Incorporation of user interface and usability engineering in software process
5	10453: ELSA Experimentation of a Logical Approach to the Specification of Automation Control Systems	Italy ENEL CRA, CISE Technologie Innovative, TXT Ingegneria Informatica, Politecnico di Milano	01/1994 18 months	Formal specification and object orientation
6	10476: ENG–SODEPRO Experimentation of a New Software Development Process, Oriented to Software Quality	Italy Engineering Ingegnaria Informatica	01/1994 18 months	Quality engineering
7	10760: FAME Framework for Management and Design of Multimedia Applications in Education and Training	Greece FIRST Informatica, Benaki Museum, Lambrakis Research Foundation	06/1994 18 months	Incorporation of multimedia development in software process
8	10836: PRAMIS System and Software Project Management and Management Accounting Methodology	Spain Labein UK CCL	05/1994 18 months	Management accounting for software projects
9	10936: ISORUS Implementation and Evaluation of a Software Reuse Methodology	Spain ELIOP, Universidad Politecnica de Madrid, COYPSA	12/1993 18 months	Reuse

- *Tool deficiencies.* AEs were fairly vocal in identifying shortcomings in the tools they attempted to use. A pretty damning overall judgement was that tools are 'uncertified, unreliable and immature'! One is tempted to be depressed: to judge from the apparent quality of their products, those who build tools to support the software process must themselves have pretty bad processes! The following is a summary list of deficiencies actually experienced.

  – Many tools do not live up to their claims. For example, tools claim to support standard file formats but do not, leading to the need for file translation.
  – Many tools have poor training and support. There are consequent problems finding/forming qualified staff.
  – Tools do not scale up well to tackle large projects.
  – The tool evaluation and selection process is unduly difficult. Description and documentation of tools needs to be better.
  – There is often poor cooperation between tool and method developers.
  – There are too many delivered defects.
  – Change to another programming language or target hardware is often difficult.

- *Communicate with vendors.* This is an important and underestimated area of communication, and can be a critical focus for SPI. Successful and mature software developers understand their critical dependence on vendors, and will often devote great effort to selecting them, developing close relationships with them, and often making them partners in a process which crosses company boundaries. This can result in vendors having a better understanding of customers' needs. It can also lead to a vendor having confidence in the long-term nature of its relationship with a customer, and accordingly being prepared to give special attention to meeting its needs. The overall outcome can be better tools, and a vendor–customer partnership in SPI.

1.5 THE CASE HISTORIES

The earlier sections of this chapter have presented aspects of ESSI, and some lessons learned by AEs in general. It is now time to turn to some specific AEs, who have volunteered to contribute to this book accounts of their individual projects – their aims, their experience, and some of their immediate conclusions.

Table 1.2 summarises the eight projects which contribute the case histories in Chapters 2 to 9.

These eight projects represent a valuable range, diversity and richness of experience, spanning six European countries and their national cultures. One important point needs to be made before the reader embarks on the eight chapters in which the projects present their case histories. Some of those chapters incorporate a good deal of complex technical detail, about applications and/or about development methods. It is judged that the detail is necessary if readers are to gain more than a superficial grasp of what the AEs were setting out to do, and why it was significant for the companies concerned.

Some very brief summary observations are offered in the final chapter of this book. Until then, however, let the eight AEs speak for themselves.

2

Application Enabler Technology for Factory Automation*

Maurizio Morisio[a], **Carlo Leonardi**[b], **Giuseppe Menga**[a]

[a]*Dipartimento di Automatica e Informatica Politecnico di Torino, Torino, Italy*
[b]*Digital Equipment Corporation, Milano, Italy*

2.1 INTRODUCTION

The AEFTA (Application Enabler Technology for Factory Automation) experiment, which involves Digital Equipment Corporation, Politecnico di Torino and SYCO, with a staff of seven, develops a factory automation product using BASEstar Open (1990) and object technology, notably OMT (Rumbaugh *et al.* 1991), G++ (Menga *et al.* 1993) and C++. The goal of the application experiment is to verify if object-oriented (OO) technology, through the reuse opportunities which it offers, improves productivity and quality in the factory automation context.

Software Development in Digital

The Digital Equipment Corporation Engineering Centre in Italy develops a number of products that encompass software technology in the areas of databases, CASE and manufacturing (Computer Integrated Manufacturing or CIM). The CIM component of the Centre focuses on the implementation of BASEstar Open, a framework for factory automation which is portable across multiple hardware and software platforms. Together with all the components of the Centre, the CIM group is constantly pursuing the following objectives.

- Reduce the number of defects in released products, by improving software quality assurance in all phases of the software development process.
- Increase the reuse of software artefacts.
- Improve the ability to control costs and schedule overruns.
- Facilitate and support compliance with ISO 9000 standards.

The current practice leaves to the implementor and to company policies the verification of the compliance of a software component with the initial specifications and with the real needs of the customer (internal or external to the company) and the documentation of the process from the initial analysis to the final implementation. In Digital the development process is divided into phases, each of which is entered only after technical and financial approval, and is exited only after all exit criteria are met. All the phases must be supported by a number of documents of increasing detail, which are written as a separate activity by the Project Leader, and their constant update to the current status of the project depends on the balance with other tasks that are the responsibility of the Project Leader.

The satisfaction of goals and the analysis of the current state are supported by a Software Development Metrics Program that has been in effect across all Digital Software Groups in Europe since 1990. Typical examples of the identified metrics are: planned versus actual completion dates, business performance for each product, cumulative number of

* This work was partially supported by the European Commission, DGIII/A, under contract ESSI AEFTA n. 10070.

telephone calls to the service centre to require bug fixing (perceived quality), and actual number of faults fixed by the maintenance group.

The BASEstar Open product, relating to a sensitive area of Information Technology, is particularly affected by two deficiencies that are still embedded in the current process: time-to-market and software quality. These issues are mainly generated by the current use of an implementation technology that uses the C programming language, has no provisions for embedded documentation and is also lacking in analysis and design support and verification.

The application experiment deals with the production of an application using BASEstar Open. With the current technology such an application is basically a set of C programs using BASEstar Open services in the form of a number of calls to C procedures. As pointed out in the previous paragraph, this technology has many drawbacks: poor quality of documentation of analysis and design phases, and limited responsiveness to customer needs in terms of time-to-market. The experiment uses object-oriented technology to verify if it can improve these factors.

2.2 DESCRIPTION OF THE APPLICATION EXPERIMENT

In this section we describe the application experiment. The first subsection explains how the experiment was designed, and the following subsections describe in more detail some crucial parts of the experiment; that is, the product produced, the technology under observation and the measurement method.

2.2.1 Experimental Design

The experiment was designed using the DESMET (Law 1994, Kitchenham *et al.* 1994) methodology.

DESMET (Determining an Evaluation methodology for Software MEthods and Tools) is a methodology for evaluating methods and tools in software engineering. One starting point of the authors is very similar to that of ESSI: the IT community desperately needs controlled and quantitative evaluations of its methods and tools, as very few of these have been made in past years.

In the DESMET approach, the first step is the selection of an evaluation method, by using defined criteria. Roughly speaking, the method can be a *formal experiment*, a *case study* or a *survey*; and the evaluation can be *qualitative* or *quantitative*.

A formal experiment is based on replication. Many subjects (i.e. software engineers) are required to perform the same task(s) using the different methods/tools under evaluation. The assignment of tasks to subjects is an experimental design choice, and should be unbiased. If this hypothesis is satisfied, statistical techniques can be used to evaluate the results.

In a case study there is no replication. The tasks are performed once; statistical techniques cannot be applied. A case study is indeed useful if it is performed in a real-life environment, while rarely are there resources to execute formal experiments outside academies using students as subjects.

In a survey, organizations that have used the method/tool in the past are required to provide information on it. The information is then processed using statistical techniques.

According to this classification, AEFTA is a quantitative case study where the experiment is conducted once, in an industrial environment.

In a case study, the method/tool under observation, the experimental hypothesis, the subject, the response variables, the state variables, the control variables and the control object have to be identified.

The method/tool observed is, in general, the object-oriented approach and the technology supporting it; in fact the method/tool is a complex object that will be detailed in Section 2.2.3.

The experimental hypothesis is a predicate over the method/tool observed that must be accepted or rejected at the end of the experiment. In our case it is 'the method/tool improves the quality of the product and productivity, through the reuse opportunities offered by OOT'. This hypothesis is very broad and will be refined in Section 2.2.5.

The subject is the person(s) performing the experiment. In our case it is the staff of software engineers involved in the project. They are always considered as one single subject, except in one case in which they are partitioned according to experience in OO development (Section 2.3.3).

The response variables are factors that are expected to change as a result of applying the method/tool. In the case of AEFTA they are the quality of the product and productivity. In Section 2.2.5 they will be detailed to the level of quantitative metrics.

The state variables are the elements of the experiment that could influence the result and are not under the control of the observer. They are: the product to be developed (see Section 2.2.2) and the staff. The staff can vary as regards experience of the domain (factory automation), experience of the technology (OO, BASEstar Open, G++) and skill.

The control variables are the elements of the experiment directly under the control of the observer. As we are in an industrial environment, there are no control variables.

The control object is a project not using the method/tool under observation. The control object provides a baseline against which the results can be compared. The control object is the project, run in Digital in 1992, that developed a C version of the product. In the following, the control object will be called the C project, while the product developed during the experiment will be called the C++ product, or simply the product.

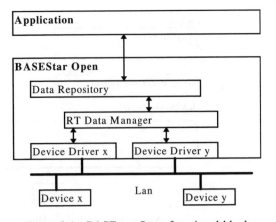

Figure 2.1 BASEstar Open functional blocks

2.2.2 The Baseline Project (State Variable)

In this section we describe the product developed in the AEFTA experiment. In ESSI terminology this is called the baseline project, that is, the real-life project on which the method/tool is tested. According to the DESMET terminology, the product to be developed is a state variable that could influence the result of the experiment but is outside the control of the observer.

The AEFTA baseline project develops a factory automation product using BASEstar Open (1990).

BASEstar Open is, in factory automation terminology, an application enabler. It is composed (see Figure 2.1) of a real-time data manager, a data repository, a data acquisition module and a device control module. It provides uniform and transparent access to devices on a network. In the case of factory automation, the most common domain of use of BASEstar Open, devices are the basic elements of a plant: PLCs (Programmable Logic Controls), NCs (Numeric Controls), robots, and terminals to communicate with human operators. Through BASEstar all these devices can be read or written in a uniform and simple way from a plant management application.

Figure 2.2 shows BASEstar Open as a layer between the operating system and devices distributed in a network. The application interacts with BASEstar Open through procedure calls in C. At run time a BASEstar process monitors the devices assigned to it and answers calls from the application. BASEstar is available for different operating systems (VMS, UNIX, Microsoft Windows NT). Figure 2.2 also shows the typical hardware/software architecture of a plant: a number of computers and devices connected by a network, and a distributed plant management application running on those computers and controlling the devices. Figure 2.3 shows the evolution of BASEstar Open to a C++ library (more detailed explanations are in Section 2.2.3)

The product developed is a manufacturing cell controller. The cell is composed of four machines, 10 buffers, a loading/unloading bay and a number of pallets moved by a transport system (a conveyor) connecting the machines with the buffers and the loading/unloading bay. The cell receives shop orders to be produced. A shop order settles the type and the number of pieces to be produced. The piece type, in turn, determines the sequence of operations to produce the pieces. An operation can be performed on

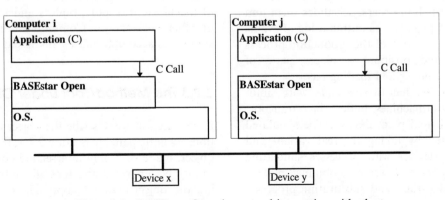

Figure 2.2 BASEstar Open layers and interaction with plant

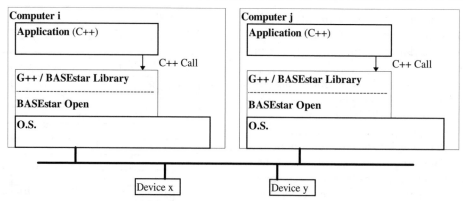

Figure 2.3   BASEstar Open layers and interaction with plant – OO style

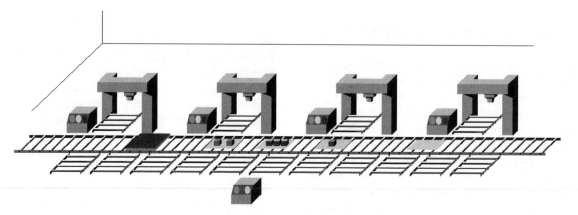

Figure 2.4   The cell controller: snapshot of the screen with the cell state

more than one machine, but each machine is usually not able to perform all possible operations. Therefore a piece is operated upon by many machines: this is the routing problem (route a piece to the next machine on which the requested operation is possible) that the cell controller must solve. Moreover, more than one shop order is usually assigned to a cell: this is the scheduling problem (choose the piece on which the next free machine will operate) that the cell controller must solve, too.

The cell controller (see Figure 2.4) receives as input a number of shop orders, schedules them and routes pieces, and produces as output a log of events and a graphical animation of the production process including state and position of pieces, state of machines, state of buffer and loading bay.

The cell controller has two variants: with simulated plant devices (machines, buffers, bay, transport system), and with real plant devices. The simulated variant is obtained by taking the real variant and substituting real devices with processes simulating them. Conversely the real variant is obtained by taking the simulated variant and substituting processes with real devices. Usually the simulated variant is

produced and tested in a software house, then the real variant is installed in the factory. Since ESSI projects are dedicated to software projects, the experiment finished with the simulated variant.

The simulated cell controller has two versions: concentrated on a single workstation, and distributed. In the concentrated version, the cell controller and the simulators of devices are on the same workstation and communicate through primitives of the operating system. In the distributed version, the cell controller is on one workstation, and the simulators of machines, transport, buffers and loading bay are on other workstations. Communication among workstations is accomplished by BASEstar Open.

2.2.3 The Method/Tool Under Observation

In this section we describe the object under observation. As anticipated in Section 2.2.1, this is a complex object, made of highly interrelated components that cannot be separated and that all contribute to defining the object-oriented approach in the context of AEFTA. Therefore their effect on the experiment cannot be isolated. We identify two main components: the production process, including formalisms and languages used, and the supporting tool. They are described in the next sections.

2.2.3.1 The production process

The process (see Figure 2.5) is composed of three phases (this is also called the macroprocess): simulated concentrated, simulated distributed, distributed. The simulated concentrated phase produces a running version of the product, simulated and concentrated (as defined in Section 2.2.2). The simulated distributed phase produces a running version of the product, simulated and distributed. The distributed phase produces a complete manufacturing cell (as already mentioned this was not part of the ESSI experiment). In a project any number of iterations of the three phases are allowed.

Each phase undergoes the subphases analysis, design, coding and test (this is also called the microprocess). Analysis, starting from a previous analysis document or more informal documents, produces a new analysis document. Design, starting from an analysis document and a previous design document, produces a new design document. Coding and test, starting from a design document, produces C++ classes, assembles them in a product and tests it. Analysis and design use the OMT formalism, coding uses C++.

Any number of iterations of the subphases are allowed during a phase. An iteration fixes faults or extends the document on which it works.

If we forget iterations, the simplified, linear process used in the project is the following.

Phase simulated concentrated An analysis of system requirements was performed; then a design was derived and the product was coded and tested. The product was developed on a UNIX workstation and ported to a personal computer running Microsoft Windows (with no code changes).

Phase simulated distributed Analysis, design, coding and testing were repeated. In fact only minor modifications were made to obtain the distributed version from the concentrated one. As stated in Section 2.2.2 the distributed version uses BASEstar services.

BASEstar Open offers its services in a procedural way (calls to C procedures). In an object-oriented world the same services should be encapsulated in a set of classes, offering the service of distributed messaging, and packaged in a class library. The advantages of this approach are the homogeneity in the overall design and the availability of the library to future projects. In fact the project took this approach and developed a BASEstar Open C++ library, integrated in the G++ tool.

We can state that the experiment actually consisted of two subprojects: (1) development of the product; (2) development of the BASEstar Open/C++ library.

The process used to develop the library consists of one phase, while the subphases are the same as those defined above: analysis, design, code and test. Figure 2.6 shows the temporal relations between the two subprojects. Figure 2.7 shows the library (called G++/BASEstar Library) and its integration in the G++ tool. Figure 2.3 shows BASEstar Open as a layer between the application and the operating system, in the OO style of a C++ library.

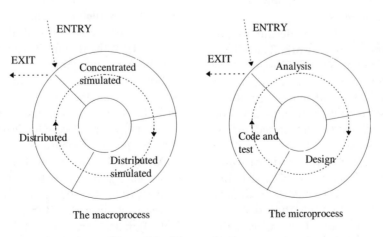

Figure 2.5 The production process

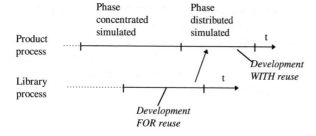

Figure 2.6   Product and library processes

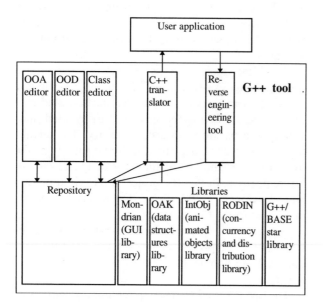

Figure 2.7   The G++ tool

can be translated into C++ code. The tool relies on an external compiler, linker and debugger. Moreover, the translation into C++ can be directed either towards a concentrated concurrent environment based on Windows NT or UNIX; or towards a distributed environment based on TCP/IP. During the experiment this functionality was enriched with the possibility of translating towards a BASEstar Open distributed environment.

In the backward sense the tool reverse-engineers C++ code to Class, OOD and OOA models.

A documenter tool formats models into predefined or user-defined paper documentation.

The tool is completed by a number of class libraries, one for data structures and related algorithms, one for building GUIs portable on MS Windows and X, one offering concurrency and distribution services, and others. The class libraries are used internally by the tool for the automatic translations. For instance, the data structure library is used for translating OMT relationships; the concurrency and distribution library is used for translating the dynamic model and to support the distribution of classes.

BASEstar Open was integrated in the tool as a class library, used by the tool itself to support the distribution of classes. From this point of view, G++ becomes a development environment for BASEstar Open applications.

2.2.3.2 The tool

G++ (Menga *et al.* 1993) is not the GNU compiler but a homonym CASE tool supporting OOA/OOD, a concurrency/distribution model, generation of C++ code and a large set of libraries.

The tool (see Figure 2.7) stores models in a repository, on which editors and tools work. The editors are: an OO Analysis editor, an OO Design editor (both using an extended OMT formalism), and a class design editor (it allows the attributes, operations and relations of a class to be defined as pseudocode or C++ code). The editors are integrated in the forward and backward sense.

In the forward sense it is possible to derive automatically an OOD model from an OOA model, and Class models from an OOD model, including dynamic information. The first translation does not add any value; the second translation suggests the translation of relationships. Finally, Class models

2.2.3.3 Process and tool

It can be seen that the production process is strongly influenced by the use of G++.

The subphases in the microprocess (analysis, design, code and test) basically match the models supported by the G++ editors.

The phases (concentrated, distributed) also reflect the ability of the tool in offering high-level services to distribute an application.

Forward and backward translation facilities push the software engineer to iterate rapidly and continuously between analysis, design and coding. For this reason the microprocess has very few temporal constraints among subphases.

Also, reuse (which will be discussed later) is supported by the tool. It is used by the tool itself to perform automatic translations; it is supported by the tool since the libraries are integrated in the tool. For instance, the same OOA/OOD editors can be used to browse and adapt the libraries.

2.2.4 Confounding Factors in the Experiment

In this section we discuss the factors that could have a confounding effect on interpreting the results of the experiment.

2.2.4.1 The control object

During the design of the experiment it was decided that the control object would be a 1992 Digital project, dedicated to developing a C version of the product. This seemed to be a natural and useful choice, making the experiment a sort of formal experiment with two replications, one in C, one in C++.

During the development of the product it became apparent that a number of drawbacks existed (see Table 2.1).

For business reasons, a number of functionalities not provided by the C product were added to the C++ product. In particular, the user interface is much more sophisticated and features graphical animation.

The C product was developed by the developers of BASEstar Open. On the contrary, the developers of the C++ product are BASEstar Open beginners. The C product was developed by experienced C programmers. The staff of the C++ product was composed of experienced OO programmers and beginners.

The C product was developed with a 'code and go' process. No analysis, design or test phases were performed; the only documentation was the source code. On the contrary, the C++ product was developed with a defined process, and analysis, design and testing documentation were produced. The development environment for the C product was composed of a text editor, a compiler, a linker and a debugger. The

development environment for the C++ product was a sophisticated CASE tool.

During the C++ product development, a library was developed, to be reused both in the project and in future projects (this is called development FOR REUSE, see later). Accordingly the C++ product was developed using this library (this is called development WITH REUSE, see later). No such techniques were used in the C product.

Because of all the above-mentioned differences, we believe that the two projects, unfortunately, are not comparable. The only available measure on the C project (total effort) is not comparable with the analogous measure on the C++ project.

2.2.4.2 Learning

The experiment included a learning phase in OO technology for OO beginners on the staff (approximately half the staff). Normally this is a high-risk factor: the effort dedicated to learning could make the experimental project show far worse results in productivity and elapsed time than the control project. We believe the composition of the staff (half OO beginners, half experienced in OO) reduces this risk. In other words, the staff could be ideally considered as composed of OO intermediate people.

2.2.5 Response Variables and Measures

In this section we describe the measures used to monitor the experiment. The definition of these measures corresponds to defining in detail the response variables part of the experimental design. According to the GQM approach (explained below), the definition of measures depends on the goals of the project. In

Table 2.1 Comparison of C and C++ projects

	Staff experience	Development environment	Process	Product	Reusability
C product	BASEstar and advanced	Text editor, compiler, linker, debugger	Code and debug	Concentrated	No
C++ product	BASEstar beginner, C++ intermediate	Integrated CASE tool	Analysis. design, code, test	Concentrated version+ distrbuted version; some functionalities added (graphical animation)	Yes

our case the goals of the project correspond to the experimental hypothesis. Therefore we use the GQM approach to define response variables and the related metrics starting from the experimental hypothesis. This approach is part of a more general measurement method. Below we describe the measurement method, the goals and response variables, and the measures defined.

2.2.5.1 The measurement method

The method used to measure the software process considers measurement as a (sub)process of the software process. The measurement process consists of the following activities:

1. modelling the software process using OMT,
2. defining goals for the project,
3. formalizing goals in measures defined on the process model,
4. designing the technological support for measures (procedures, repository and tools),
5. implementing the technological support,
6. operating the measurement process,
7. assessing the measurement process, and modifying it, if needed.

For a deeper description of the method see (Morisio 1995); tools and techniques for data collection, storage and analysis are described in (Aarsten and Morisio 1996).

Activity 1 is the definition of the process model, since measures are defined on it. The process is modelled in OMT, using mainly the object model, in which activities, products and roles are modelled as classes (see Figure 2.8).

The process model defined here has a different flavour from the one presented in Section 2.2.3. Here the focus is on measuring, therefore the model is descriptive and no temporal information is represented (except duration of activities). Class **Process Phase** models phases defined in Section 2.2.3. Subphases are not modelled as classes. Instead documents are modelled (see Figure 2.9). Work done on a document of a certain type belongs to a certain subphase. For instance, work done on **Analysis Document** belongs to an analysis subphase. Class **Process Activity** models work done by a single person, and is the basis for computing and analysing effort. Specializations of **Process Activity** (Figure 2.10) provide a classification of efforts by type (creation, modification, verification, presentation, discussion, . . .) rather than by phase/subphase. This allows subphases to overlap and to be iterated.

The next activities (2,3) are the definitions of goals and measures. The well-known, top-down, Goal Question Metric (GQM) approach (Basili and Rombach 1988, Basili 1995), refined in standard IEEE1061 (IEEE 1992) and in AMI (AMI 1992), is used.

The starting point of GQM is simple. Given a software project, measuring everything on it is costly and

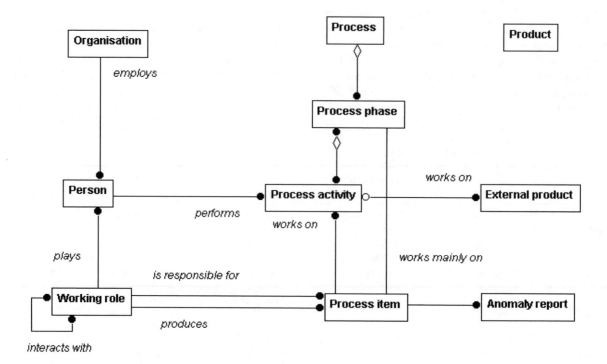

Figure 2.8 Process model

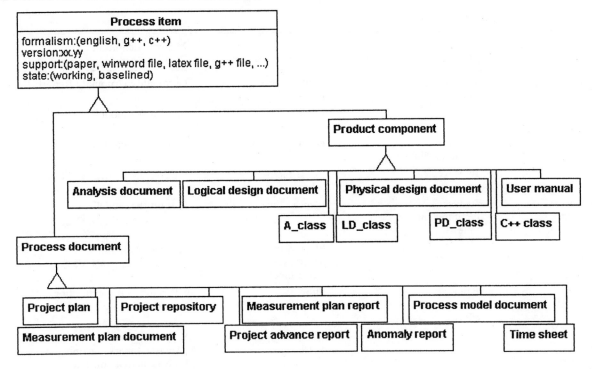

Figure 2.9   Specialization of process item

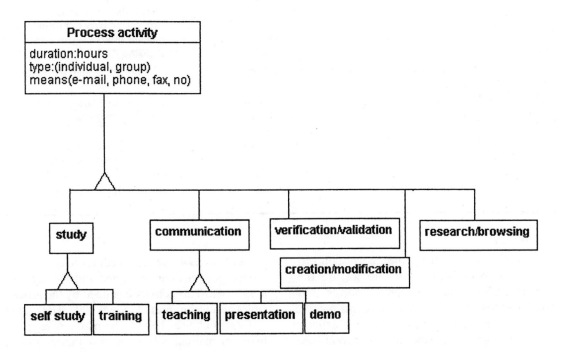

Figure 2.10   Specialization of process activity

useless, since this generates a mass of data in which it is easier to drown than to find useful information. Measurement must be focused, both to spare resource and to guide analysis of data. Focus can be achieved with a top-down approach: defining the goals of the project, deriving from them more detailed subgoals, and so on until a subgoal is so fine-grained that it can be measured. Goals, subgoals and measures define a graph: the same measure can be an indicator for many subgoals; the same subgoal can appear in the decomposition of many goals. Refer to Table 2.2 for an example.

Table 2.2   Goals, subgoals and measures

Goal	Subgoal	Measure name	Measure definition [U of measure]
Improve quality	Reduce faults	Faults before release	Cardinality (Anomaly Report) [ ]
		Faults after release	(not on the model)
	Improve maintainability	Documentation level	(not on the model)
	Improve reuse	Reuse factor	(not on the model, see Section 2.2.5.3)
Improve productivity	Reduce development time	Elapsed time	(not on the model)
		Elapsed time per phase (cycle time)	Process_phase.finish − Process_phase.start [day]
	Reduce development effort	Effort	Σ Process_activity.duration [person hour]
		Effort per phase	Σ Process_phase {Analysis}.works_mainly_on. Process_activity.duration [person hour]
		Effort per phase (ex. Analysis)	Σ Process_item {Analysis Document}. Process_activity.duration [person hour]
		Productivity	size/effort (see Section 2.2.5.3)
	Improve reuse	Reuse factor	(not on the model, see Section 2.2.5.3)
Analyse the reuse process	(none)	OO learning effort [person hour]	Σ G++.Study.duration + Σ C++.Study.duration
		Reuse effort	Σ G++Library.study.duration + Σ G++Library.research /browsing.duration [person hour]
		Economic analysis	(not on the model, see Section 2.2.5.3)

In our case the goals of the project correspond to the experimental hypothesis. Therefore we use the GQM approach to define response variables and the related metrics starting from the experimental hypothesis. As regards terminology, we will equate, in the following, goal and experimental hypothesis, response variable and measure.

Measures, defined according to Fenton's measurement framework (Fenton 1991), are formalized as scripts on the process model in an OMT query language. For instance (see Table 2.2), total effort is the sum of the duration of all instances of **Process Activity**; effort per subphase is the sum of the duration of all instances of **Process Activity** relating to **Analysis Document**.

In activities 4 and 5, procedures to collect, store and analyse measures are designed and the required tools are chosen. This activity is guided by the general principles and techniques of (Jones 1991, Hetzel 1993).

Design choices have to be made as regards: automatic or manual collection of data; design of collection procedures, sheets and forms; design of the schema of the database dedicated to store measures; design of analysis procedures and choice of techniques to present the elaborated results.

In the case of AEFTA the automated procedures are: definition of the process model, definition of measures, definition of the database for measures, elaboration of raw data into measures. The manual procedures are: collection of process data (effort, faults) through paper time sheets and fault report sheets, insertion of process data into the database, definition of the algorithms to transform raw data into measures.

Operationally, most process measures, and in particular time sheets and anomaly reports, were collected by hand by software engineers. Time sheets were filled in every day and collected weekly. The measurement manager verified each of them with the author during the first four weeks, then only occasionally and in case of possible misunderstandings.

The tool chosen to support the automated procedures is G++; the same tool used by the measured development process.

The definition of the process model uses the OMT analysis editor of G++; the definition of measures uses the annotation feature of the editor.

The database for measures is generated from the process model using the C++ code generation facility of the tool and the library to add persistency to classes; the translation is done automatically, except for the addition of persistency, which is manual.

The elaboration of raw data into measures is done in terms of C++ function members belonging to the persistent classes. The definition of these function members is done by hand starting from the definition of measures on the process model, but could easily be automated.

The advantages of basing the process measurement on a process model are: clear and unambiguous definition of measures, better understanding of the definition of measures by the staff, therefore improved reliability of the data collected and of the measures extracted from them.

The advantages of using the OO approach applied to measuring the process are: sharing of tools, training, know-how and mindset with the rest of the project; possibility to define a process model and a set of measures which evolve easily; less effort in the implementation of the technological support for measurement.

2.2.5.2 Goals, subgoals, measures

As stated in Section 2.2.1, the overall goal of the experiment is to verify if object-oriented technology improves quality the of the product and productivity, through the reuse opportunities which it offers, in a factory automation context. Table 2.2 shows the decomposition of this goal until measures are defined, the result of activities 2 and 3 in the measurement method.

The goal Improve quality is decomposed into Reduce faults, Improve maintainability and Improve reuse. Reduce faults is measured through the number of faults identified before and after the release of the product. Faults before release were not properly collected (see Section 2.4.2). Maintainability is considered as the other meaning of quality, and is measured, during development, as the availability and quality of documentation. Reuse is considered as an enabler for quality: the hypothesis is that reused documents and code are more reliable and maintainable. Moreover, reuse can be measured during development.

The goal Improve productivity requires the measuring of size and effort. Elapsed time and effort per phase are measured too. Again, reuse is considered as an enabler to improve productivity.

Reuse is a focal point of the experiment. For this reason a third high-level goal was added, Analyse the reuse process. The corresponding measures are reuse effort, OO learning effort, the reuse factor, and the economic analysis of introducing reuse.

2.2.5.3 Measures, definitions

In this section we define measures that are not defined on the process model.

Size Size measures used are Logical Source Statements (LSS) and Physical Source Statement (PSS). LSS and PSS are computed according to the IEEE 1045 standard (IEEE 1992). Briefly summarizing the definition, PSS is the number of physical lines of the file minus blank lines and comment lines. LSS is the number of executable statements ended by ';'.

Reuse factor The measures and terminology used here are taken from Frakes and Terry (1996) and Bieman and Karunanithi (1993). We compute the reuse factor on three reuse levels (defined as the level of abstraction of reused items): source code (both LSS and PSS), functions and classes. The first two are common in the procedural world, the last is typical of the OO approach.

The reuse factor is defined as follows.

$$reuse\_factor = 100 \cdot \frac{reused\_items}{total\_number\_of\_items} \quad (2.1)$$

A reused item is not modified, i.e. it is reused verbatim. Total number of items is the sum of reused and newly developed items. According to Bieman and Karunanithi (1993), this is a system perspective on reuse. Bieman also defines a client and a server perspective. In our case the servers are the libraries of classes which are part of the G++ tool, and the clients are the classes developed during the project. According to Frakes, this is a measure of external reuse, in the sense that all reused items are developed outside the project and are part of the G++ libraries. The same concept is defined as public reuse in Fenton (1991).

As regards leveraged reuse (i.e. reuse through inheritance), we consider it on the same level as the other types of reuse and we define that class A reuses class B if

1. A declares an instance of B, or
2. A inherits from B, or
3. A uses a member function of B.

In all cases A needs to know the interface of B. This means that in actual code the file containing the definition of class A must #include the header file of class A (B.h).

Reuse is considered to be transitive: if A reuses B and B reuses C, A reuses C too.

If a class is reused by many other classes, the class is counted once only. The rationale for this choice is economic: the class is paid for (whether developed or bought) once.

If a class is reused, all its LSS, PSS and member functions are considered to be reused. This choice was taken for the sake of simplicity in counting.

All measures were taken using a commercial package: PC-Metric/C++ v. 4.0 by Set Labs Inc. To determine the set of classes reused (according to the definition above), the output of the C++ compiler preprocessor was filtered using a simple AWK program.

Economic analysis We use the model proposed by Gaffney and Durek (1989) to analyse the cost of reusing software components.

$$C_{DEV} = C_{REUSE} \cdot R + C_{NEW} \cdot (1 - R) \qquad (2.2)$$

where

C_{DEV} = actual cost of development

C_{REUSE} = cost of development if the application were developed with reuse only

C_{NEW} = cost of development if the application were developed with new components only

R = reuse factor

and dividing by C_{NEW},

$$C = b \cdot R + 1 \cdot (1 - R) \qquad (2.3)$$

where

$$C = C_{DEV}/C_{NEW}$$
$$b = C_{REUSE}/C_{NEW}$$

The target of a reuse initiative is to reduce C, which depends on having $b < 1$.

While R (Reuse factor measure in Table 2.2) and C_{DEV} (Total effort measure in Table 2.2) are known, our goal is to estimate C_{REUSE} and C_{NEW} and therefore b. To estimate C_{REUSE} we assume

$$R \cdot C_{REUSE} = C_{ACQUISITION}$$
$$+ (OOlearning\_effort + reuse\_effort) \cdot c_h \qquad (2.4)$$

where c_h = cost per person hour.

To estimate C_{NEW} we use (from Equation 2.2)

$$C_{NEW} = \frac{C_{DEV} - C_{REUSE} \cdot R}{1 - R}$$

Therefore

$$b = \frac{C_{REUSE}}{C_{DEV} - C_{REUSE} \cdot R} \cdot (1 - R) \qquad (2.5)$$

2.3 RESULTS OF THE EXPERIMENT

In this section we present the values of the measures defined for the experiment.

2.3.1 Size

Figure 2.11 and 2.12 show the size of the application, computed in LSS, PSS, member functions and classes. The two former measures are functional, the two latter are object-oriented. Many size measures are used since there is no consensus on a single one. We use them all as indicators of size.

Besides the total number of items of the application (rightmost column), the number of newly written items is shown too (leftmost column). Total − new gives the number of reused items. For, instance the application is made up of 118 classes; 28 are new, 90 are reused.

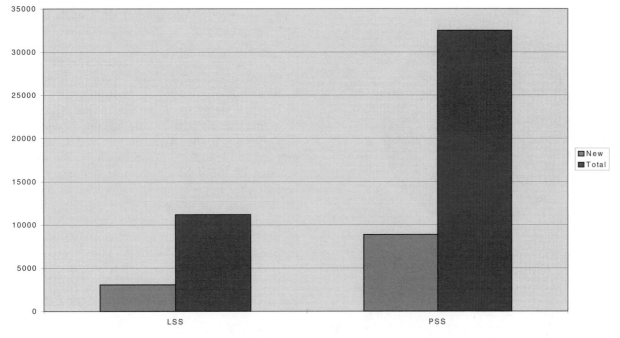

Figure 2.11   Size of the application (LSS, PSS)

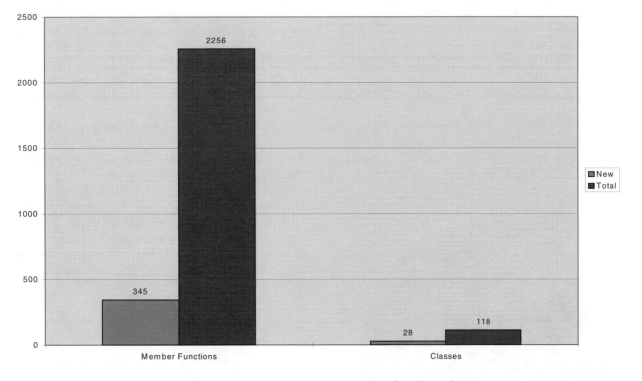

Figure 2.12   Size of the application (member functions, classes)

2.3.2 Effort, Duration

Figure 2.13 shows the effort per phase. Only technical activities are considered (analysis, design, coding and unit test) and learning (defined as studying the OO approach in general, studying OMT and C++, browsing class libraries, studying any document). Learning is not a technical activity but appears since it is an enabler for doing technical activities. As can be seen, it accounts for a heavy 20%. The figure on learning will be essential for the economic analysis of reuse.

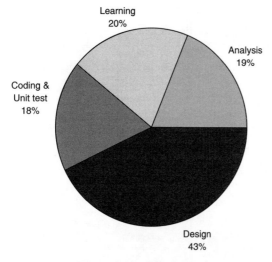

Figure 2.13   Effort per phase

Analysis and design together account for a surprising 62%. A shift of effort from coding to analysis and design is common in OO projects, but we think in this project this figure is partially explained by the CASE tool used. Its capabilities of automatic translation from analysis to design to code let the software engineer work at a higher level of abstraction. Moreover, in class design it is possible to write C++ code (such as function prototypes, data types, function bodies). This activity was counted as design and not as coding.

Figure 2.14 shows, in percentage terms, the duration of each phase. The concentrated simulated phase is performed twice. The first iteration, consisting mostly of analysis and design, delivered a first proto-

type of the application, running on a single machine and featuring nearly all the functionalities. The second iteration added the graphical user interface and fixed a number of analysis faults. The distributed simulated phase is performed once; it fixed other faults and distributed the application.

The first iteration of the first phase is no faster than that one for similar applications developed in C. This is due to the longer analysis and design activities and to the use of a new technology. But the next versions of the product are released much faster. Usually in C applications the next releases require a much longer time to be delivered, probably because of the difficulty in managing the growing complexity of the application, which sometimes causes older versions to be thrown away.

2.3.3 Object-oriented Technology Transfer

As was apparent from Figure 2.13, learning required an important effort during the project. The software engineers working on the project belonged to two distinct categories: experienced in OO technology (more than three years' experience in C++ and G++) and beginners (less than three months' experience in C++ and no experience in G++). There were no staff members with intermediate experience. It is therefore interesting to analyse their performance regarding learning.

In Figure 2.15 100% corresponds to the effort spent in learning plus technical activities (analysis, design, coding and test). These activities are then grouped into OO learning (studying C++ and OMT both in self-study and training, browsing and studying class libraries), non-OO learning (mainly GUI and BASEstar Open), and no learning (which corresponds to technical activities). The distribution of effort is again depicted according to the type of staff, OO experienced or OO beginner. Notice that,

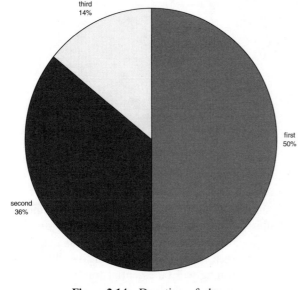

Figure 2.14   Duration of phases

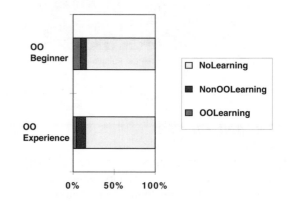

Figure 2.15   Learning effort vs. OO experience

in absolute numbers, the total OO learning effort for beginners is around twice that for experienced staff.

The first observation from these data confirms the meaning of words: beginners need much more time to learn (approximately twice as much; in percentage terms, 10% and 5%).

The second observation is less intuitive. Experienced staff have a non-zero effort dedicated to learning. In this case, learning accounts mostly for browsing and studying class libraries. We believe this 5% is a typical prerequisite for reusing components. Moreover, we believe this 5% could be, in general, much higher. First, the experienced staff developed the class libraries of G++, (except for the BASEstart Open library developed in this experiment). An experienced developer with no such knowledge of the libraries will need more time to study them. Second, the effort expended in browsing/ searching class libraries was underestimated. In fact all staff reported that, since these activities are inter-mixed with other activities (such as coding and designing), they found it difficult to remember precisely how long they spent on them when filling in their time sheets.

2.3.4 Reuse

In Figure 2.16 the external reuse factors are presented. The figures are high, ranging from 75% to 85% according to the reuse level at which they are computed.

This result can be read as a clear confirmation of the advantages of the OO approach and of the possibilities of reuse. The product is functionally rich (simulation, scheduling....), usable (GUI), complex (concentrated and distributed) and has been developed by writing only 28 new classes, or around 8900 PSS. The external reuse factor takes a system point of view. In the following, we take a client and a server point of view.

On the client perspective we analyse the origin of reused items. In Figure 2.17 a column represents all the items of the application that are reused, and the G++ class library from which they come.

Five class libraries exist: Mondrian for GUI building, Rodin for concurrency (processes, thread of controls and their scheduling), OAK for data structures (lists, hash tables, etc.), IntObj to build highly specialized interaction objects used for animation, and G++/BASEstar (a special version of the G++ distribution framework that uses BASEstar Open as network support). Since class libraries group classes by type, the figure shows which functionalities or services are most reused. For instance, of all reused classes, nearly 40% come from the Mondrian library and 40% from the OAK library (when computed in number of classes, see the rightmost column of Figure 2.17). In other words, 80% of reuse is due to classes from the information technology domain.

Figure 2.18 shows, for each library, how many different items are reused. This is a measure on the server side of the reuse relation. In terms of number of classes, Mondrian, OAK and G++/BASEstar are

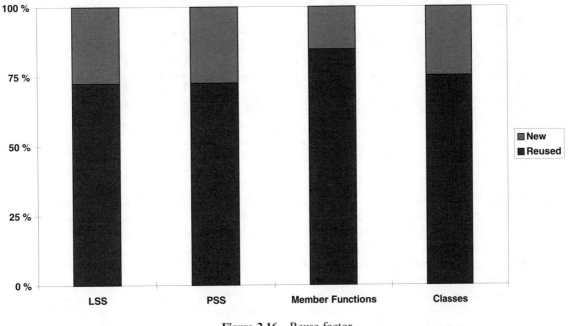

Figure 2.16 Reuse factor

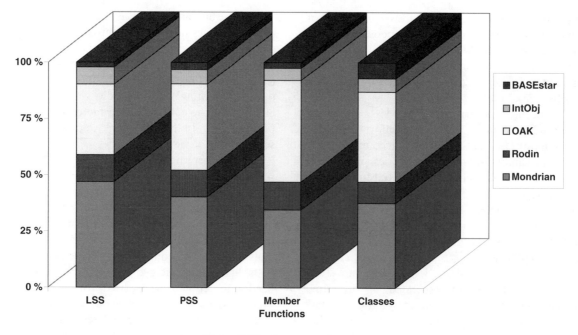

Figure 2.17   Reuse per class type

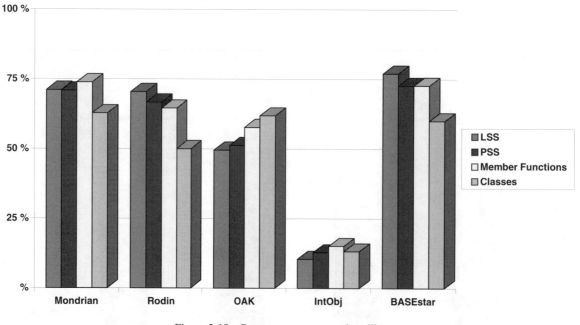

Figure 2.18   Reuse coverage per class library

the ones from which most items (around 70%) are reused. However, this result has very different interpretations, which depend on the nature of the library.

A GUI-building library such as Mondrian is a framework of highly interrelated classes and services that are reused as a whole. Whatever GUI you build (one window, one menu – or five windows, 50 menus), the same number of classes will be reused. In other words, this score is more a property of the library than of the

application being built. We believe this phenomenon is not peculiar to this GUI library, but general.

A data structures library such as OAK is a container of similar classes, not strongly interrelated. In this case, the 70% means that the application uses a large variety of data structures. The score depends on the particular application built and cannot be generalized. The same observation holds for the Rodin and IntObj libraries.

G++/BASEstar is a library of classes containing knowledge about the domain of the application and not, like the other libraries, about information technology. Moreover, it was developed during the project (more precisely it was developed *for reuse* in a previous part of the project while a latter phase developed the product *with reuse* of it, see Figure 2.6). Here 70% could suggest that the library was useful and was developed to be reused in future projects too. In any case, more observations from future projects using it are needed.

If we consider the size, in classes, of each library (around 55 for Mondrian and OAK, 10 for BASEstar, 16 for Rodin and 38 for IntObj), the reuse factors of Figure 2.16 are mostly explained by reuse for GUI building and data structures.

2.3.5 Economic Analysis of Reuse

First we apply Equation (2.5) to the whole project. A value of b < 1 indicates that reuse gives an economic advantage. In our case with R = .75 we obtain b = 0.2. Since the variables in Equation (2.5) can be very imprecise, a sensitivity analysis relative to the threshold value of b = 1 is important. This value is obtained with a variation of −50% of R, or with an increment of 100% for C_{REUSE}. Since we are confident that their precision is better than these variations, we conclude that there was an important economic advantage in applying reuse in this project.

This is not always true the first time reuse is applied in an organization. The result can be explained by the low cost of the G++ libraries (equivalent to around two person-months) and of the FOR reuse project developing the G++/BASEstar library (two person-months).

2.4 LESSONS LEARNED

The first goal of the experiment (Improve quality) could not be proved quantitatively. Nevertheless, the application is running to the satisfaction of the users. The second one (Improve productivity) was satisfied thanks to the use of off-the-shelf libraries. For custom-made libraries, no meaningful conclusion can be drawn until more data from other projects is available. The reuse process was successful, as demonstrated by the high reuse factor.

In the following, a qualitative analysis of the project is performed.

2.4.1 Successes

The project developed the specified application on time, using a new technology for the first time and achieving a high reuse rate, and therefore an improvement in productivity. We believe this can surely be defined as a success.

The reasons for this success can be summarized as follows.

- The staff was mainly composed of OO beginners, but they were assisted by some software engineers who were experts in all technical aspects (the programming language, the CASE tool, the class libraries).
- The working plan allocated time for learning, both in dedicated training classes and in discussion and brainstorming.
- Time was allocated for analysis and design, without immediate pressure on coding.
- An incremental life cycle was used, starting from a kernel subset of the application, then extended incrementally. This life cycle was supported by the CASE tool used.
- Reuse was planned and enabled: time and personnel were planned to achieve reuse, the staff experienced in OO knew the libraries available very well, and the same staff developed the new library.

2.4.2 Problems

A number of analyses on the quality of the product were planned, but were not performed.

- It was planned to collect (manually) fault reports and change requests, and to analyse them in order to assess the quality of the product. In fact, during and at the end of the project very few of these reports were available and it was clear that they were not representing what actually happened. This was caused by a sloppy definition of the rules for issuing the reports. The situation did not change after these rules were improved. The use of a CASE tool which really eased changes promoted at best the evolutionary incremental life cyle. But the lack of integration between the CASE tool and configuration management meant that software engineers were not forced to issue the reports.
- It was planned to execute static analyses on the product to assess its quality. This analysis was not satisfactory because the static analysis and metrication tools for C++ available on the market

today are, in fact, C tools and do not capture the essence of object oriented-design and programming.

- It was also planned to compare the project with a similar one, already carried out at Digital using BASEstar Open and the C language. The comparison was not meaningful, because the processes (life cycle, tools, people) are too heterogeneous; and because productivity measures, expressed in lines of code per person per month, are not comparable if the programming language is changed.

2.5 FUTURE PLANS FOR FURTHER SOFTWARE PROCESS IMPROVEMENT

The AEFTA experiment led the management at Digital to take the following decisions for further software process improvement.

1. Improvement of productivity
   - As far as possible, use the OO approach and off-the-shelf libraries in future projects.
   - Use the G++/BASEstar library in future BASEstar Open projects, monitor reuse from this library and refine the economic analysis. Use this new data to take decisions about building other proprietary custom libraries intended for internal use.
   - Develop competence centres around the libraries. In the AEFTA project, even the experienced OO staff, who participated in developing the libraries, needed a not negligible portion of project effort to achieve reuse. This is due to both the complexity and the size of the libraries. The same members of staff reported that, although proficient in using a certain library (e.g. data structures), they nevertheless needed considerable time to feel the same proficiency in using another library of the same type. Therefore we believe that a company should build competence centres around libraries, or types of libraries, to best exploit the competences of their staff.
2. Improvement of process control
   - Instead of lines of code per person per day, define other productivity metrics, independent of the programming language and capable of taking reuse into account. Analyse the impact of such new measures on all related management activities (pricing policies, cost accounting, . . .).
   - Automate and enforce as much as possible the production of change requests and fault reports. The improved reliability of change requests and fault reports is expected to improve the quality assessment of both the process and the product.

REFERENCES

Aarsten A. and Morisio M. (1996) Using object oriented technology to measure the software process. *Aquis 96*, Florence, January.

AMI, Applications of Metrics in Industry (1992) *AMI Handbook, a quantitative approach to software management* (London: CSSE, South Bank Polytechnic).

Basili V.B. (1995) Applying the GQM paradigm in the Experience Factory. In Fenton, N., Whitty, R. and Iizuka I. (eds). *Software Quality Assurance and Measurement* (International Thomson Press).

Basili V.B. and Rombach H.D. (1988) The TAME Project: Towards improvement-oriented software environments. *IEEE Transactions on Software Engineering*, **14**(6), June.

Bieman J. and Karunanithi S. (1993) Candidate reuse metrics for object oriented and ADA software. *IEEE-CS 1st Int. Software Metrics Symposium*.

DEC. (1990) *BASEstar Open Introduction*.

Fenton N. (1991) *Software Metrics – A Rigorous Approach* (Chapman & Hall).

Frakes W. and Terry C. (1996) Software reuse and reusability metrics and models. *ACM Computing Survey*, **28**(2), June.

Gaffney J.E. and Durek T.A. (1989) Software reuse – key to enhanced productivity: some quantitative models. *Information and Software Technology*, **31** (5 1989); 258–267.

Hetzel B. (1993). *Making Software Measurement Work* (QED).

IEEE (1992) *IEEE 1061 Standard for a Software Quality Metrics Methodology*.

IEEE (1992) *IEEE 1045 Standard for Software Productivity Metrics*.

Jones C. (1991) *Applied Software Measurement* (McGraw-Hill).

Kitchenham B.A., Linkman S. G. and Law D.T. (1994) Critical review of quantitative assessment. *Software Engineering Journal*, March, pp. 43–53.

Law D. (1994) *DESMET Methodology – Specification of Requirements and Architecture* (Manchester: National Computing Centre), vol. 2.

Menga G., Elia G. and Mancin M. (1993) G++: an environment for object oriented design and prototyping of manufacturing systems. In Gruver, W. and Boudreaux, G. (eds). *Intelligent Manufacturing: Programming Environments for CIM* (Springer Verlag).

Morisio M. (1995) A methodology to measure the software process. *Proceedings of the Annual Oregon Workshop on Software Metrics*, Portland, OR, 5–7 June.

Rumbaugh J., Blaha M., Premerlani W., Eddy F. and Lorensen W. (1991) *Object Oriented Modelling and Design* (Addison Wesley).

3

ALCAST – Irish Company Experiences with ESSI

Anne Downey[a], Fran Keating[a], Janet Byrne[b], Fergal O'Sullivan[c]

[a] Q · SET, Galway, Ireland
[b] The Voluntary Health Insurance Board, Dublin, Ireland
[c] CSK Software, Dublin, Ireland

3.1 INTRODUCTION

3.1.1 What ALCAST Is

The initial aim of the **A**utomated **L**ife **C**ycle **A**pproach to **S**oftware **T**esting (ALCAST) project was to improve manual testing practices and then automate them in two finance/insurance sector organizations. This aim was expanded during the course of the project to include improving review processes.

The ALCAST consortium consisted of three companies: the Voluntary Health Insurance Board (VHI), Quay Financial Software (CSK) and Quality Software Engineering Technologies (Q·SET). The main interest groups for this project are companies that test software as part of their product development life cycle, and those that need to automate the process or parts of it, using tools.

The incremental marginal costs of the project were 100% grant-aided by ESSI, (the European Systems and Software Initiative), an accompanying measure to the EU research and technological development programme in the field of information technologies (1990–1994). The pilot call went out in April 1993 and there were approximately 960 applications to the ESSI office for funding. Thirty-six of these were from Ireland, with four successful applicants, of which ALCAST was one.

3.1.2 Goals

The goal of ESSI is to promote improvements in the software development process in industry, so as to achieve greater efficiency, higher quality, and greater economy. This is to be accomplished by applying state-of-the-art software engineering in a wide range of industries, on the basis of a thorough analysis of each individual company. By enhancing the software production process, improving the efficiency, the quality and the cost-effectiveness of software, there will be a substantial added value to all sectors of activity in which software is regarded as a key component. Given the extremely broad base of software-related activities in European industry, the consequent knock-on effect aims to have a significant impact on European competitiveness. A key condition of the ESSI programme is the dissemination by the participants of the results of the improvement projects, across borders and across industry sectors.

VHI wanted to improve software quality through systematic testing and to reflect this by reducing corrective maintenance. It specifically wanted to:

- introduce an enhanced formalized testing life cycle;
- focus on error prevention rather than detection;
- automate the standards and procedures process as far as was possible;

- use Groupware to improve communication/workflow;
- reduce system revisits due to ineffective testing.

CSK recognized that effective software testing was pivotal in terms of customer and distributor confidence and thus wanted to integrate testing into its Groupware-based development processes. In addition, CSK wanted:

- formal test planning with input from marketing and customers;
- the test life cycle to be integrated with the CSK workflow system;
- automation of regression testing;
- knowledge of the reliability of released software discovery of errors earlier in the life cycle.

Q·SET was the subcontractor to the ALCAST experiment and its main goals were:

- to help improve the partners' software engineering practices and processes through training interventions and direct implementation support;
- to record the real-life experiences of a software testing improvement initiative, for dissemination to the other organizations with which it works, and therefore help them to replicate the ALCAST successes;
- to install, develop and evaluate workflow management software, Q·SYS Groupware[1].

3.1.3 Tasks

During Phase 1, software testing practices in VHI and CSK were first assessed against current best practice, or, in effect, what was currently available in the area of automated tools in the industry. CSK conducted a survey of these tools, using 'demo' copies, and teams were formed to spend up to two days evaluating each tool, and then report on findings. (See Appendix 3.2 for the combined evaluation reports.) Having identified key areas for improvement, the V Model was implemented as a process framework and then further enhanced using the Systematic Test and Evaluation Process (STEP)[2] methodology.

In Phase 2 of the project, VHI piloted an on-line test environment with automated defect tracking and change management. In CSK, support for STEP was included in their existing corporate information system, and automation of both regression testing and static analysis took place.

3.1.4 Costs and Resources

The ALCAST project ran from January 1994 until June 1995. Over the period of 18 months, VHI involved 18 people, CSK involved 12 people and Q·SET involved a maximum of four people. The total grant provided was ECU 369,203. Both VHI and CSK enlisted the help of a senior company executive as the project sponsors. An 'end-of-project' dissemination event was held in Ireland (estimated 150 companies attending) and the report on which this chapter is based was distributed in booklet form to Q·SET customers (numbering more than 7000).

3.1.5 Results

The project was regarded as a success in all three companies. The partners achieved their stated goals, and plans are in place for company-wide implementation. VHI reduced pre-release defects costs by 40% and post-release maintenance costs by 30%. CSK reduced the number of defects by 50%, despite an increase in application complexity of 30%.

3.1.6 Conclusions

The main conclusions were as follows.

Re. specific ALCAST lessons
- Testing should be done at all stages, including the project requirements stage.
- The STEP methodology has proved effective when tailored for individual company needs.
- Test automation is beneficial but has a significant learning curve.
- Metrics should be kept simple and usable.
- Training for best practices is essential to ensure the success of a company-wide implementation.

Re. general project management issues
- Improvement must be managed as a mainstream project in a company, with equal priority to core business projects.
- Expertise in tools and automation is a company asset which should be organized into a team structure and used as a resource on projects.
- The initial assessment in the cycle of **A**ssess, **I**mprove and **M**easure is critical for gauging the success of the project.

3.2 BACKGROUND INFORMATION

3.2.1 ALCAST Consortium Members and their Roles

VHI is a self-financing, not-for-profit health insurance organization that was set up in 1957. It insures 1.3 million members, which is approximately one-third of the population of Ireland. Its products include various levels of insurance for hospital in-patient health care, in-patient professional fees, and primary health care. Membership is based on the principles of community rating, open enrollment and lifetime cover. VHI interacts electronically with most of the larger industries and services in Ireland for member billing and subscription collection purposes, and with most of the providers of health care – hospitals and consultants – for claims assessment and payment purposes. Throughout the term of ALCAST, VHI, as Prime User, interfaced with the ESSI office, piloted improvements in testing and automation, and participated in dissemination events.

CSK's products are InVision, a real-time digital information delivery and presentation system, and InVision+, a suite of integrated dealer analytic tools with money markets, capital markets and risk management applications. The company was established in 1985 and is the dominant supplier of digital dealing systems in Ireland. Today it employs over 70 staff and has over 50 clients in 15 countries, with life assurance companies, investment banks, stock-brokers, money brokers, treasuries and large corporations ranking among its client base. During the term of ALCAST, CSK, as a Partner, piloted improvements in testing and automation, and participated at dissemination events.

Q·SET is an international supplier of training and software, specializing in software quality and global quality management systems. It provides public courses, in-house courses, software to automate the workflows and documentation associated with quality management systems, and support to implement software engineering change. Customers of Q·SET include the world's leading software companies, in-house software development teams and purchasers of software. Q·SET has experience in applying ISO 9001[3]/TickIT[4] to software engineering and it provides Capability Maturity Model (CMM)[5] assessment services. Having worked prior to ALCAST with both VHI and CSK on improving their software quality processes, Q·SET was aware of each company's strengths and objectives in the area, and was well placed to facilitate, steer and coordinate the consortium's proposal for ESSI funding. Q·SET, as a Partner, piloted Groupware technology, provided tailored training courses to VHI and CSK, and held dissemination events to publicize ALCAST results.

3.2.2 Communication between the Partners

Project progress, findings and information were shared between the member companies at an informal level by telephone and e-mail, and latterly via Lotus Notes[6], and at a more formal level by regularly convened meetings. A steering committee with representatives from all three companies managed the overall project.

3.2.3 Internal and External Dissemination

All material prepared for external dissemination was also available internally. A mid-term ALCAST booklet and a final report were produced and distributed to all the ALCAST pilot projects, and also at the mid-term dissemination event, which was attended by over 150 Irish companies. The material was also distributed to selected Q·SET customers with a specific interest in improving their software testing. Project information was also disseminated to project members through the customized training sessions.

At VHI, the project results, findings and information were communicated internally to the ALCAST pilot project teams at monthly team meetings. More general information relating to ALCAST was presented to the Software Development and Technical Services Department at the end of each measurement phase. ALCAST has also been communicated at an organizational level using management presentations and reports.

Internal dissemination at CSK was widespread because the creation of a new Product Quality Assurance Department was coincident with the introduction of the STEP methodology. This group was trained in the implementation of STEP. All information about the pilot development projects was available to everyone in the company via Lotus Notes (the CSK corporate information system). This dissemination will be further amplified by the newly formed Special Interest Group focusing on development testing and also by the assimilation of CSK by the world-wide CSK group. Experiences of the ALCAST experiment can now be disseminated to a wider internal and external audience, and sister companies have already expressed an interest in CSK's improved methodologies and processes.

In both VHI and CSK, the people involved in the pilot development projects were also trained in the implementation of STEP. Modified versions of the STEP testing methodology have been adopted for the individual companies, and dissemination of this has been assisted by the inclusion of procedures covering STEP in, respectively, the software development, and on-line quality, procedures manuals.

3.3 STARTING SCENARIO

None of the participating organizations had undergone a formal assessment (TickIT or Bootstrap[7] or CMM). The typical process of software development in VHI at the outset of the ALCAST project is outlined in the following steps.

- The Business Planning Department defined the scope of projects.
- A feasibility study was completed in some cases.
- Resources were assigned when the project was approved and prioritized by Executive Management.
- The traditional project life cycle was followed for projects developed using 3GLs; 4GL systems were developed using Rapid Application Development (RAD).
- In both cases a requirements-gathering exercise was prepared and signed off.
- For medium to large systems, outline and detailed designs were produced.
- The project plan included a detailed plan for all phases of the development life cycle.
- Program specifications and test plans were produced manually without the support of automated tools.
- Testing was done after coding, and in most cases Unit/System/Acceptance tests were carried out.
- User manuals, operations and data control manuals were produced before implementation.

CSK's typical software development process steps, at the outset of the ALCAST project, were as follows.

- Marketing defined the scope of projects.
- Resources were assigned when the project was approved and prioritized by senior management.
- The standard CSK development life cycle was followed. This is a form of the traditional Waterfall model and is tailored according to the project needs. Typically it produces a Project Plan, Requirements Specification, Architectural and Detailed Designs, Code, Software Release Notes, System and Integration Test Results, Alpha and Beta Test Results.
- Informal unit testing was done during coding.
- Code reviews, coding standards and guidelines were used to ensure production of quality code.
- For an Alpha release, the software and documentation was delivered to the product QA group where an independent spiral of 'test and fix' would be used, following both formal and informal test specifications.
- For a Beta release, software was installed on selected client sites. This phase provided acceptance and real-use testing.
- For a full product release, the software was placed on the order list.

3.3.1 Technical

VHI currently uses a Bull Mainframe system for its core business applications and a Digital VAX and Alpha for its client/server applications. The client/server applications include Oracle, Teamlinks E-Mail, Calendar Manager and MSOffice, among others. VHI has a LAN running on EtherNet and a WAN which connects the branch offices, hospitals and the Dutch Insurance Network to Head Office in Dublin. The development languages used include COBOL, Visual Basic, SQL and Oracle.

Development languages in CSK include C, C++ and Visual Basic, with development environments covering Windows, Win NT, Windows '95, OS/2 and most UNIX platforms. EtherNet and Token Ring networks are in use, supporting NETBIOS and TCP/IP connections. All CSK employees have access to Lotus Notes as part of the corporate information system, with remote links set up for several customer and distributor sites.

3.3.2 Business

VHI has operated in a monopoly situation since inception, but the possibility of competition became a reality due to the impact of the 1994 Third European Directive. As a result of this, the issues facing the software development function included:

- reaction to market forces and competition by faster development and implementation of systems;
- reduction of maintenance costs;
- minimizing of manual procedures by the developers, to allow them more time for technical work,

in order to keep pace with the rapid advances in technology;

- design and implementation of an automated approach to system testing, in order to reduce administration costs and development time.

CSK software is seen as 'mission-critical' by its customers, and so the main issues facing the software development group at the outset of ALCAST included the need to:

- deliver stable, resilient and portable products in a timely manner, to keep pace with competitors;
- reduce maintenance costs by ensuring quality in the products from the start;
- reduce development costs and time scales by implementing an automated approach to system testing.

The only constraint imposed on the ALCAST project was that the experiment should not be too disruptive for the pilot project teams involved. It was not given higher priority over core business projects.

3.3.3 Organizational

VHI's part in the project was managed by Technical Services Department, with a Business Analyst working almost full-time on the project. This person liaised with the Quality Analyst from Software Development. A number of staff changes (due to business changes) took place during the project. These changes necessitated additional work on ALCAST in terms of communication and restarts. CSK's part in the project was managed by the Process Improvement role in the company reporting to the Managing Director. Following the appointment of a Production Manager to oversee all software production, the Process Improvement role reported to the Production Manager. The CSK Steering Group for ALCAST consisted of a Senior Development Manager, the Product Quality Assurance Manager, who has responsibility for product quality, and the Quality Assurance Manager, who has responsibility for process and workflow.

3.3.4 Cultural

VHI is a mature organisation, which has undergone many technological changes and developments in quality software practices over recent years. There is a good mixture of young and experienced staff in the IT division. The company was ready to

implement new methods and software engineering best practices, provided that they were not overly disruptive.

CSK is a relatively young but fast-growing organization, recognized for producing high-quality solutions. Its workforce is in general young and enthusiastic with a good mix of technical and business skills. Its adoption of Lotus Notes as an enabling technology has been well received.

3.3.5 Skills

The pilot project leaders involved with the experiment had varying degrees of experience in taking projects from requirements to implementation phase. Some had test experience. The members of the teams ranged from very experienced to moderately experienced programmers, with skills in one or more of the development languages. The ALCAST team included senior managers from a development and technical services background. The team at CSK had some Notes development expertise as well as exposure to Software Process Improvement (SPI) and quality management systems. The VHI team had experience in both traditional and Rapid Application Development (RAD) methodologies.

3.3.6 Management of the Project

Q·SET's approach to Project Management was used in the first instance. This is a six-phase methodology which covers every stage from project establishment to evaluation and post-mortem; based on this approach, Table 3.1 outlines the initial project stages. (It is not possible to detail every issue and finding in the project stages, e.g. at 'Project Stage Vision 1' on Table 3.1, CSK decided that the correct direction for it was to:

Implement a life-cycle approach to Testing;
Find suitable tools to support the Testing process;
Incorporate Testing into the CSK Lifecycle and
    Development Management.)

3.4 EXPECTED OUTCOMES

Apparently, the ALCAST consortium was the first group of companies in Ireland, and possibly Europe, to use groupware software in the implementation of a software engineering quality system. The partners expected to benefit from more effective and efficient quality systems, and greater user

Table 3.1   Initial ALCAST Project Stages

Project stage	Stage description	Stage timing
Project Initiation	Start the ESSI Project and the spiral of continuous software testing improvement	Jan. 94
Status 1	Assess the initial status of software testing capability against the chosen benchmarks	Feb. 94
Vision 1	Decide the required future vision of software testing capability (e.g. full system, integration, unit testing and reviews supported by testing tools and Groupware)	Mar. 94
Plan 1	Understand all that needs to be done to achieve Part 1 of this vision (e.g. system testing supported by regression and capture/playback tools)	Apr. 94
Design 1	Decide what gets done when and by whom to achieve Part 1 of this vision and pilot the changes on the selected projects	May – Jun. 94
Implement 1	Implement the training plan, utilizing the successful improvements on the project in question	Jul. – Aug. 94
Manage 1	Monitor the progress and start the cycle of improvement for Part 2 of the vision	Sept. 94
Status 2	Assess the status of software testing capability against the chosen benchmarks after the implementation of Phase 1 of the improvements	Oct. 94
Report 1	Produce the booklet reporting on Phase 1	Nov. 94
Vision 2	Revise the required future vision of software testing capability (e.g. full system, integration, unit testing and reviews supported by testing tools and Groupware)	Nov. 94
Plan 2	Decide what gets done when, and by whom to achieve Part 2 of the vision (e.g. unit testing supported by static and dynamic analysis tools and supporting the testing process with Groupware)	Dec. 94
Design 2	Decide what gets done when and by whom to achieve Part 2 of this vision and pilot the changes on the selected projects	Jan. 95
Implement 2	Implement the training plan using the successful improvements on the projects in question	Feb. – Mar. 95
Manage 2	Monitor the progress and finish the cycle of improvement started by ESSI and begin another cycle of improvement sponsored by the candidate companies	Apr. 95
Status 3	Assess the final status of software testing capability against the chosen benchmarks	May 95
Report 2	Produce the booklet reporting on Phases 1 and 2	Jun. 95
Project Completion	Wind up and report on the ESSI project	Jun. 95

participation in the continuous improvement of their software engineering processes.

All of the ALCAST partners considered that Testing warranted serious attention, and that the project's success depended on concentrating on both product and process quality. So ALCAST was considered to provide an ideal basis for motivating each company's software engineers to contribute effectively to future quality software engineering initiatives, and ESSI's aim of encouraging and shaping quality software engineering initiatives bestowed significant benefits.

All companies involved in ALCAST wanted to adopt a life-cycle approach to software testing which would provide benefits as follows:

- lower maintenance costs due to less frequent changes to live systems;
- uniformity and consistency of approach to the testing process;
- higher quality systems for end-users;
- more end-user confidence in the software development process;

- enforcement of the review process;
- continuity of approach as software development staff change;
- reduction in the number of bugs caused by oversights in testing;
- more automation in testing, leading to greater accuracy as well as a decrease in the time and costs of testing;
- improved communication and workflow with the use of Groupware tools.

As mandated by ESSI, ALCAST experiences and results would be disseminated through two 'Information Events' and an interim and a final report, and the information reused by other organizations throughout Europe. However, due to the marketing and training activities of Q·SET through its European network, the dissemination would be on a wider and more comprehensive scale, and the dissemination activities would be extended to include training courses, implementation support programmes, and publications.

3.5 WORK PERFORMED

As the project spanned 18 months, it was agreed that a two-phase approach would be used. Adopting AIM (Assess, Improve and Measure), Q·SET's modified version of the Deming Cycle of Continuous Improvement[8], the pilot projects were to be assessed to gauge the current status of testing capability. Improvements would be designed and implemented, and the effects of these improvements would be measured.

Prior to the project, the status of testing in both companies was as outlined in Section 3.3.

3.5.1 At VHI

VHI selected three pilot projects which were scheduled for implementation over the lifetime of ALCAST. These projects were considered to be representative of the type of work carried out in the Software Development Department, in terms of the business objective, platform type and development language.

A metrics programme was put in place to provide a baseline to compare the results before and after the project, in order to test and demonstrate the effects of changes to the Software Testing Process, and to assess where VHI stood in terms of industry best practice.

The initial metrics concluded that 56% of all issues reported related to testing, and that VHI was in line with the industry norm. The focus was on error detection, the timing of testing was after system design, coverage was largely unknown and visibility of testing was poor. Metrics proved difficult and time-consuming to collect from the start, and posed a number of questions, e.g. what exactly differentiates corrective maintenance from enhancements? If a change is necessary due to something that should have been discovered at the design stage, to which category does it belong?

In order to change the focus to error prevention, and to include good test visibility and coverage, the STEP testing methodology was selected and adapted to integrate with the development life cycle in VHI (see Figure 3.1).

A Testing User Manual was written for the project teams involved, and a *How to Collect Metrics* document was designed, with metrics being collected by the project teams on a weekly basis. (See Appendix 3.1 'Metrics at VHI – User Aids'). Informal and then formal reviews were introduced. A condensed *How to Hold Reviews* document was designed.

The tools evaluated were *STEPMaster*[9], *Q·SYS Groupware* and *SQA TeamTest*[10], the last of which was found to meet VHI requirements in the short term, with *Q·SYS Groupware* having potential in the medium term. (See Appendix 3.2.)

Workshops on Test and Risk Analysis were held. (See Appendix 3.3 for "How to" guides.)

V H I T e s t i n g L i f e - C y c l e

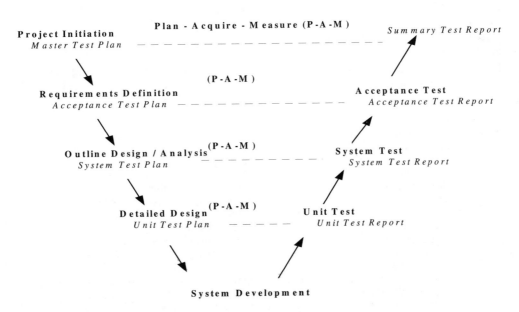

Figure 3.1 Tailored STEP diagram at VHI

Standards for developing software were enhanced to cater for new technology and updated practices, during the ALCAST Project.

The following sources of data were used to measure progress:

- helpdesk records, change management software and metrics forms designed by the ALCAST team;
- metrics data was collected on a weekly basis from the project teams;
- project leader discussions were held at the end of each phase;
- interviews with project team members were held monthly as 'open forum discussions';
- formal reviews of documents produced during Phase 2;
- Software Development work report sheets.

3.5.2 At CSK

The STEP methodology was selected and tailored to integrate with the chosen development life cycle. The newly formed Product Quality Assurance department was sent on a three-day STEP training course, with follow-up workshops in-house to assess the implementation progress. Support for STEP was added to the CSK development workflow in Lotus Notes and applied on pilot projects. (See Appendix 3.2 for a view of the forms implemented in Notes.)

A number of tools to support automated regression testing were identified, short-listed and evaluated, and finally one, WinRunner[11], was selected and deployed on a project. Analysis of the data at the end of Phase 1 showed that implementation of the STEP processes, at the system and integration test levels, was successful in finding bugs. However, these bugs should be caught earlier in the life cycle. Therefore Phase 2 focused on implementing STEP during the earlier development stages. This involved the following.

- Coaching in testing techniques was given to selected development projects.
- Tools to support development testing processes were identified and evaluated. (See Appendix 3.2.)
- Workshops on Test and Risk Analysis were held. (See Appendix 3.3.)
- A Special Interest Group (SIG), to support the improvement and dissemination of development testing, was set up.
- Metrics on testing were gathered from the Notes databases.

3.6 TECHNICAL ENVIRONMENT

Refer to Appendix 3.2 for details of the tool evaluation tasks carried out at both VHI and CSK. Table 3.2 presents a summary of the application of the tools considered.

Q·SET had a strong interest and experience in software development process improvement, software testing, reviews and measurement, and contributed in the following ways:

- tracked the progress of the ESSI programme and coordinated the ALCAST proposal;
- designed a project management plan;
- tailored its publicly available courses to meet ALCAST-specific needs;
- provided training and implementation support, including workshop and coaching sessions;
- attended and chaired Steering Committee meetings;
- organized dissemination events;
- authored the mid-term booklet;
- customized Q·SYS Groupware.

Table 3.3 sets out the training and implementation support designed for and provided to the VHI and CSK by Q·SET.

Table 3.2 Summary of the application of the tools considered by CSK

Tools	Application area
WinRunner/XRunner (CSK)	GUI Regression Testing
PR QAC/C++ (CSK)	Source Code Quality/Readiness for Testing
Cantata (CSK)	White-box testing
STEPMaster (VHI)	Test environment support for STEP
SQA TeamTest (VHI)	Defect Tracking and Change Management
Lotus Notes (VHI)	Groupware platform
Q·SYS Groupware(VHI)	Documentation and workflow automation
Purify, Quantify (CSK)	Memory and performance testing
Pure-Coverage (CSK)	Code coverage testing

Table 3.3 Q·SET's Training and Implementation Support

Course	Content
SEI CMM (Software Assessment Training)	Software Engineering Institute Capability Maturity Model
STEP Testing Methodology	Systematic Test & Evaluation Process
Test Techniques	General
Metrics training	Why, what, how to gather and analyse
Formal Review Process (VHI)	Review process
Lotus Notes Introduction (VHI)	Lotus Notes basics (external trainer)
Lotus Notes Administration (VHI)	Lotus Notes advanced (external trainer)
Test Methodology implementation	STEP workshop
Test Methodology advanced implementation	STEP workshop
Development Testing Coaching	Test Analysis and Planning
Risk Analysis	Failure Modes Effects Analysis, Cause Effect Analysis and Likelihood analysis

3.7 PHASES OF THE EXPERIMENT

The phases of the experiment, including the major milestones on the project, are described in Table 3.1.

3.8 RESULTS AND ANALYSIS AT VHI

3.8.1 Technical

3.8.1.1 Corrective maintenance was reduced by 30%

A metrics programme was put in place at VHI to provide a baseline in order to test and demonstrate the effects of changes to the software testing process, i.e. compare 'before and after'. Initially it was hoped that the department's corrective maintenance would be reduced by 50%. This was overly optimistic as only two of the pilot projects had phases which were sent into production during the ALCAST Project. It is hoped that this figure will be realized when the improvements have been fully implemented. Unfortunately, this will only be measurable after projects have gone into production. The improvement was partly attributable to ALCAST, partly to the separate standards project and partly to the increased awareness of software quality by the staff in the Software Development department.

3.8.1.2 Defect fix-cost pre-release improved by 40%

The pilot project metrics revealed increased defects being found at the early stages of the project, i.e. 15% at June 1995, compared to 0% in the initial measurement phase in early 1994; 7.5% was measured at the end of Phase 1 (December 1994). This

was due largely to informal and later a more formalized review process which was implemented by the pilot project teams. VHI considered this to be a very positive move towards error prevention and lower fix-costs per defect. See Figure 3.2 for detailed graphs. The results gathered by Boehm and reported by Tom Gilb in [15] show how each phase has a fix-cost,

% of TEST & REVIEW DEFECTS found by PHASE at January 1994

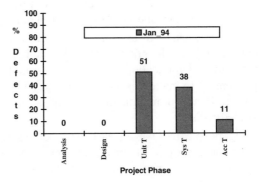

% of TEST & REVIEW DEFECTS found by PHASE at June 1995

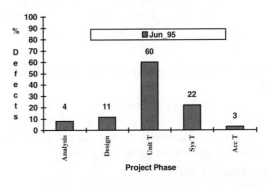

Figure 3.2 Defects (% by Phase) at VHI

which increases significantly when it occurs in the later stages of the development cycle. Applying these results to this case, the VHI pre-release defect fix-costs have fallen by 40%.

3.8.2 Adoption of STEP

The project leader discussions and the interviews with pilot project team members highlighted the fact that STEP was having a beneficial effect, and there was little resistance to taking it on board as part of the standards. The main findings in these discussions were the following.

Benefits of introducing STEP for the Software Engineering Process

- People felt more confident that they were doing a better job of test coverage.
- Moving between projects had become easier as the improvement in documentation standards resulted in a shorter learning curve, in terms of becoming familiar once again with each project.
- There was more inter-project communication with a central keeper of useful documentation and information for dissemination to all interested projects.
- Users are now more actively involved with project requirements review and acceptance test planning.
- Projects are starting to examine risk, both in the context of risk to the project internally, and risks in the delivered applications. There is still room for improvement to make this analysis more systematic and to focus on minimization strategies for the identified risks.
- Forcing people to take an early view of testing strategy on a project has meant an improvement in the way requirements are presented, gathered and reviewed.
- Having invested time and effort learning how to apply the test methodology STEP, people starting on new projects or phases are seeing real-time savings the second time around. Reuse of test plans and code review checklists for generating tests is common.

Weakness of introducing STEP for the Software Process

- All expressed the view that utilizing metrics was the only way to determine the success or otherwise of the project. However, improvements must be made in the process of gathering them.
- Comments on metrics
  - Gathering metrics is difficult.

- There must be a simple set of metrics.
- Five minutes is the maximum time it should take to complete a form.

Current testing practice

- Test coverage is perceived to have improved.
- The involvement of users in the development of acceptance and system tests is widespread, due to an awareness of the need for early test planning.
- The defacto standard on projects is to have three levels of testing – unit, system and acceptance.
- Desk checking before test execution has been used to good effect.

Current technical review process

- Formal reviews are common.
- 'Error guessing' checklists (a prioritized list of the most common pitfalls on projects which the project teams designed) are starting to be used on projects.
- Ill-defined projects have been postponed after formally reviewing requirements with end-users. This might not have been discovered until the design phase, if we had not tested our requirements so formally.

Feedback on measurement form

- Each entry area on the form must be clearly defined.
- It is all or nothing – to compare one project with another, similar categories of data must be captured.
- Project teams must be aware of the objectives for metrics-gathering.

Preparation time for testware documentation decreased when team members started second and subsequent pilot project phases, i.e. reuse. Having put the testware in place on the initial pilot phase, they were then able to reuse this. System controls and test planning have moved to significantly earlier phases of the development life cycle, with an additional increase in planning activity. Test checklists, which had been informal, have evolved into full test plans with built-in schedules and risk evaluations.

3.8.3 Formal Reviews

A formal review process was introduced and many documents were formally reviewed during Phase 2. The general consensus is that these documents are of high quality and greatly improved on the original versions produced in earlier phases. The review records collected during the review allow for easy metrics-gathering and subsequent analysis.

3.8.4 Tools and Automation

In the area of tools and automation, many actions were taken. Lotus Notes was evaluated and purchased. However, there were some problems experienced during the installation. It was planned to use Notes for inter-company communication on the ALCAST project, but this only became possible towards the latter stages of the experiment.

Q·SYS Groupware was evaluated with a view to controlling access to on-line standards for the Software Development group and to controlling the workflows involved in generating such standards. The product was found to be useful and provides significant opportunities in the medium term, particularly once familiarization with Lotus Notes is achieved (see Appendix 3.2 for more details on this evaluation).

Having chosen STEP as a testing methodology, the Lotus Notes application, STEPMaster, which implements STEP on-line, was evaluated. The consensus of opinion is that while the tool is useful and is a natural fit for STEP, it requires a significant amount of effort for developers to get 'up to speed' with the product and it is unlikely to be used in the short term. It is, however, an ideal environment for larger test groups using STEP.

SQA TeamTest was found to be very user-friendly and a useful tool for defect tracking and change management and will be used on subsequent projects in the department. (See Appendix 3.2 for more details.)

3.9 RESULTS AND ANALYSIS AT CSK

3.9.1 Technical

3.9.1.1 Adoption of STEP and WinRunner

Work performed at CSK centred on the introduction of a STEP-based test methodology, the piloting of an automated test tool (WinRunner) and the enhancement of development test techniques. A modified version of the STEP methodology (piloted under ALCAST) is being 'rolled out' and adopted as the standard testing methodology in CSK. This roll-out is being accomplished using Lotus Notes, allowing the test methodology to be a seamless component of the development life cycle, with the elements readily available to all parties involved in each project. This has provided a solid foundation for the introduction of automated testing with WinRunner which is currently in progress. Another benefit is that gathering statistics on testing and software defects, e.g. defect open and closure rates, overall defect levels etc., is now straightforward.

3.9.1.2 Development testing

Significant efforts were made in the assessment and improvement of what was subsequently called 'development testing' in CSK. (Most companies refer to this as unit testing.) Developers test as part of the implementation phase. Normally the testing is informal and is part of a Code/Debug/Fix implementation cycle. Developers often claim that they are not 'testers', especially in an organization where there is a separate test group.

In the second phase of ALCAST, CSK wanted to put more structure on development testing and see if this increased the efficiency and benefits of this phase to the company. So a full audit of testing activity on a typical development project was carried out, with the following conclusions.

1. The developers were doing some element of all of the 'classic' test phases, as seen in the V Model, and the phrase 'Development Testing' was coined to describe this method of testing.
2. It was apparent that there was a strong need for training in all of the testing areas, and that this training had to be timed correctly, i.e. at Test Planning stage.
3. The type of training had to be almost 'one to one' sessions, on an individual project basis, and had to be specifically geared towards the needs of the 'Development Testers'. In one experiment, team members who believed that they had completed unit testing were coached in test techniques and risk analysis. In a three-hour session (1.5 hours teaching and 1.5 hours of an exercise listing test concerns) the group of three people created a set of test objectives and identified 32 test concerns, but they were convinced that none of the tests would fail. Execution of these tests revealed three major defects (i.e. system crash), and six minor defects, as well as 10 enhancement suggestions. The defects were fixed. When the code was shipped to the customer site, no defects were found. This was not the case for a similar project, the control group in this experiment, in which the team members received no coaching
4. The type of project was not a major factor.
5. Development testing must be put as a separate task into any development plan.
6. At the start of the development testing phase, use an experienced external or in-house tester/expert to give the coaching.
7. Formal Development testing is efficient.

8. A development testing SIG (Special Interest Group) has been set up internally to disseminate the positive results and to tailor the coaching for widespread use in the company.

3.9.1.3 Tools

Evaluation of static analysis tools, for source code quality and readiness for testing, was included as part of the analysis of development test efforts. Memory and performance test tools were also evaluated and implemented. These included Purify, PureCoverage and Cantata.

3.9.2 Defects Reported from the Field Fall by 50%

(See Section 3.1.5.)

Measurement of software defects and configuration issues occurring in the field have shown an improvement in product quality during the 18-month term of ALCAST. (Details are given in Figures 3.3 and 3.4). Note that the complexity of released product has risen during the same timeframe, as witnessed by the increase in 'configuration' issue calls to the client helpdesk. The CSK bug trend has fallen by 50%.

3.9.2.1 Metrics for process improvement

See Figure 3.3.

Question: Is the Quality of the product Improving?
Answer: Yes.
Justification: Fewer bugs for customers.

Explanation The data was gathered from the CSK Customer Support Desk database. Two classes of support call were compared.

- CSK bug – this is a call which results from a BUG/DEFECT in the released software.
- Configuration issue – a query about how the products should be interconnected with other products or components. As would be expected, these calls relate to the complexity of the product.

For the purpose of this data analysis, we use the complexity issue as a reference to show that even though the complexity of the products was increasing the bug level was dropping. The exported data from

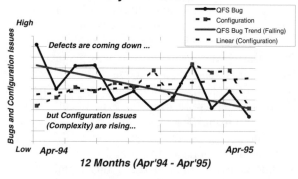

Figure 3.3 Metrics for process improvement

our helpdesk application was imported into Excel and graphed. Trend lines were also graphed.

3.9.2.2 Metrics to help testing

See Figure 3.4.

Question: What modules (function or file) are the most important to test or inspect, and how are they differentiated?
Answer: Use McCabe's Cyclomatic Complexity. In this case it indicates using E:alpha, A:delta and A:gamma in that order.
Justification: Identifying the more complex modules or files.

Explanation McCabe's Cyclomatic Complexity for various modules is shown as V(G) in the graph.

The data was first collected by running a static analyser (e.g. HP_Mas) on the files which could extract complexity data (e.g. McCabe) for each module. The extracted data was then imported into Excel and graphed as a bar chart.

Note that a cyclomatic complexity of 10 is the de facto threshold below which code is 'not complex', and above which code is 'complex' and requires:

1. more development effort;
2. more testing effort due to the likelihood that it contains defects.

Even though 'E:alpha' and 'A:delta' have very high complexity values there may be a good reason for it. The important thing is that you check and verify that there is.

Av V(G)

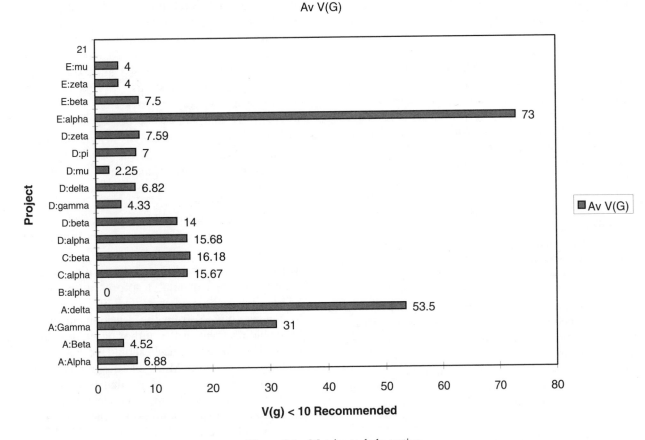

Figure 3.4   Metrics to help testing

3.10 EFFECTS ON BUSINESS

3.10.1 In VHI

During the ALCAST project period, two of the projects which had software sent into production have needed to carry out only minor corrective maintenance post-release. Both of these projects are considered business-critical. Management is encouraged by this result. Users are actively participating in development, technical reviews and test planning as a result of increased awareness and visibly better products.

3.10.2 In CSK

The use of state-of-the-art testing methodologies and techniques is viewed positively by customers and within the industry.

The initiatives sponsored by ALCAST have assisted CSK in obtaining ISO 9001 certification.

The documented test procedures for products serve as a repository of test information, and eliminate the need to start afresh with each product test cycle. They also allow new tests to be added on while defects passing through the test cycle are discovered. This also means that other groups, both internal and external, can participate in the testing effort while maintaining the required level of quality and control.

The decrease in software defect levels (see Figure 3.3), has resulted in a saving in maintenance costs.

3.11 EFFECTS ON ORGANIZATION

In VHI, a steering team has been set up to implement ALCAST improvements and to introduce the STEP testing methodology, metrics, reviews and the test tools to a wider group within the Department. It consists of the training leader, the ALCAST project leader, the user manager and business analysts and tool evaluators who were involved in the project. The tailored version of STEP has already been included in the Software Development and Procurement Standards and this was taken on board enthusiastically by the development staff. Project milestones and deliverables are identified in advance with formal reviews included in plans. This allows more accurate resource scheduling and maximizes the potential to prevent defects entering products.

At CSK, ALCAST has been managed by a steering group, but the initiatives which have emerged are being led by a team focused on each initiative, chartered to spread across the company the expertise they gain. For example, a team of experts will exist in CSK whose function will be to provide automated tools knowledge to development projects. They will be a department-wide resource. Quality improvement initiatives will be fully fledged projects in the future, with priority equal to or higher than core business projects. CSK has a positive and proactive approach to quality, and during the period of the ALCAST project, there was a separate project to implement a quality management system for certification to ISO 9001. It is felt that the two initiatives complemented each other by creating a positive synergy.

Based on the regular monthly meetings, it is now known that people outside of the ALCAST project in both companies have an improved awareness of the need for testing, and how it should be used at all stages of the software development life cycle, not just from unit testing onwards. They are also aware of the concepts of testware and a test life cycle.

3.12 EFFECTS ON SKILLS

As well as improving their knowledge about testing, reviews and metrics, participants also learned good project management skills. They are now familiar with state-of-the-art testing methodologies and have exposure to the CMM Assessment and Inspections, which may form the basis for further work in this area in the future. Experience has been gained in various state-of-the-art tool evaluations and use, and implementation cycles. From a personnel point of view, this exposure to new tools and the latest trends in the industry tends to motivate individuals and encourages them to remain with the companies.

3.13 KEY LESSONS

3.13.1 For Technology

3.13.1.1. STEP methodology

- Implementation of STEP is better if it is carried out at the initiation and requirements–gathering stage of a project. A master test plan can be put in place and the full benefits of STEP, i.e. the early detection and prevention of defects in the product,

can be realized. VHI found that implementing STEP on projects which were already at unit testing stage was more difficult. Planning the implementation, and documenting it, later on in the development life cycle imposed an extra burden on the project teams because, at that stage, it was more difficult to step back from the product to creatively analyse risk and prevent defects.

- The terminology used in the 'as delivered, vanilla flavored' STEP methodology can be confusing for an Irish software development audience. It was designed in the United States and contains unfamiliar terminology such as 'inventory', 'acquire' etc. However, this aspect of the STEP methodology can be tailored for a particular application.

- STEP should be customized by writing a user manual or departmental test procedure. If the STEP approach is documented, it is necessary to achieve 'buy-in' from the development group, by including them in the authoring of this document. The document itself should be kept short and to the point. Most of the requests for changes to the STEP user manual were for test plan templates, test procedure templates and checklists which were tailored for the companies' business. Generating a reference manual with all of this tailored information before the methodology is implemented was quite difficult and required much effort. An iterative approach was used, where a generic manual was put in place. All of the comments and suggestions from the developers and testers using it were gathered in a single repository. Version 2 of the manual is in place at VHI. CSK Notes implementation continues to evolve.

- It is critical to get the test person/group/project involved at the earliest possible opportunity in the requirements–gathering stage on the software development project. This pays dividends directly in cost savings and indirectly in boosting morale, building effective technical teams and educating staff.

- The STEP testing methodology is established in the three organizations and has started to filter out to non-ALCAST projects. The following critical success factors have been identified for the successful implementation of the STEP methodology.

  1. Significant initial effort in familiarizing the entire project group with the methodology.
  2. Formal training for developers in planning and execution of unit testing.

3. Early involvement of the quality assurance/ testing department in the development life cycle, ideally at requirement stage.

4. Easily accessible central storage of test plans, objectives, procedures, data and results.

5. Developers must take ownership of the testing process.

6. There should be objective or independent test processes in addition to testing by the development group.

7. Rigorous enforcement of standards and controls at each phase of the life cycle e.g. if there are no test plans, there will be no sign-off or progression to the next phase of the development life cycle.

8. Formal documented guidelines for test procedures.

9. Formal documented guidelines for the review process.

10. Testing standards and guidelines should be developed by, or at least have significant input from, the development group.

3.13.1.2 Metrics

- Metrics–gathering, although it was well planned, proved to be difficult. This was an extra task for each project member during their normal working week, and too much information was being gathered on a small form. It was only when analysis of the data was attempted, that it was discovered that the different pilot projects were collecting different types of data. The metrics–gathering form was difficult to follow. Even the simplest definition proved to be a stumbling block; for example, what exactly is a defect, given that a defect at the requirements–gathering stage of a project is completely different from a defect discovered during test execution? In addition, the length of time required to fix defects in the early stages is measured in terms of minutes and seconds. Defects found at the acceptance testing stage can take days or longer to fix. People on projects found this distinction a little difficult to come to terms with when they were completing the metrics forms, in the early stages of the project. Some took the view that, since defects were simply corrections in a document, which required only a little time to fix, there was no need to record many of them. This important data must be captured to measure the success of the initiative.

- Metrics should be kept simple, few in number and easy to collect. Some sample data should be taken

in the initial stages of the project, and then taken all the way through to plotting the results on a graph. Some analysis against target baselines should be done before spending time gathering lots of data. The project teams adapted the aphorism coined by one of the team members on this point, 'If the results don't fit the theory, change the theory!'

- Measuring improvement is difficult. A thorough assessment should be done before improvement, and findings documented, with as many side-effects as possible identified. Numbers and facts should be gathered at the start. Using the **A**ssess **I**mprove **M**easure method, the 'measure' stage can produce definite conclusions about the success, or otherwise, of the project members' efforts.

- At CSK, metrics for testing were gathered as a part of the normal activity in Lotus Notes. This did not cause any upheaval, as having the documents online effectively automated the gathering of data. Standard metrics definitions were designed for use throughout the software development group. These metrics templates included a short name for reference, a description, an observation on how the metric is collected, how often the metric should be collected and how it is used. The template (shown in Figure 3.5) also included items like range, history, expectations, relationships with other metrics, validation, and problems with this particular metric. Based on the literature search conducted and meetings with development

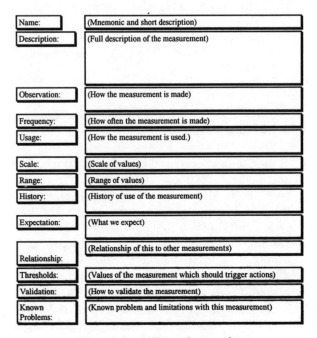

Figure 3.5 CSK metrics template

Table 3.4 CSK metrics choice

Name	Short Description
KLOC	Thousands of lines of code (new or modified) per project or system
DEVDEF	Total number of defects reported during development
SPECDEF	Percentage of defects attributable to the System Specification
REQDEF	Percentage of defects attributable to the Requirements
L1DEF	Percentage of defects reported during Level 1 Testing
RELDEF	Reported defects after Product Release
DEFDEF	Percentage of defects attributable to previous defect corrections
$DEVDEF	Cost of defects found during development
L2DEF	Percentage of defects reported during Level 2 Testing
$RELDEF	Cost of defects found after product release
ARCHDEF	Percentage of defects attributable to the Architectural Design
EOM	Ease of maintenance of the final product
RELRATE	Rate of release of new product versions
DESDEF	Percentage of defects attributable to the Detailed Design
RESU	Resource usage – i.e. the extra resources required to meet project requirements
PSLIP	Project slippage
L4DEF	Percentage of defects reported during Level 4 Testing
CODEDEF	Percentage of defects attributable to the code
L3DEF	Percentage of defects reported during Level 3 Testing

managers (the prime customer for the metrics) the list of measurements/metrics shown in Table 3.4 was initially chosen by CSK.

- CSK identified the following critical success factors for the successful implementation of a metrics programme.

  1. Keep metrics simple and usable.
  2. Collect only what will be used.
  3. Collect metrics at acceptable frequencies, ensuring currency/time limits while reducing administrative overhead.
  4. Educate people as to why each piece of data is needed.
  5. Automate metrics collection where possible, ideally as part of the development or testing process.

3.13.1.3 Automation

- Testing tools are essential in a modern, responsive development environment. In particular it has been shown that they can significantly increase the rate of error detection and reduce the test cycle time. However, testing tools are not easy to use, are associated with a high capital cost, and require a step-learning curve before they can be effectively deployed.

- A formal evaluation of a tool for a particular task is essential. It provides a snapshot of the latest technology available and identifies requirements very clearly, which makes good engineering

sense. This evaluation process also promotes ownership of the tool when the choice is finally made, and this in turn makes implementation much more likely to succeed.

- The following critical success factors have been identified for the successful introduction of tools and automation.

  1. Set realistic expectations in terms of costs and functionality of current testing tools.
  2. Have a formal multi-disciplined evaluation exercise of tools and methods.
  3. Promote a willingness to adapt the process to accommodate the limitations of tools.
  4. Invest in significant initial and ongoing training.
  5. Clarify a manual process before automation.
  6. Ensure technical architecture compliance with the company environment for all software tools purchased.

3.13.1.4 Groupware

- The Groupware platform, Lotus Notes, quickly becomes an everyday working environment and has proven its usefulness as a communications medium. The Lotus Notes applications used by VHI, i.e. Q·SYS Groupware and STEPMaster, have generated a lot of interest. VHI experienced some technical problems with Lotus Notes, both in communicating with CSK and on the installation, but has overcome this. CSK successfully incorporated the various applications supporting the testing methodology into their existing mature Lotus Notes–based corporate workflow system. (See Appendix 3.2 for more details.)

3.13.2 For Business

3.13.2.1 Project management

- There were lessons to be learned from both the project management of ALCAST itself, and the impact which ALCAST had on the management of the pilot projects in each organization. With regard to the impact on pilot projects, positive feedback from Project Managers has a visible effect on the progress of the implementation. It is important that Project Managers realize that the extra effort required by this new Testing methodology is, first of all, planned for and, secondly, explicitly included in the project plan. The use of STEP tends to shift the efforts of those involved in Testing towards the earlier phases of the project. This means that the panic at the end of the project schedule is reduced! The same resources are used in testing but the effort is shifted to earlier phases.

- Many good ideas are generated at group follow-up after training/workshop sessions, and these should be captured and recorded for use by software development management. Many of these ideas relate to other areas in the department and are positive benefits from the ALCAST project. It was useful to summarize the follow-up sessions in a simple set of minutes that were distributed widely outside ALCAST after each follow-up session.

- The clustering of three companies together, all working towards a common set of project goals, provided real synergy. This was especially useful when the 'going got tough'. ALCAST was not a mainstream project in any of the partner companies, so its priority sometimes lagged, and, like any software group, its people/time resources were sometimes called on for higher priority tasks. Having other groups in different companies helped to solve this problem, by sharing information and solutions, and taking up the slack on ALCAST administrative tasks, etc. The project gained a momentum and maintained it, even if individuals had to step off 'the merry-go-round' for short periods.

- Exposure to the EU has been a useful experience for the project team. Both the positive (risk sharing and funding, the challenges, the incentive, the information base) and negative (red tape, contracts, delayed payments) have been encountered.

- The synergy of three companies also provided a useful benchmarking within the group. Pilot projects have been comparing results and this friendly competition tends to move everyone forward.

- ESSI definitely reduced the risk of piloting new methodologies. The risk has been reduced for each company by spreading it across the group, seeking external expert advice, and having the major costs borne by ESSI. Of course, this is one of the objectives of ESSI, i.e. to share the risk burden. It makes good project management and engineering sense and appeals to management who have budgets close to their hearts!

- However, the ALCAST Project was perceived to be too long (18 months) for focused pilot projects in process improvement. It can be difficult to sustain interest and justify investment of resources over such a long period of time.

- The following critical success factors have been identified for the successful project management of improvement initiatives.
  1. Good project management skills are essential.
  2. Treat process improvement initiatives as core business projects.
  3. Attempt to ensure that the process improvement project is synchronized with other development projects within the organization, to minimize disruption and to take advantage of project management experience.
  4. Manage process improvement initiatives as a series of small tightly managed subprojects.
  5. Early visible successes are critical to maintain momentum for the duration of the longer projects.
  6. Formal management buy-in, ideally at a senior level (e.g. CEO), at the start of the project is essential.
  7. Highly visible, ongoing practical support from senior management is also vital to success.

3.13.2.2 Customers and competitors

- During investigations and benchmarking within ALCAST, it was found that the industry norm is not synonymous with best practice. Best practice in this instance is that a company has a defined test life cycle (at least a version of the V-Model together with some of the concepts of STEP). The Test life cycle exists in parallel with the software development life cycle or is tightly integrated within it. In addition, test procedures exist for the generation of Acceptance tests, System tests, Integration tests and Module/Unit tests as required by individual projects. These procedures should be supplemented by company-defined guidelines and checklists, to ensure a systematic approach. All staff involved in testing should have formal training which, at the minimum, covers black-box and white-box test techniques. In fact, the industry norm seems to be that there is no test training provided and testing is the last task on a project, susceptible to the effects of schedule slippage by the other development activities.

- The participating companies feel that they are ahead of their competitors in the area of testing as a result of their participation in this initiative. Some customers have already approached VHI and CSK on their testing process and supporting infrastructure.

- Q·SET has subsequently installed QSYS Groupware in 16 countries in four continents. A significant number of these Q·SYS installations were a direct result of the Irish dissemination event and the ALCAST reports. Many inquiries have come from finance, food and drinks and insurance sector organizations.

3.13.2.3 Training

- The training of staff in the latest industry best practices has obvious benefits for both the company (problems get solved) and the staff (loyalty and motivation are promoted). Training that is planned and implemented in a structured way avoids the risk of failure and the frustrations of staff, who may feel they effectively have to train themselves by reading through manuals and any other available resource materials.

- The following critical success factors have been identified for the successful implementation of the process improvement initiative.
  1. New skills require training, and the level of training should not be underestimated in the interest of gaining financial approval.
  2. Formal training sessions off-site are best.
  3. Training in both process and tools is important, and should be phased appropriately with process training coming first.
  4. Aim for early success with all initiatives to reinforce training.
  5. Plan for ongoing training apart from the initial tasks. A 'train the trainer' approach or special interest groups (SIG) provide a productive way of achieving this.

6. Coaching, together with formal training, improves morale by provision of individual attention, and ensures a more rapid uptake of new methodologies and procedures.
7. Process improvement should not be seen as a way of introducing productivity measures.

3.14. STRENGTHS AND WEAKNESSES OF THE EXPERIMENT

3.14.1 Strengths

The initiative has been shown to make good business sense. This project provided the opportunity to work with other software companies, and to identify and implement software best practice in the area of testing. The introduction of formal technical reviews has been effective. All participants now have a more accurate, automated and consistent approach to testing. The test life cycle is now documented and is a well-proven element of the software quality system.

3.14.2 Weaknesses

The project had too wide a focus, i.e. too many small initiatives. It would have been better divided up into a number of shorter subprojects. The project duration was such that it suffered the normal problems associated with long-term projects, i.e. staff changes, motivation, changes of direction etc. The project plan was not strictly adhered to. A more complete Risk Analysis would have alleviated this. Introduction of the metrics programme was the least popular with the project teams because its objectives were not well understood. An opportunity was missed in both companies to do a formal Capability Maturity Model Assessment. This was due to the level of disruption to staff.

3.15 CONCLUSIONS AND FUTURE ACTIONS

- The test process has improved in all companies as a result of the ALCAST experiment. Both VHI and CSK agreed that the number of defects reported has fallen. While it is acknowledged that other process improvement activities may have contributed to this substantial decrease, the most constantly cited reason is that the improved testing was now preventing the more obvious defects and more effectively detecting the more complex ones.

- Process Improvement projects by their nature (i.e. change) need special skills to manage them effectively. Improvement projects require all the resources available to the mainstream projects in a business. It requires equal or higher priority.

- Test analysis and management worked well in CSK with their implementation on Notes. The manual process was effectively put in place in VHI but the automation of this on STEPMaster suffered because the manual process was still being implemented and was not fully understood at the time. The opportunity now exists to automate this working manual process.

- There needs to be a well-controlled environment for the introduction of new test tools. It is intended to put a team of experts in place that will be available as a department asset for projects to call on when required.

- Complexity tools worked well, but the notion of complexity needs to be linked with business risk to make it effective from a management point of view.

- The set-up costs for each tool should be considered separately as they distort project costs. For example, in the case of CSK, much work has been done on the infrastructure required to support WinRunner and so at first glance it would appear that Winrunner implementation was an excessive cost for ALCAST. But as many generic functions have now been written which will apply to all future projects that use Winrunner, in reality this cost is shared amongst this project and those future projects.

3.15.1 Cluster of Companies

- The cluster of companies worked because the consortium members had no fixed expectations of each others' capabilities; and, obviously the situation would be different if the same group were to work together on another project. More emphasis on communication between pilot project participants would be required, with communication milestones and events included on the project plan. Special interest groups or other such fora were suggested for future consideration. For clustering to work, the maturity of each organization should be similar. The costs were certainly reduced by clustering.

- Some felt that there were too many threads to the ALCAST improvement initiatives. This led to a thinning of ALCAST resources and a reduction in the effect of each improvement. Improvements

could not be attributed to single initiatives. Timing of improvement is critical. The 'changes' (i.e. ideas, training, procedures, etc.) have to fit into the schedule of the project being piloted.

3.15.2 Metrics Conclusions

Many lessons were learned during the project about metrics-gathering in general. It is important to measure the right things. Managers and developers require different information to be gathered.

- There is no magic solution to setting up a measurement programme to support a process improvement programme which delivers timely information to help managers manage.

- The following are the main keys to a successful metrics programme.

  - Find out what information is needed, and use it to determine goals of the measurement programme.

  - Let everyone in the department know that metrics are being collected.

  - Explain why you are measuring.

  - Provide feedback/results on metrics to the people who are collecting metrics.

  - It is extremely difficult to come up with a statistically provable figure for corrective maintenance.

  - Always keep in mind that *'You don't have to do this – survival is not compulsory'* (Deming).

3.15.3 Future Actions

VHI will automate defect tracking for all software development projects, and introduce formal reviews, metrics, test change management, and tool expertise within IT.

In CSK, 'life-cycle testing', with adoption and efficiency tools, is now standard company-wide, and more readily available metrics help to find problems earlier. The defect detection focus continues – Support and Documentation groups enter projects earlier to join Quality Engineering and Development groups, and improved inter-group communication happens from project initiation to release/post-release stage. This multi-discipline approach reduces defect-injection, and increases defect-removal earlier in the life cycle. The Product Quality Assurance group now has quarterly 'conferences' at which actions to improve software and personal processes are assigned.

Q·SET, in the course of its training activities, will continue to disseminate information on ALCAST, ensuring that as many as possible learn of the benefits of software process improvement.

ACKNOWLEDGMENTS

This chapter has been written with the assistance of the ALCAST (**A**utomated **L**ife*c*ycle **A**pproach to **S**oftware **T**esting) staff at CSK, VHI and Q·SET. The authors gratefully acknowledge their help.

The views expressed here are subjective and are based on our unique circumstances, requirements and evaluations.

This chapter contains Registered Trademarks, Trademarks and Service Marks which are owned by their respective companies or organizations.

Members of the ALCAST Project gratefully acknowledge the financial help provided by the ESSI Group at the European Commission without which ALCAST would not have happened, and also thank the VHI and CSK project sponsors for their commitment to the success of the project.

APPENDIX 3.1 METRICS AT VHI – USER AIDS

PROJECT MEASUREMENT FORM – HOW TO FILL IN

COLUMN	DESCRIPTION
Total Project	Total Effort spent on the project during week
Testing Effort	Any effort designing testware, writing test plans, executing tests.
Reviews	Any group discussion, document review, desk check or peer review that results in some action for change to the item reviewed or discussed. Should not include spelling/grammar errors

DEFINITION OF A DEFECT

Defects Found	**The definition of a defect changes for each phase of project as shown below**
Requirements	Any change to the requirements document forced by designing tests, writing test plans or executing *prototype* tests. E.g. Rephrasing an ambiguous statement.
Plan Development /Analysis	Any change to the project plan forced by designing tests, writing test plans or executing *prototype* tests. E.g. Adding extra people.
System Design	Any change to the design models/architecture forced by designing tests, writing test plans or executing *prototype* tests. E.g. Including extra data flow paths/controls/screen layouts.
System Development	Written code/user interface/documentation forced by designing tests, writing test plans or executing *prototype* tests. E.g. Including extra code to do range checking.
Unit Test Execution	Any change to the previous delivered items forced by executing unit tests. E.g. Any of the above examples.
System Test Execution	Any change to the previous delivered items forced by executing system tests. E.g. Any of the above examples.
Accept Test Execution	Any change to the previous delivered items forced by execution of acceptance tests. E.g. Any of the above examples.
Maintenance Corrective (Mini Project)	Any change to the previous delivered items forced by designing (Mini Project) tests, writing test plans or executing tests (prototype).
Maintenance Enhance (Mini Project)	Any addition/change to the previous delivered items forced by designing tests, writing test plans or executing tests (prototype).

MEASUREMENT FORM

TOTAL PROJECT	TESTING				REVIEWS			
PERIOD COVERED: FROM __/__/19 TO __/__/19	TOTAL PROJECT EFFORT (Hrs)	TOTAL TEST EFFORT (Hrs)	DEFECTS FOUND (No.)	DEFECTS CORRECTED (No.)	TIME TO FIX (Hrs)	TOTAL REVIEW EFFORT (Hrs)	DEFECTS FOUND (No.)	DEFECTS CORRECTED (No.)	TIME TO FIX (Hrs)
PROJECT INITIATION									
PROJECT APPROACH									
REQUIREMENTS/M. & A. T.P.									
ANALYSIS/System T.P.									
DESIGN/Unit T.P.									
SYSTEM DEVELOPMENT									
UNIT TEST EXECUTION									
SYSTEM TEST EXECUTION									
ACCEPTANCE TEST EXECTN									
PROJECT EFFORT TOTALS									

PROJECT NAME: PROJECT WORK or MAINTENANCE. (E/C):   SIGNED: DATE:

1. Total Project Effort = TOTAL TEST EFFORT + TOTAL REVIEW ERROFT + NORMAL DEVELOPMENT TIME
2. Total Testing Effort = must include TIME TO FIX
3. Total Review Effort = must include TIME TO FIX
4. M/A/S/U T.P. = Master/Acceptance/System/Unit Test Plan
5. WHAT IS A DEFECT??? = REFER to "HINTS and TIPS" provided

Refer to xxxxxxx for any problems/suggestions related to these metrics

'HINTS and TIPS' for Metrics-gathering

1. Anything worth fixing – *record it*.

2. Use your *judgement*.

3. Bugs found in the *early* project phases will normally:
   - be found by reviews
   - take minutes/*seconds* to fix.

4. Note that testing in the early phases is *prototyping* only – (not the formal execution) – where prototype tests are tests issued to check functionality etc. of a query or form, rather than the integrity of the formal test data.

5. Formal test execution occurs in the last three phases, i.e. Unit Test onwards.

6. Remember to fill in the defects corrected during current week even if the defects were captured during a previous period.

7. All bugs recorded in Change Management should appear on this form, but not all bugs on this form will be recorded on Change Management.

   Note 1: All of the changes marked up on reviewed documents must be counted on the form, but in general will not go to change management.

   Note 2: Only record defects that are within your power to fix.
   E.g. Ignore system crash

8. Include time spent by user when filling in the form.

9. Defects recorded on the Measurement Form are where defects are found. Defects recorded in Change Management are where defects were introduced.

10. Testware: Can be broken down into
    - 1. Environment
    - 2. Plans
      - gathering test data
      - creating test directories/files/JCLs
      - getting equipment together

METRICS FOR TODAY
(fill in each day)

COMMON TEST ERRORS	NUMBER OF OCCURRENCES	TIME TO FIX
Illegal Decimal Data		
Subscript out of Array		
Incomplete/Incorrect Spec.		
Coded Incorrectly		
Uninitialized Variables		
Control Loop Incorrect		
Out of Range Data		
Unreachable Code		
Memory Leaks		
File Access Incorrect		

METRICS FOR TODAY
(fill in each day)

COMMON REVIEW ERRORS	NUMBER OF OCCURRENCES	TIME TO FIX
Technically Incorrect		
Data Missing		
Missing Diagrams		
Objective Not Met		
Sentence Poorly Phrased		

APPENDIX 3.2 TOOLS EVALUATION

At VHI

The evaluation of:
- *STEPMaster* will only be of interest to those who use the STEP methodology and who need a tool to support this methodology.
- *SQATeamTest* is relevant to those who operate in a Windows environment and who want to automate aspects of testing like Capture/Playback and Defect Tracking
- *Lotus Notes* will be of interest to those considering a Groupware communication and workflow environment.
- *Q·SYS Groupware* is of interest to those documenting a Quality Management System which includes procedures, standards and quality records.

Evaluation of STEPMaster

STEPMaster is a software support package which facilitates and enables the effective use of the STEP process. It consists of four interrelated Lotus Notes databases. Three of the databases, *Planning*, *Acquisition* and *Measurement*, are set up for each new major project (or for a group of related small projects) and directly support the three phases of STEP: *Planning* (developing master and detail test plans); *Acquisition* (developing and acquiring test objectives and procedures, the test environment and test sets); and *Measurement* (executing tests and tracking and reporting results). The fourth database, *Forum*, provides information pertaining to all projects using STEP and is used to support and coordinate the test improvement effort throughout the organization.

Positive
- Documentation can be centrally stored and shared.

- Change management system is included, called issues management.
- User manual provided is good.
- Screens can be printed.
- Provides templates for many documents.
- Numbers each document with a prefix of user's initials.
- Tests stored in STEPMaster can be reused.

Negative
- No help keys listed on screen, e.g. PF4 to exit.
- Presumes knowledge of Lotus Notes.
- User interface is not attractive.
- Error messages can be misleading.
- Page numbers are missing from manual provided.

Evaluation of SQA TeamTest

SQA TeamTest is a team testing environment for GUI client/server applications. It automates test development and execution, and provides team workflow tracking and report. It consists of two major components, *SQA Manager* and *SQA Robot*, integrated by a shared network repository.

1. SQA Manager: an information management tool to help track software testing information through all phases of the development test and revision cycles.
2. SQA Robot: an automated testing tool for windows applications, which would have needed a lot of effort to evaluate. Not considered in this context.

VHI concentrated on the Manager part of the tool to help automate the change management of testing.

SQA Manager (Defect Tracking and Trend Analysis)
- Allows all defects to be stored, accessed and managed centrally.

- Provides for simple and user-friendly documentation of incidents.
- Automatically detects failed test prints and eliminates manual entry of defects (for GUI development only when using *SQA Robot*).
- For manual testing on other platforms, provides powerful method of managing and analysing (through excellent redefined and customizable reports) large amounts of test data, so tool is not limited to GUI client/server applications.
- Provides for team testing coordination allowing for incidents to be assigned to individuals.
- Tracks status of defect through workflow cycle (the cycle can be customized to suit the process existing within an organization).
- Provides operational security defining access and operational limits to defects (again a useful option for standardizing internal tracking process).
- Could be used for defect tracking of software, in both development and live states.

Evaluation of Lotus Notes

VHI had some problems initially installing Lotus Notes. Some of these were as follows.

- Our version of TCP/IP was not compatible.
- Advised that we would need to buy NETBIOS.
- Our current version of Pathworks would need to be upgraded to Version 5 (large job).
- OS/2 did not fit with our current architecture.
- Could not replicate to partner company– discovered that a specific modem file was needed.

The main features that VHI found useful in Lotus Notes were as follows.

- Built-in electronic mail.
- Easy to define and compose new document or form types.
- Basic text editing and word processing facilities.
- Easy to change and rearrange already defined forms.
- Easy to view and locate forms and data in multiple ways.
- Special support for categorizing and classifying documents (expand and collapse).
- Markers for read and unread documents.
- Provides a document management system.

Evaluation of Q·SYS Groupware

Q·SYS Groupware covers all areas of ISO 9000, as well as other quality standards such as TickIT, FDA[12] and SEI CMM. It provides templates for all quality documents and tracks and controls these documents. It is an on-line review process which routes and manages the review and approval of quality documents using Lotus Notes features. The system is on-line, visible, easy to use and accessible.

Positive aspects
- There is a logical hierarchy to the database layout, i.e. 15 databases covering all the main areas of a quality management system.
- Allows easy importing of existing standards and procedures documents.
- Makes extensive use of workflows and thus allows processes to be built into the databases.
- Help available on every field with suggestions on what should appear there.
- Many keyword lookups allowing the user to quickly fill in forms.
- Intelligent links to other databases in the system, e.g. QSYS automatically looks up the Employee database when you select a review team for a document.
- Easy-to-follow review process (built-in workflow) for documents.
- High visibility of current status of everything from audit results to corrective actions to authorized procedures etc.

Negative aspects
- Implementing all of the functionality of QSYS is beyond the scope of this current project.
- Problems with our Notes platform hampered this full evaluation.
- Requires familiarity with Lotus Notes which we are only getting now.

At CSK: Corporate Information System – Lotus Notes

CSK has made a strategic decision to use Lotus Notes to build efficient workflow solutions which support its business of creating and supporting high quality software.

We see Lotus Notes not as an application but as an enabling technology. Currently in CSK we use Notes to support all company processes.

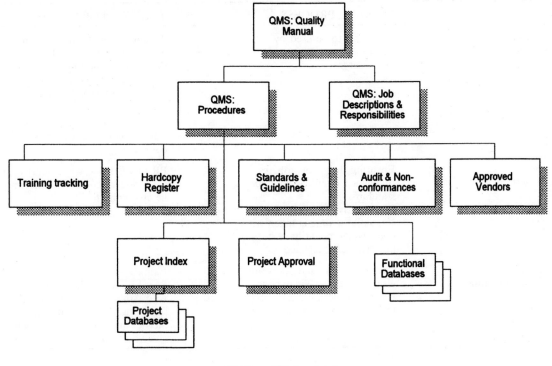

QMS and Notes databases

Tools to support the testing process at CSK

WARNING – Tools evolve faster than almost any other type of software so it is very important that any organization considering using tools to support an already defined process contact the vendors for the latest information. Other sources for information on tools include:

- the Ovum test tool report;
- the test tool report published by SQE in the USA;
- Internet news groups such as comp.software.testing.

TEST AREA	MANUAL PROCESS	TOOL SUPPORT in CSK
Regression Testing Testing to ensure that latest modifications have not caused previously working functionality to develop problems	Can be very time intensive. If the product is such that regular releases or updates are unavoidable, then regression testing of a complex product can become the major component of maintenance cost. One CSK product required seven person weeks of manual regression testing. You expect regression tests to pass.	Mainly due to the need for open system multiple platform support. CSK selected WinRunner.
Test Management Knowing which tests have run, which have failed etc. Knowing what defects have no corresponding test	Very difficult	In CSK we use Lotus Notes to manage tests but most GUI test tools (e.g. WinRunner, SQA) will include a test manager module.

(Continued overleaf)

TEST AREA	MANUAL PROCESS	TOOL SUPPORT in CSK
Development Testing Testing by a developer before independent system testing	Test tools to be used by developers need to be easy and fast to use.	A suite of test tools from Pure Software are well liked by developers. The tools are licensed per developer and currently are available for UNIX only. Purify – Tests memory leaks Quantify – Tests performance PureCoverage – Shows execution coverage
Static Testing Testing code without executing it	Ensuring that code adheres to predefined interfaces and coding standards. The effectiveness of code reviews can suffer if time is taken with items which could have been automatically detected.	PR QA C/C++ will inspect C and C++ source code. The rules can be customized.
Dynamic Testing Testing code by executing it	Usually drivers and stubs are written as throw-away code. Using a tool allows a company to regard drivers and stubs as code.	**Cantata** Based on a test definition file. Adds stubs and driver code to functions. After execution, metrics and code coverage will give you feedback.

APPENDIX 3.3   RISK ANALYSIS 'HOW TO'

Risk Analysis

You now have a list of test worries/objectives. Where do you start testing? At the top of the list? What happens if time is short? What does the customer care about? What is likely to fail?

You must test the high-risk areas of the system first with the intention of finding as many defects as possible, as early as possible.

The following are some techniques for prioritizing your tests. You should use all three as they complement each other. Taking a bottom-up *and* a top-down approach together will ensure that no risks are missed.

The three dimensions of risk

1. Causal Analysis : 'what might cause ...'
2. Effects Analysis : 'what might result from ...'
3. Likelihood Indicators : "what are the chances of ..."

Customer Observed Disasters

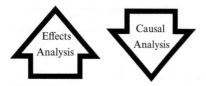

System Failures and Human Errors

1. Causal analysis This technique is also known as Cause–Effect Analysis and is a top-down approach. Start by trying to list all of the disasters the user of this system might see while using this product. Don't worry about likelihood just yet. List even the obscure disasters. Estimate a cost to the customer of these disasters occurring based on lost revenue, rework costs, downtime etc. Then try to link these disasters with your product to see what software failures would cause these disasters. Test for these failures in this prioritized order.

2. Failure modes and effects analysis (FMEA) This technique is bottom-up and is based on the hardware analysis technique FMECA which tries to estimate the reliability of a piece of hardware (Mean Time Between Failures).

This time, start with a list of all the ways your software could fail. Again, don't worry about the likelihood of these failures occurring. List them all for the moment. Try to work out what the user of the product would see for each of these internal failures. Again estimate a cost to the customer of these disasters occurring based on lost revenue, rework costs, downtime etc. Test for these failures in this prioritized order.

| List all the system failures and human errors | Build causal chains starting from product failure or human error and see what could happen | Disasters as observed by the customer |

● How many ways can users or operators make an error?

| inaction | incomplete | ill-timed |
| wrong | extra | more? |

3. Likelihood indicators This is not an 'exact science'! You will have to use your judgement when working out the likelihood of something happening. Remember that it's better that you test for a rare event than have the customer see it first – Murphy's Law ('if anything can go wrong, it will go wrong') applies!

There are three areas that should be considered when trying to estimate how likely a particular customer-observed disaster could be.

1. Errors: what are the signs that a user will make a mistake?
   ● User error history
   ● User attitude and moods
   ● User product knowledge
   ● Task complexity or monotony
   ● Product usability
   ● Degree of product change
   ● General error statistics

2. Faults: what are the signs that the work product is faulty?
   ● Product evaluation and fault history
   ● Author error likelihood indicators
     –Author error history
     –Author attitude and moods
     –Author product knowledge
     –Task complexity or monotony
     –Degree of product change
   ● General fault statistics

3. Failures; what are the signs that the work product will fail?
   ● Product failure history
   ● Testing results
   ● Fault likelihood indicators
   ● General failure statistics

Risk Analysis Session: Pilot Project

The following table is a sample from a full analysis table generated using the Cause–Effect technique by a group comprised of developers, testers, client services and customer representatives.

	Customer potential disaster	System failure to cause this disaster	Relative cost estimate (000s, 00s, 0s)	Likelihood (H, M, L)
1.	Calcs – Values Dates problems	Date mismatch	Thousands	HIGH
2.	Calcs – User error	Poor naming convention Speed of response Non-standard UI Training Documentation	Thousands	HIGH
3.	System Crash ● Reload (Windows) ● Restart (NT, UNIX) ● User error ● Market conditions ● system load ● rate itself (e.g. near 0)	Memory allocation Disk usage Hard-coded arrays (stack) Boundary overruns Coding standards not followed See also user error under the calcs section	Hundreds	HIGH

(*Continued overleaf*)

	Customer potential disaster	System failure to cause this disaster	Relative cost estimate (000s, 00s, 0s)	Likelihood (H, M, L)
4.	Start-up performance	.INI file access Poor feedback to user	Hundreds	HIGH
5.	Page-RIC mismatch (Does RIC take priority)	Configuration (user setup) Comment: a policy of 'what you see is what you use' is required	Tens	HIGH
6.	Layouts • Saving • Opening	Backward compatibility problems File access differences between platforms Display characteristics	Tens	HIGH
7.	Calcs – Holidays problems	Database corruption Updates to database mismatch	Thousands	MEDIUM
8.	Calcs – Bank specific calc completed incorrectly	'Incorrect' requirements	Thousands	MEDIUM
9.	Calcs – Requirements mismatch	Communications Politics	Thousands	MEDIUM
10.	Rate templating errors • no rate output • intermittent errors	Coding error Configuration problem (.INI file) Reuters page format changes	Thousands Tens (no rate)	MEDIUM
11.	Platform	Portability issues	Hundreds	MEDIUM
12.	User Validation and Permissioning (UVP)	User naming incorrect Reported incorrectly	Tens	MEDIUM
13.	etc.	etc.	etc.	etc.

END NOTES

[1] Q·SYS Groupware
A global quality management/business improvement system, which combines the benefits of Lotus Notes and Extranets (Inter- and Intranets).

[2] STEP
Systematic Test and Evaluation Process. An established industry methodology which incorporates the best testing practices of a broad client base and the system engineering philosophies of ANSI and IEEE Software Testing Standards. It has three phases:
Plan (including the Master Test Plan and the detailed 'Level' test plans)
Acquire (gathering a test inventory or set of objectives, and test procedures for each objective)
Measure (including the execution of each test procedure and its subsequent review)

[3] ISO 9001
One of a series of international quality standards which details requirements of a Quality Management System between a supplier and a purchaser, and which most closely pertains to the software development industry.

[4] TickIT
A quality management system certification scheme, originated by UK industry and sponsored by UK industry. It is 'ISO 9001 for Software Development'. It aims to increase the understanding and adoption of minimum best practice as set out in the international quality standard ISO 9001:1994, by setting training standards for TickIT Auditors and providing specific guidelines for suppliers and purchasers (The TickIT Guide).

[5] Capability Maturity Model
The Software Engineering Institute (SEI) at Carnegie Mellon University is a US government-funded body whose function is to improve software practice. Their model of progress has five levels from ad hoc in Level 1 (which applies to most companies) to optimized in Level 5 (which applies to few companies).

[6] Lotus Notes
The leading groupware communications tool, based on a set of databases with common access. Client/server architecture with servers available for most platforms.

[7] Bootstrap
An assessment method for software engineering companies developed under European funding and 'owned' by the Bootstrap Institute.

[8] Deming
W. Edwards Deming (b.1900), a quality 'guru', whose work (e.g. *Out of the Crisis*, MIT Press), on the concepts of process control and statistical quality improvement has greatly influenced quality in software processes.

[9] STEPMaster
This is a Lotus Notes application which implements the STEP methodology. It has database support for the three stages in STEP, i.e. Plan, Acquire and Measure.

[10] SQA TeamTest
This is a Windows test environment which includes test planning, capture playback and defect tracking. The defect tracking element was used on this project. Supplied by Systems FX (UK).

[11]WinRunner
A windows capture/playback tool for regression testing. One of a suite of tools available from Mercury Interactive.

[12]FDA
The US Food and Drug Administration, whose guidelines have been extended to address the need for awareness of quality and safety in software for medical devices.

REFERENCES AND BIBLIOGRAPHY

[1] Bernadette Leonard, Fergal O'Sullivan, Sharon Gormley, Margaret Grene, The ALCAST Presentation at CQS Rome

[2] ALCAST Steering Team, ALCAST Project Folders.

[3] National Standards Authority of Ireland, ISO-9001:1994

[4] Bache, R. and Bazzana, G. (1993) *Software Metrics for Product Assessment* (McGraw-Hill).

[5] Goodman, P. (1993) *Practical Implementation of Software Metrics* (McGraw-Hill).

[6] Software Product Evaluation, ISO 9126.

[7] Standards for Software Productivity Metrics, IEEE Std 1045–1992.

[8] Standard for a Software Quality Metrics Methodology, IEEE Std 1061–1992.

[9] AMI (1994) *AMI – a quantitative approach to software management*, ISBN: 0-9522262-0-0.

[10] Grady, R. B. and Caswell, D. L. (1987) *Software Metrics: Establishing a company-wide program*, ISBN: 0-13-821844-7.

[11] Grady, R. B. (1992) *Practical Software Metrics for Project Management and Process Improvement*, ISBN: 0-13-720384-5.

[12] Hetzel, B. (1993) *Making Software Measurement Work – Building an Effective Measurement Program*, ISBN: 0-471-56568-7.

[13] Sanders, J. (1994) *Software Quality – A Framework for success*, ISBN: 0-201-63198-9.

[14] HP_Mas (University of Idaho and Hewlett-Packard) ftp cs.uidaho.edu/pub/setl

[15] Gilb, T. and Graham, D. (1993) *Software Inspection* (Addison-Wesley).

The Internet contains in excess of 1000 worldwide electronic discussion groups, several of which are devoted to Software Engineering, Quality etc.

- Newsgroups
  - comp.software-eng – Software Engineering Discussion Group
  - comp.testing – Testing of Software Discussion Group
- Internet Mailing Lists
  - ami-request@aaf.alcatel.at – Ami Method Discussion List
  - iso9000@vm1.nodak.edu – ISO 9000 Discussion List
  - quality@pucc.prince.edu – Quality Discussion List
  - ttn@soft.com – Testing Technologies Newsletter
- Internet FTP/ WWW Sites
  - ftp.sei.cmu.edu
  - sei.cmu.edu

4

Addressing The Missing Element in Software Process Improvement: User Interface Design

D. Bell and A. Gupta§[a], and E. Spencer§[b]
[a]*Philips Research Laboratories, Redhill, Surrey, UK*
[b]*EDS, Hook, Hampshire, UK*

EXECUTIVE SUMMARY

Software Process Improvement is widely recognized to be vital for future success in the software industry. Usability is also very important as increasingly software is used by a wide and varied customer base – both in the office and the home; from diagnostic and planning tools, to mobile phones and even shavers containing embedded software. As the tools and products become ever more complex, we must ensure that users are not alienated from them but feel comfortable and in control, are able to operate them safely, accomplish their tasks efficiently, and even derive pleasure and joy from their use.

The fields of software development and user interface development are different disciplines in their own right. The former is largely an engineering discipline whereas the latter draws from the fields of psychology and design. This difference introduces problems in multidisciplinary development teams, relating to communications, organization, and management.

In this project, we evaluated a user interface development method which explicitly sets out to overcome these problems. MUSE (Method for USability Engineering) (Lim and Long 1994) structures the activities undertaken by human factors professionals when analysing and developing user interfaces.

Additionally, it identifies important stages during product development when the human factors and software teams should exchange information, and suggests a notation in which to do so.

This project was funded by the CEC. Philips Research Laboratories, Redhill, was the prime partner, leading a consortium consisting of EDS Defence Ltd, Philips Analytical X-Ray and Electrowatt Engineering Services Ltd. The Ergonomics and HCI Unit at University College London, and Philips Corporate Design, were subcontractors. Each partner applied MUSE on a separate software development activity. Philips used it to guide the user interface design of an X-Ray diffraction system and EDS a tool to aid vehicle route planning. In this paper, the collective experience of Philips and EDS is described.

Our main findings are that, overall, MUSE offers a number of distinct benefits for the formalization of human factors in the system life cycle.

- It provides a process model that extends throughout the life cycle, and documentation templates and notations that benefit both user interface and software design.
- It contributes to improvements in verification, validation and product quality.
- It can be beneficially adopted (and adapted) to play a useful part in an organization's Software Process Improvement plan.

---

§NB: The names of the authors are listed in alphabetical order.

- The increased awareness of human factors issues that results from its adoption helps elicit user-centred user requirements.
- It can be used by software engineers, though preferably not without the involvement of professionals trained in human factors.

This project should interest:

- those in the software development community who are involved in designing Graphical User Interfaces and improving the usability of their software products;
- those who are developing or using state-of-the-art software engineering methods (who might be interested to see how their methods could be augmented);
- human factors experts involved in the specification and development of software systems.

Further details of these, on MUSE, and the work carried out, are described in the following sections.

4.1 INTRODUCTION

4.1.1 Objectives

Users increasingly base their judgement of the functionality and quality of a product on their perception of its user interface. The identification of techniques that improve the interface are therefore of great interest. By addressing issues early on in the design cycle we hope to reduce our redesign and maintenance costs. Most importantly, by improving the integration between the user interface and software development processes (Figure 4.1) we hope to support the implementation of good human factors practice. Alternative views of an integrated cycle are given in (Browne, 1994), (Bass and Coutaz, 1991), (Sutcliffe and McDermott, 1991), (Catterall, 1991), (Macaulay *et al.*, 1990), (Curtis and Hefley, 1994), (Hix and Hartson, 1993) and (Wasserman *et al.*, 1986). Software process improvement is increasingly based on models such as the Capability Maturity Model for Software (Paulk *et al.*, 1993). It cannot be emphasized enough that such models do not address the user interface design process at all.

The aims of this project were:

- to apply MUSE and evaluate its ability to enhance the design of end-user interfaces, and especially the human–computer interaction of graphical user interfaces;

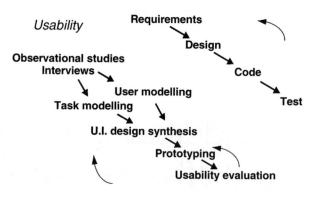

Figure 4.1 A simplified view of the user interface and software development processes

- to gain familiarization with integrated methodologies that allow usability criteria to be addressed at an early stage of the development life cycle;
- to assess the costs and benefits of applying MUSE to improve software engineering practice as it concerns human–computer interactions;
- to disseminate the results of the application of MUSE and its associated costs and benefits.

4.1.2 Abbreviations and Acronyms

BIUSEM	Benefits of Integrating Usability and Software Engineering Methods
CEC	Commission of the European Communities
CTM	Composite Task Model
DoDD	Domain of Design Discourse
ESA	Extant Systems Analysis
ESSI	European Software and Systems Initiative
GTM	Generalized Task Model
HCI	Human–Computer Interaction
HF	Human Factors
ITM	Interaction Task Model
MUSE	**M**ethod for **US**ability **E**ngineering
PSL	Pictorial Screen Layouts
SE	Software Engineering
SoRe	Statement of Requirements
STM	System Task Model
SUN	Statement of User Needs
TD	Task Descriptions
UI	User Interface
XRD	X-Ray Diffraction

4.1.3 The Companies Involved

4.1.3.1 EDS

EDS is today the largest and most successful information technology (IT) services company in the world. Over the past 30 years it has matured into a global organization of over 90 000 people dedicated solely to providing comprehensive IT services to its customers. EDS possesses vast experience in the areas of system integration, project management of major undertakings worldwide, management consultancy services, system design and development, problem and change management.

EDS Defence UK is a wholly owned company within EDS, and provides defence IT services both within and outside of the UK, covering operational and non-operational systems. It offers a full range of services including system integration, project support, consultancy and system management. In the nature of the defence environment, it is involved in leading-edge technology as well as delivering proven systems.

4.1.3.2 Philips Electronics

Philips Electronics of the Netherlands is one of world's leading electronics companies, with sales of over US $40 billion in 1995 and some 265 000 employees worldwide. Its products include lighting, consumer electronics, recorded music, components, semiconductors, communication systems, medical systems, industrial electronics, domestic appliances and personal care products.

Philips Research is a corporate organization with laboratories in five countries. The UK laboratories in Redhill conduct research in software engineering, interactive systems, cordless communications, liquid crystal displays and large-area electronics. Philips Analytical X-Ray is a product group within Philips Industrial Electronics with an international business in leading-edge equipment for materials analysis using X-Ray techniques. Philips Corporate Design is a centre-of-excellence in ergonomics and in various design disciplines including product design, graphic design and interaction design.

4.1.4 The Domains of Application

4.1.4.1. EDS

The target system in EDS' use of the MUSE method (Method for USability Engineering) was a tool to support vehicle route planning. MUSE was used to specify the Human–Computer Interaction (HCI) design for the tool. The purpose of the tool was to aid route planning in support of a mission involving one or more vehicles. For the purpose of the study, route planning was considered to cover the generation of a path for each vehicle to follow in the performance of a mission. Although the tool's requirements focused mainly on mission planning for aircraft, the tool was required to be adequately generic to support mission planning for other vehicle types.

4.1.4.2 Philips Electronics

In Philips we investigated the design of a software system to assist users with experiment design, results interpretation and visualization, for materials analysis in the X-ray Diffraction domain (XRD). The user group varies from school leavers employed in a process control function, to laboratory technicians who are adept at handling conventional problems, to researchers growing novel materials or developing new analytical algorithms. A range of software packages have been produced in-house in the past, each of which supports different analyses; there is a need to integrate the packages. Powerful new algorithms make solvable previously intractable problems, by users with diminishing domain expertise; there is therefore a need for a supporting user interface and consequently a need to design and specify the user interface.

NB: In this chapter, we each focus on our independent use and evaluation of MUSE, and not on technical details relating to the target system. We have therefore excluded further details of the target domains, concentrating instead on how we applied the MUSE method to the design of our target systems.

4.2 WORK PERFORMED – APPLICATION OF MUSE

Due to limitations of space, we cannot explain the MUSE method in this chapter. A short overview is provided in Appendix 4.1, or the reader may refer to (Lim and Long 1994) for definitive information. NB: Familiarity with MUSE, to the minimal extent provided in Appendix 4.1, is a prerequisite to understanding this section.

Although the following sections make detailed observations about MUSE, for those readers with limited contact with the MUSE method and nomenclature we recommend going directly to Section 4.3.

4.2.1 EDS

A short overview of the results of the EDS component of the study is provided here. For fuller details the reader is referred to (BIUSEM, Annex C).

4.2.1.1 Phase One – Information elicitation and analysis

Extant Systems Analysis (ESA) stage This stage focused on obtaining a number of views of the mission planning problem. Three Task Descriptions of existing systems, TD(ext)s, were created:

1. A TD(ext) for the automobile route planning tool, AutoRoute™
2. A TD(ext) for the aircraft mission planning task that is performed manually
3. A TD(ext) for a computer-based tool, developed by EDS, that replaced the manual mission planning method

Excerpts from the TD (automated mission planning) and the General Task Model (mission planning) are shown in Figures 4.2 and 4.3 respectively.

Two extant Generalized Task Models were generated: a GTM(ext) for AutoRoute and a combined GTM(ext) for the manual and computer-based aircraft mission planning task (based on TD(ext)s 2 and 3). The Statement of Requirements, SoRe, is a formal list of requirements for the target system. In this study, the list is relatively long, providing a significant flow of information for the target system design.

The MUSE method identifies several optional ESA stage documents, collectively known as R(ext). These include the full complement of MUSE documents from all phases that describe the *extant* systems in further detail. Although not required within the planned scope of the study and optional in the method, one of the R(ext) documents, the Domain of Design Discourse (DoDD(ext)) syntax diagram, was created. These documents were created in an attempt to address a need to understand the scope of the extant systems during the creation of the TD(ext)s for the on-line systems. They were helpful in providing a one-page description of the entire scope of the extant systems. These were particularly useful in learning the system domain.

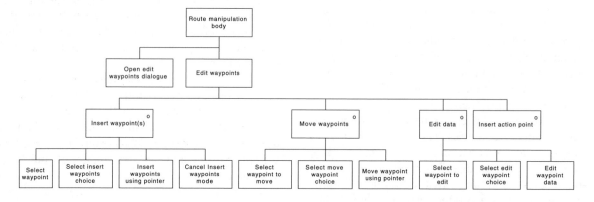

Figure 4.2 Excerpt from a Task Description (automated mission planning)

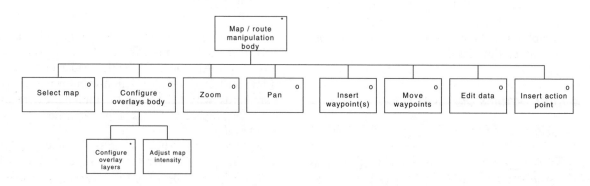

Figure 4.3 Excerpt from a General Task Model (mission planning)

Risk of losing good design features At the creation of the GTM(ext)s, the 'device-specific' features of the extant task descriptions were removed. There was some concern at this stage that the good HCI design features identified as tasks in the TD(ext)s would not be carried forward for consideration in the target design. To ensure that this information was not lost, the promising HCI design features were included in the target Statement of User Needs (SUN(y)), at the recommendation of UCL. This is a modification of the MUSE process.

Generalized Task Model Stage The detailed SoRe enabled a comprehensive GTM(y) to be derived. Although the principal flow of information to the GTM(y) is from tasks identified from the SoRe, the knowledge of the extant tasks helped significantly to group and order the tasks into a meaningful order and structure. The GTM(x) was created by synthesizing promising features of the ESA stage documents.

Translating functional focus of SoRe to task of GTM(y) Generating the GTM(x) involved creating task descriptions from the SoRe. Owing to the functionally oriented nature of the requirements in the SoRe, some translation was required in attempting to derive user tasks for the GTM(y). This was found to require some customization of the basic MUSE procedure: the order and structure of the extant tasks, as identified in the GTM(x), were used to provide a meaningful structure to the tasks identified from the SoRe. Without this structure, organizing the unrelated tasks from the SoRe would have been more difficult. The resulting GTM(y) was reasonably well defined owing to the detailed nature of the SoRe.

Auditability of design and requirements In creating the GTM(y), two goals were borne in mind at all times:

- to ensure that all of the requirements were addressed in the GTM(y) (or ensure that those that are not appropriate are *not* subsequently lost);
- to ensure that all of the design features in the GTM(y) could be traced back to requirements in the SoRe.

The method does not explicitly address the second goal. To facilitate this, an extra column was added to the supporting tables for the GTM structured diagrams to identify the requirement number that prompted the task node. Also, additional tables were created listing requirements that were addressed in the GTM(y) and requirements that were not addressed in the GTM(y). Ensuring completeness and auditability took a significant time in the GTM stage.

Nomenclature The GTM stage document derived from extant systems documents is commonly known as the GTM(x) although it is identified as the CTM(x), Composite Task Model, in the MUSE book. GTM(x) is a less confusing term – it is created in the GTM stage, not the CTM stage, and is equivalent to the GTM(y). In this chapter it is referred to as the GTM(x).

4.2.1.2 Phase Two – Design synthesis

Statement of User Needs stage The focus of the target statement of user needs SUN(y) was on recording good HCI design ideas from the extant systems analysis stage. Few user needs and problems were recorded there. The target domain of design discourse provides a one-page scoping for the target system and recorded system terms. Although not required in the plan for the study, the object and actions list was created to identify all of the system objects and actions available with them. This was deemed to complement the DoDD(y) by providing further semantic information.

The SUN(y) in the current study was small. Had the SoRe been smaller, there would have been a greater emphasis on the information flow from the ESA stage and the SUN(y) would have compensated by containing more user needs, i.e. requirements. The main focus of the SUN(y) was therefore on good HCI design features that were identified in the TD(ext)s but were removed when creating the GTM(ext)s. Few extant problems and specific needs were explicitly identified. The information that would have been contained in the SUN(ext) was derived informally from observations within the TD(ext)s.

The DoDD(y) and, to a lesser extent, the objects and actions list are the documents that should contain the information identifying the conceptual objects and their attributes in the target system. These are perceived to be useful in the subsequent design of the HCI (phase 3).

Object and attribute information was collected prior to the creation of the DoDD(y) but was seen as information to guide the creation of the DoDD(y) rather than information that should be included in it. This information was therefore not included in the DoDD(y) semantic net or the supporting table.

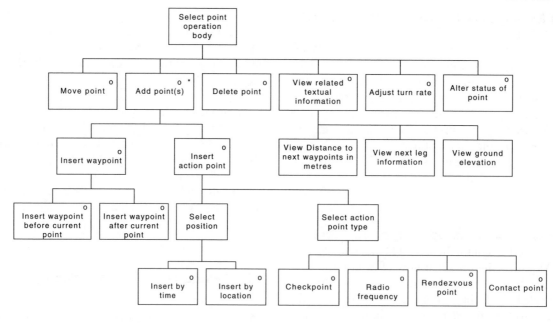

Figure 4.4   Excerpt from the Composite Task Model of the target system

However, the list of objects and attributes was appended to the DoDD(y).

Composite Task Model stage The target composite task model, the CTM(y), is the first MUSE document that potentially identifies the whole breadth of the task for the target system. Design information is synthesized from the SoRe via the GTM(y) and from the GTM(x). An excerpt from the CTM(y) is shown in Figure 4.4.

CTM(Y) information coming primarily from GTM(Y)
The target composite task model, the CTM(y), is created by combining task information derived directly from the SoRe with task information de-

rived from extant systems in the ESA stage. In the current study, the SoRe was well defined, so GTM(y) offered a comprehensive description of the target system. The main flow of information for the CTM(y) therefore came from the SoRe, via the GTM(y), as shown by arrows labelled '1' in Figure 4.5. Some task descriptions were expanded or qualified using components of the GTM(x).

If the SoRe had been less well defined, it is felt that the main flow of design information would have come from extant systems analysis via the GTM(x), as shown by the arrows labelled '2' (in Figure 4.5).

System and User Task Model stage In the target System Task Model, the STM(y), the task descrip-

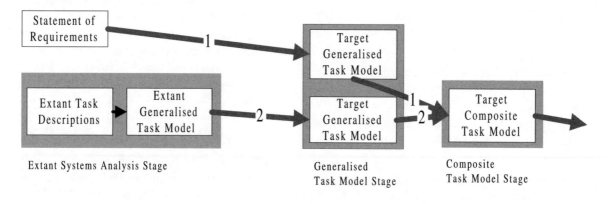

Figure 4.5   Balance of information flow, with well-defined SoRe (1) or a less well-defined SoRe (2)

tions in the composite task model were decomposed to a level where human and computer components of the on-line task were differentiated. No significant wholly off-line tasks were identified, so no target User Task Model was created. This was a deviation from the planned activity.

Revealing incomplete tasks   The STM(y) was useful in revealing where complementary tasks were missing. Although the CTM(y) should have described the complete design, some further tasks were identified that naturally complemented some tasks in the design, e.g. moving and removing map annotations in addition to creating them. Such complementary tasks are not explicitly identified in the requirements and may, quite reasonably, not be explored as part of the ESA stage. Therefore their inclusion in the CTM(y) could only result from a thorough analysis and review of the task set.

Document size   During decomposition, the STM(y) grew significantly in size. Managing the resulting diagrams proved difficult with the tool used here. There was a need to organize nodes to meet the constraints of page size. This contributed significantly to the time spent generating this document.

4.2.1.3 Phase Three – Design specification

Interaction Task Model stage   During the interaction task model stage, the computer leaves of the STM(y) are removed and the human leaves decomposed further to include 'device-level' interactions.

Level of decomposition of the ITM(y)   The level of decomposition of our Interaction Task Model, ITM(y), was not always as deep as recommended by MUSE. Generally the mouse or keyboard-level interactions were not described. Basic interactions such as selecting an item on the screen were assumed to be straightforward and would use standard widgets based on the style of interface to be designed. This represents a design decision that was made but not represented or documented (until the HCI specification).

Iteration between the PSL(y) and the ITM(y)   It was found that the design decisions that had to be made in the generation of the ITM(y) were facilitated by envisaging the screen design, i.e. sketching the Pictorial Screen Layout, PSL(y), for the current task. The procedures indicate that the PSL(y) should not be derived until the generation of the ITM(y) is complete. In practice, we found that the

notation of the ITM(y) did not support the design decisions made during the ITM(y). The PSL(y) was more appropriate in showing the design implementations and revealing inappropriate design decisions. In some cases the ITM(y) was reordered as a result of the generation of the PSL(y).

Interface Model stage   The interface model stage involves the generation of a set of descriptions which specify the behaviour and appearance of screen objects. The procedure used to derive the Interface Model was to create the static screen display descriptions in the PSL(y)s and describe the non-standard screen objects in the screen. NB: Where an interface style is selected for a given design (e.g. MS Windows, OSF/Motif) the description of standard widgets as part of the ITM is believed to be a redundant exercise.

Display Design Stage

Auditability of design   As the display design is produced it is possible to trace back from screen designs, PSL(s), to 'interaction units' demarcated in the ITM(y), but the auditability between screen objects and tasks (and therefore requirements) in the ITM(y) is not as straightforward. To facilitate this, a column was added to the descriptions of the screen objects to identify the ITM(y) node(s) from which it was derived and, where applicable, the requirements that generated that task node.

Multiple interaction methods   Graphical User Interfaces enable the user to perform the same action (task) in several different ways. In the current study, the UI was required to support action selection using a menu bar, pop-up menus, toolbar/palette or direct manipulation. The ITM(y) could decompose each task to show the interaction using each method. The value of doing so is questionable and was not attempted.

Combining screen designs   The generation of PSL(y)s from interaction units in the ITM(y) ensures that the dialogue supports an identified task. However, many of the tasks use very similar information at the HCI and in some cases it is logical to combine screens so that one window supports more than one task. It is felt that it would be beneficial to add an activity in the display design stage that methodically identifies screens that are very similar and may be combined.

This concludes the brief overview of the activities at EDS.

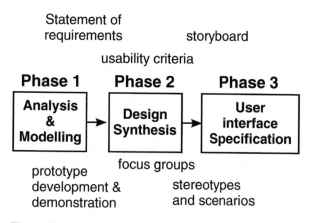

Statement of
requirements   storyboard

usability criteria

Figure 4.6 An overview of the design activities undertaken around MUSE (Philips)

4.2.2 Philips Electronics

A short overview of the application of MUSE by Philips Electronics is provided here. For fuller details the reader is referred to (BIUSEM, Annex E).

Figure 4.6 shows the three phases of MUSE (the blocks in the figure) surrounded with the names of additional human factors (HF) and user interface (UI) design activities that we undertook in Philips in order to arrive at a high-level UI design. These are now described briefly.

4.2.2.1 Phase One – Information elicitation and analysis

The Existing-Systems Analysis stage After the development team had received the initial project brief, an analysis and design activity was planned according to the MUSE method. The task analyses were chosen in order to provide a comprehensive foundation of task descriptions (TDs); we wanted to cover a broad range of tasks, and we wanted these to be performed by a representative sample of the target user group.

Eighteen task analyses were performed by the human factors team, complemented by discussions with experts in X-Ray Diffraction (XRD) to help build our knowledge of the domain.

Transcription of task analyses The task analyses were documented as Structured Diagrams using the notation suggested (but not prescribed) by MUSE in conjunction with tables to record selected highlights (e.g. design sparks, problems identified with the task, or information about some object or fact

of the domain). The structured diagram and table form a Task Description. The structured diagrams were first drawn up on an electronic whiteboard. This permits their development as a team effort, it being easy to iterate over the task description till we were happy that it captured all the aspects observed, and at the right level. Final copies were produced using a tool, *Select Yourdon*, while the tables were constructed in Microsoft Word. These task descriptions were verified with the task performers in order to ensure that they accurately represented the task analysed. Figure 4.7 shows how the Task Descriptions contributed to the generation of subsequent design documents, and gives an overview of the relationships between the activities undertaken during Phase 1 of MUSE.

Understanding and developing user requirements In order to constrain the design of the target system, clearer requirements than had been available in the project brief had to be defined. For the purposes of the MUSE activity, a set of initial software requirements were derived which made some assumptions about the target user group and the likely functionality of the system. These were needed because a user interface can only be designed with knowledge of (or in conjunction with) the functional design of the system. Knowledge of the target user group is also needed to aid decisions made regarding the look and feel of the interface.

The high-level description of the concept provided an outline of the functionality to be provided by the system. Further possibilities for system functionality were suggested by task performers themselves during task analyses, or arose from discussions among the team. The ideas associated with each analysis were collated into a table of Design Speculations and this provided much source material for the Statement of User Needs (SUN). Non-functional requirements of the system were also considered, including applicable user interface guidelines and interoperability requirements.

The core requirements for the concept system were compiled into a Statement of Requirements (SoRe) and the non-functional requirements (primarily user needs) were fed into the companion document – the SUN. Though MUSE does not give them great emphasis (or even a clearly defined structure), these two documents are essential components of the MUSE process and are frequently required for discussion of the target system.

The derivation of user needs was a process which commenced in Phase 1 rather than in Phase 2 as MUSE defines it, because we saw the derivation of

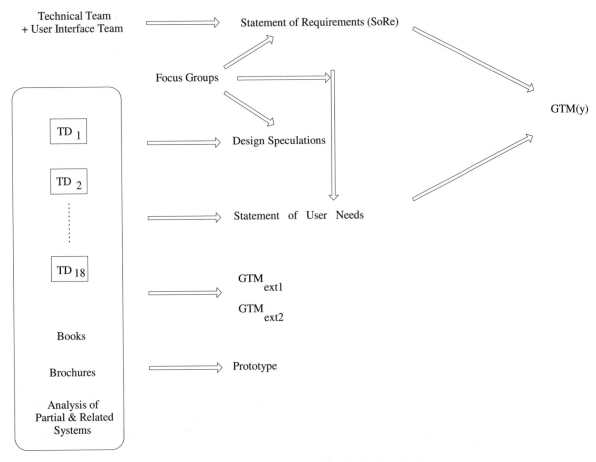

Figure 4.7 Activities undertaken in Phase 1 of MUSE (Philips)

the SUN as a way to clarify the requirements and model of the target system.

Usability requirements exposed during task analyses and observations regarding potential usability improvements were documented in tables associated with each task description.

Generalized Task Models The Generalised Task Models (GTM) of *existing* systems are suffixed with (*ext*) while the models related to the *target* system are suffixed with (*y*) in order to differentiate them (hence the labels GTM(ext) and GTM(y)).

The general models of each existing system, GTM(ext)s, present a high-level description of the union of the tasks undertaken with that system. The generalized models of existing systems were verified by asking the performers of the original tasks (from which they were derived) to check that the high-level descriptions reflected what they had done, i.e. that the task which was analysed could be undertaken within the high-level description presented.

After gaining knowledge of current systems from the task analyses, we were able to generate a high-level description of the target system – the GTM(y). The SoRe and SUN were prime sources of information for constructing the GTM(y), and the associated table for the GTM(y) captured many of the same requirements and design guidelines. The GTM(y) by its nature is high level, but it was sufficient to represent the outline of a design for the purposes of discussion within the human factors team in subsequent stages of MUSE.

4.2.2.2 Phase Two – Design synthesis

This phase contained two distinct stages:

1. the construction of a model composed of existing and desired task behaviours;
2. the allocation of tasks between system and user.

Figure 4.8 shows how the results of the Phase 1 activities (high-level descriptions of existing and desired task behaviours) fed into the activities undertaken in Phases 2 and 3 of MUSE.

This section provides details of the activities undertaken during Phase 2 of the MUSE method.

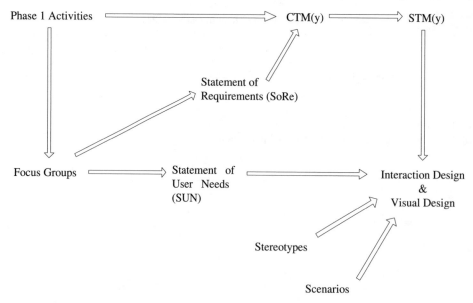

Figure 4.8 Relationship between activities Phases 1, 2 and 3 of MUSE (Philips)

Focus groups In order to obtain feedback on the conclusions we had reached on users' needs and the technologies that might be utilized to meet those needs, we arranged two focus groups. Design ideas for the target system were presented and their validity tested by discussion in a focus group held with experts. The focus group exposed new candidate solutions and provided expert feedback on the desired functionality of the intended system. User needs and design ideas were discussed in a focus group with the sales managers in order to get feedback and input from people with knowledge of a range of users.

The requirements of the system (SoRe) and the high-level model of the target system (GTM(y)) were revised after the focus groups. Design ideas were collated into a Design Speculation document, and the user needs identified during Phase 1 were collated into a single document – the Statement of User Needs (SUN). The revised SoRe, SUN and GTM(y), and the high-level (generalized) descriptions of tasks, then provided material for the development of the composite task model of the target system and helped to structure the user interface.

A Composite Task Model of the target system, the CTM stage The Composite Task Model (CTM) of the target system represents a synthesis of the best user interface features found in existing systems and manual tasks, united with further desired behaviours to support new tasks and improved usability.

The CTM(x) The construction of a Composite Task Model of *existing* systems CTM(x) proved to be a very difficult stage for this project. The CTM(x) is intended to identify the human factors elements of existing systems that are deemed to be useful for porting to the target system. An attempt was made to produce a CTM(x) from the two general task models of existing systems (GTM(ext)s), but only a fragmented CTM(x) could be synthesized. There are a number of reasons for this.

1. Many of the features of existing systems were not thought to be appropriate for porting.
2. Owing to the large number of related systems, only a relatively narrow range of existing packages had been analysed.

The derivation of the CTM(y) There were some functional features in existing systems which were thought to be good enough to port through to the target design, but it was thought that basing the CTM(y) upon the GTM(y) and SUN(y), and borrowing from the GTM(ext)s and TDs, would be a more productive way to get to the target system than by trying to construct a poor CTM(x). The functionality of the target system (i.e. the allocation of tasks between computer and user) was still a matter for discussion/debate and this was another reason for going ahead with the derivation of the CTM(y) – the document upon which this discussion can take place.

The initial allocation of tasks – CTM(y)* The CTM(y) provides a conceptual model for the target system and a basis for allocating functions between human and computer based upon the SUN(y) and SoRe. Once an initial allocation of tasks has taken place, the CTM(y) is referred to as the CTM(y)*, as the structured diagrams for the CTM(y) and the CTM(y)* differ only in annotation regarding task allocation. However, the table of the CTM(y) contains information regarding decisions made about the functionality of the final system, while the table associated with the CTM(y)* was developed to contain information relating to the allocation of tasks.

A usability model for the target user groups
In order to progress the design activity, we needed further detailed descriptions of the target user group. We constructed a usability model (Jordan *et al.*) as shown in Figure 4.9. The graph plots an approximation of user performance (in terms of effort required to use the system) as a function of the number of uses of the system – for users from *three* user groups. This graph gives an indication of the expected initial performance of a user, and then shows how this should improve over time. A minimum acceptable performance level (MAP) (the criteria for system acceptance) is shown, as is expert user performance (the best performance expected

with the system). NB: The maximum system performance is the best performance one can achieve theoretically; it is therefore even beyond expert user performance.

The graph enabled us to *discuss* the different needs of the user groups; for example, a technician needs to achieve minimum acceptable performance relatively quickly, but does not need to acquire great fluency or understanding of the system. In contrast, an expert would need to be able to access 'expert' features of the system (including 'accelerators') relatively quickly, but not necessarily improve performance a great deal because we would expect them to explore new functionality and new experiments rather than repeating the same operations. We would expect a materials scientist to perform initially a little slower than (or as well as) the expert, but after a few uses of the system we would expect a materials scientist to rapidly access the functionality they will use most frequently, and thus become very efficient with the system.

The allocation of tasks between system and user The System and User Task Model stage of MUSE is the point when human-computer interactions to achieve the on-line tasks can be defined. The system task model (STM) represents the high-level functional design of the system, while the user task model is a design of the tasks that the

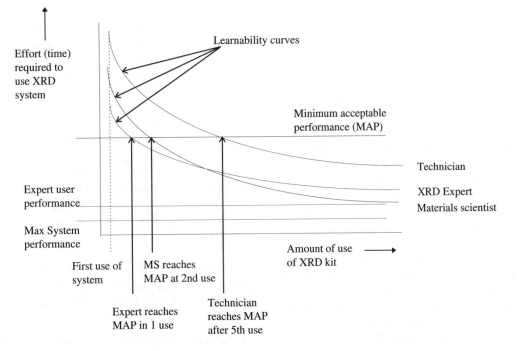

Figure 4.9 Learnability curves for different user groups

user will perform away from the system; the latter is used to support workload assessment and job re-design.

The development of the System Task Model: The STM The System Task Model of the target system, the STM(y), was derived from the CTM(y)* by decomposing the on-line tasks to describe cycles of human–computer interaction. The STM(y) suggests the form and content of potential user interface objects for user interaction, and provides a start-point for defining the content and context of feedback to the user, such as prompts, help and error messages.

The off-line tasks are captured in the User Task Model but the option of on-line activity (help or network access) for off-line tasks meant that it was necessary (for purposes of clarity) to preserve information regarding off-line tasks in the STM(y).

The development of the User Task Model The core of the User Task Model was taken from the CTM(y)* which outlined many off-line tasks. As the STM(y) developed, more detail could be added and the threading and overlapping of the on-line and off-line tasks became clearer.

4.2.2.3 Phase Three – Design specification

This phase contained two stages:

1. the design and specification of an interaction model;
2. the design and specification of visual appearance.

Stereotypes As we progressed with the user interface design of the target system, a graphic designer was involved. We described the target system to her, and showed the MUSE documents, but the designer needed knowledge of the users and their working environment in order to help her define a style for the user interface – and this information was missing from the MUSE document set.

We defined several stereotypical users from the differing user groups in order to give her an idea of the user population; the designer wanted to know about the personalities and home-life of the stereotypes as well as their skills and working lives. Based upon the users and experts we had had contact with during the analysis phases, we defined stereotypes for a materials scientist, a technician, and an expert (though the reader should note that all are fictitious).

Scenarios In order to get an impression of how the different users would make use of the target system in their daily routines, we defined scenarios of usage which were again informed by the analyses we had undertaken. The scenarios added depth to the stereotypes we had defined as well as providing a succinct insight to the functionality of the target system.

The scenarios are close to tasks which might be undertaken with the system. For example, one scenario relates to the materials scientist and involves the analysis of jet-engine parts in order to identify the reason for failure; another scenario relates to the technician and the use of XRD for testing paint in a factory.

Interaction Task Model This stage of design provides a device-level description of the user interactions required to achieve the on-line tasks described by the STM(y). Interaction design considers the user's whole experience with the system, taking a rough 'look and feel' according to error-free usage and developing it into detailed description of screen images and behaviours which include errors and error-recovery.

Storyboarding In generating an Interaction Task Model, ITM(y), MUSE recommends that the STM(y) be 'decomposed' to a level that is understood by all parties – but in our case this required us to utilize *another* notation. Due to the skills brought by the people involved (a designer, an ergonomist and software engineers skilled in UI design), *storyboards* became the main medium for interaction design of the system. The storyboards took two forms – initially screens were sketched on paper and arcs drawn between them to show transitions; then, as our ideas developed, screens were represented by stickits™ laid out on an A0 sheet of paper which allowed much more flexibility in the organization of the UI.

Successive storyboards were reviewed with respect to the SUN(y), SoRe and GTM(y), much like the ITM(y) would have been reviewed – in this way we ensured consistency with functional requirements and user needs.

Storyboard vs ITM(y) It was found to be very difficult to develop an interaction model of the target system, the ITM(y), using the structured notation, and there are a number of reasons for this.

● In order to produce an ITM(y), MUSE recommends that the on-line 'H' leaves of the STM(y) are decomposed into device-level interactions, but this produces a structured diagram with many *hundreds* of nodes where only the leaves (and possibly their parents) are of concern. With a storyboard, however, every node can be a screen and be of direct relevance to the UI.

- Design by its nature is a very iterative activity and a large structured diagram does not easily support rapid design changes. For example, any change to a leaf-node of a structured diagram means that one or more parent nodes might need to be changed; and simple reordering of screens becomes a non-trivial task when several sub-trees are involved. With a storyboard, as screens are added, removed or reordered the effects upon other screens is immediately obvious (there is no hidden high-level structure to be changed).

- The size and level of detail required by the ITM(y) makes the design task difficult because it is hard to remember the system-state and content of screens while the design evolves. In contrast, a storyboard makes the state of the system and screen content explicit and less information needs to be kept in mind to inform subsequent design steps.

In opting to use storyboards rather than a 'formal' description such as a structured diagram, we were susceptible to deviation from the earlier models (i.e. the STM and CTM) and the possibility of introducing inconsistencies. However, the design latitude offered by storyboards enabled us rapidly to explore a wide variety of design ideas, to question the earlier design decisions, and to discover improvements to our earlier thoughts.

The Interface Model In our design we limited ourselves to widgets which exist in the MS-Windows environment (or simple combinations of them) so no new widgets needed to be defined.

Dynamic aspects One of the models that MUSE recommends is a description of the dynamic characteristic of screens, capturing user tasks, system functions and screen actuation. This description is called a Display and Inter-Task Screen Actuation Diagram. It defines the points in the user–computer dialogue when error messages may be relayed to the user, when feedback may be presented and when the user will progress from screen to screen.

We considered producing such a diagram but it was felt that the benefits of the structured description were not worth the *extensive* effort required to produce it, and that the expressive power of the storyboard and screen mock-ups were ample for the task in hand.

Screen design MUSE defines the PSL (or Pictorial Screen Layout) as the structure for capturing the content and layout of screen designs. The PSL for each screen consists of:

- a drawing of the screen identifying all the objects (text, graphics, buttons, menus, and areas for presentation of feedback or error messages);
- a table detailing the screen objects, listing object names and types;
- a table containing prompts and error messages.

A sample of hand-drawn screens were produced to give an idea of the look of the system and complement the early storyboards. In the design of the prototype UI, screen mock-ups in conjunction with storyboards were the most useful tools for design discussion. Together, they allowed detail of interactions (look *and* feel) for various scenarios to be explored, and for rapid redesign to take place.

This concludes the brief overview of the activities at Philips.

4.3 KEY LESSONS

4.3.1 Comments Upon MUSE as a Whole

There is no doubt that MUSE has structured and improved our user needs analysis process, and it provides a structure for design documents which then permit integration of the activity with the software development process. Additionally, validation and verification of analyses are improved by the use of a simple graphical notation for their documentation.

However, MUSE as it stands increases the effort required for the analysis and modelling stages – and this extra effort has to be weighed up against the benefits outlined above.

The reader should note that many of the stages and design documents defined by MUSE are not mandatory or necessarily essential to the user interface design process. For any given project, the necessity of a stage and resource required will need to be assessed by the practitioner in order to maximize the benefits of the method.

As illustrated in Figure 4.10, we found the first two phases of MUSE to be very useful.

MUSE is more appropriately described as a process than a method. It provides for a series of changes, developing a set of requirements into a

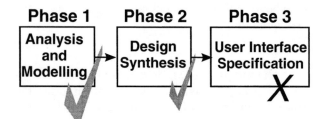

Figure 4.10   Relative benefits of the phases in MUSE

human–computer interaction (HCI) specification, but many of the actions which bring about these changes result from the use of other methods and tools external to the MUSE method (both human factors and software).

The process that MUSE provides represents one of its principal strengths. By describing the stages through which the design evolves, it offers a structure. This structure is of benefit to both human factors and software engineering. For human factors it demonstrates that control can be imposed on activities which are fuzzy due to the human element being described. For software engineering it offers tangible information which can be understood and used within the system context.

4.3.2 MUSE as a Tool for Software Engineers

MUSE is intended to structure the activities of a human factors practitioner and thus assumes knowledge of human factors techniques. We believe that this assumption is flawed both logically and practically.

Logically, there is a need for the software engineer both to understand and to *contribute to* the task-related aspects of the system. One of the aims of MUSE is to build a bridge between human factors and software engineering. This should go further than the simple exchange of documents and agreement of the basis of the design problem.

Practically there is a limited number of human factors specialists who have the appropriate expertise to undertake the design task. This issue becomes a major problem in the development of a large complex system. A single human factors specialist represents a bottleneck to the implementation, i.e. one person evolving the design being implemented by a number of software engineers. The use of more is both impractical (due to availability) and costly.

In order to allow MUSE to be used by other than human factors experts there needs to be clear guidance on where to find and how to use the scien-

tific base, e.g. the selection of appropriate guidelines, standards, methods or tools.

The ability for *non* human factors specialists to utilize a method such as MUSE is important because much user interface design and implementation is undertaken by software engineers or domain specialists. Human factors specialists are needed for new and complex user interface problems, but they are also able to provide the minimal human factors training required to enable a software engineer to undertake good usability engineering. Thankfully, we found that, after a little training, the analysis and modelling required by MUSE was undertaken successfully by software engineers.

4.3.3 Support for Communication Within the Project

At first, the terminology and notations used in MUSE can be confusing to human factors practitioners and software engineers alike. Regrettably, the papers and book on MUSE are written in an unnecessarily confusing style. But, through usage, the method and terminology can be thoroughly understood and many apparently complex procedures become clear.

MUSE supported communication between the members of the human factors team by providing a comprehensive framework for the analysis and design activities, and by defining the generation of design documents of specific content in relatively unambiguous notations. The framework also supported communication between the human factors practitioners and domain experts, who were all able to understand the structured diagrams with little effort.

4.3.4 Integrating the Software and User Interface Development Processes

There are differences in approach for integrating the software and user interface design processes (Curtis and Hefley), (Hix and Hartson). The optimal way to sequence the UI analytical and design activities and the ways in which these may be integrated with the software activities must depend on the nature of the product development project to hand. For truly innovative product development, one can make a strong case for putting a lot of effort on the UI side initially. For intensive development of more mainstream products, a process model (see Figure 4.11) that views the software and UI developments as taking place in parallel may be viable and is often stipulated by product management. We found MUSE very helpful in

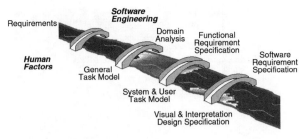

Figure 4.11 Integrating the User Interface and Software Processes

exposing clear points at which the development projects must communicate to exchange information. Additionally, as stated above, the diagrammatic notation that is suggested but not prescribed in the MUSE method goes some way toward mediating that exchange of information.

NB: In the above simplified view, by 'Requirements' we mean an initial project brief; the Requirements are actually developed during initial prototyping. We have represented the existing divide between the human factors (HF) and software engineering (SE) teams as a river and have found this metaphor powerful in many ways. First, it recognizes there is a divide. We do not feel the need to hide this divide; it is there because the disciplines, methods, tools, working cultures etc. are very different. Second, it shows that the divide can be bridged. Third, the metaphor also helps identify additional rivers *within* a discipline, i.e. the divides that exist within the HF and within the SE communities. The former has ergonomists and interaction designers, for example, and the latter has software architects and programmers – these specialists are divided within their respective disciplines.

4.3.5 Support for Validation and Verification with End-users

The construction of structured diagrams using a software engineering tool (Select Yourdon) greatly simplified the validation of diagrams, and the use of a limited set of operators to describe tasks and systems means that diagrams can be easily checked by hand if needed.

The subjects of task analysis were easily able to recognize the tasks described by the structured diagrams and were able to correct the task descriptions as required. This suggests that use of such a graphical notation will enable end-user verification in domains where usage of technical diagrams is commonplace, but we cannot conclude that task performers across a

wide variety of domains will be able to use and verify task descriptions so easily.

4.3.6 Support for Recording Domain Knowledge

The structured diagrams can capture task descriptions as MUSE defines them, but the knowledge contained by this procedural description alone is not enough for the reader of a task description to fully understand the task described. We frequently annotated the task descriptions with typical values for data entry, or domain knowledge to explain a decision taken or a task performed. MUSE indicates that such supportive information should be maintained in the table associated with each task description, but for the task analyst and reader alike it is thought that some local annotation is a better means of aiding comprehension of the descriptions.

4.3.7 Relationship to Other Human Factors Areas

MUSE is directed explicitly at the design of the HCI. The relationship of MUSE to areas where human factors has an impact is discussed as part of the method; however, explicit links between these areas is not provided. Figure 4.12 represents the areas to which human factors contributes. The focus of MUSE is shown by the shadowed boxes; developers need to pay attention to the areas not covered.

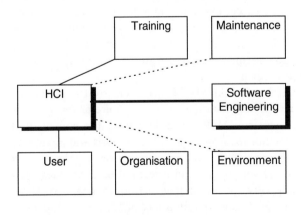

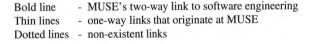

Bold line   - MUSE's two-way link to software engineering
Thin lines   - one-way links that originate at MUSE
Dotted lines - non-existent links

Figure 4.12 The scope of MUSE

4.3.8 Support for Analysis and Description of the Work Context

Greater than the need to record domain knowledge is the need to record detailed information about the task performers, the roles occupied by those people, the roles with which they interact, the teams and organizations within which they work, and the environment in which they work. This information is collected by the task analysts as a consequence of observing and communicating with task performers about their work, and this information is invaluable to the design of a suitable solution. But nowhere does MUSE explicitly describe the need to gather or record this information and no notations or design documents are defined for its capture.

At the very least, information regarding the ability of the target user group needs to be assimilated so that the content of the user interface may be designed appropriately. Furthermore, the roles needing access to the system need to be identified so that functionality may be apportioned and separate interfaces constructed if required.

4.3.9 Elicitation and Specification of Requirements

The use of MUSE is defined to begin once system requirements have been fully defined. In our experience, the human factors activity usually begins when requirements are quite vague; this caused us some difficulties as we progressed towards description of the target system. This is not an unusual situation for a software project, and a situation which MUSE needs to accommodate. Human factors methods such as task analysis are well suited to be used alongside requirements elicitation methods and may well uncover functionality for inclusion in the system requirements.

It is felt that MUSE needs clearly to specify the role of the Statement of Requirements (SoRe). Particularly, MUSE should specify the content and format of the SoRe before the analysis and modelling activities begin. MUSE should also indicate how the user-oriented requirements should be integrated with software requirements. Requirements specifications generally contain a mix of functional and non-functional attributes of the desired system, and human factors activities such as task analysis can contribute to clarification and elaboration in *both* areas. A proposed modification is shown in Figure 4.13.

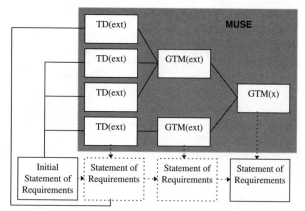

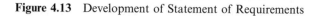

Figure 4.13   Development of Statement of Requirements

4.3.10 Interaction

None of the MUSE documents helped with the design of persistent functionality, such as menus and the options they contain, and status bars for feedback.

4.3.11 Prototyping

Software prototyping forms no part of the MUSE method, flying in the face of conventional practice in the fields of both requirements engineering and user interface development. Prototyping has been widely recognized to help in making vague requirements concrete, in generating insights on functionality or usability and in choosing between different design options, for example. Additionally, as the three phases of MUSE may be lengthy for all but the simplest of projects, it may be difficult to show any 'useful' work for a considerable period of time; a prototype serves to punctuate this lengthy process, conveying a concrete representation of the emerging design ideas. While we accept the importance of a designed and considered prototype, we nevertheless are of the conviction that prototyping cannot always be left to as late a stage as prescribed by MUSE, nor is it desirable to do so.

4.3.12 Traceability

Traceability of requirements (to identify the source of a requirement) and of designs (to identify the source of a design idea or design decision) is required. As MUSE is a design method and does not offer any tool support, neither forms are supported. Consequently, it is very tedious, if not impossible, to trace requirements to ensure they are not being violated or misinterpreted. The traceability of requirements is of fundamental importance in ensuring that the design completely meets the identified needs of the user.

Traceability can be supported by use of the tables, e.g. another column can be added to the tables in each design document, to cross-reference the requirements from the SoRe. However, there is a distinct overhead in maintaining these tables when, for example, the structured diagram is modified. Additionally, matching the requirement to the nodes in the diagram and rows in the table can be difficult. A requirement does not always correspond directly to a set of nodes in a given branch. Similarly a set of nodes may address part of more than one requirement.

The MUSE notation and tables require additional work to offer a mechanism to support effective traceability. The ability to cross-reference requirements on the diagrams would be of use as part of tool support, i.e. to be able to elect to display the requirement or not and to trace the flow of the design addressing a requirement through between documents.

4.3.13 Off-line Tasks

MUSE proposes the concept of off-line tasks (manual tasks), extracting them from the main line of decomposition and representing them in a separate document. Little action is specified for this document and the assumption is that these tasks should have little impact on the design of the HCI to meet the allocation of functions represented in the STM(y). From a broad, organizational-level perspective, this approach is flawed. The most revealing example is to consider the role of supervisor.

Supervisors frequently oversee a number of users, directing their work and tasking them to meet the changing demands of the current situation. Frequently such roles are performed with little or no interaction with the system, e.g. they are mobile. Knowledge of the tasks they perform, and of the information they need to collect in order to undertake their role, is obtained through observing their staff, the tasks they are undertaking, and the system (over their shoulder). Such supervisory roles are fundamental to overall system performance. However, MUSE does not maintain their influence in the mainstream design process. All tasks should be considered when designing the system HCI, or more correctly all roles.

4.3.14 Style Guides

MUSE does not mention the use of style guides to support the design of the HCI. Style guides are frequently identified as part of system requirements. The use of a style guide can assist in the achievement of interoperability with existing applications. A style guide offers a set of widgets with defined ways of operating that may be selected to support components or all of a given dialogue. The operation of these widgets provides the structures that can be represented as an Interface Model. These representations can then be used at the bottom-level decomposition of the ITM(y) to support consistent interaction.

4.3.15 The Creative Leap

The transition from a conceptual design to a detailed design is not supported adequately in MUSE. In the former, the Composite Task Model is felt to be the most useful model as it brings together information on tasks and systems both of the systems analysed and of the target system under development. Its comprehensive recording of logical and temporal relationships gives a very good basis on which to progress the design to the Interaction Task Model in the detailed design stage. However, the transition to the specification of the look and feel is not adequately supported. These are inherently visual and behavioural in nature yet the design documents are relatively lifeless textual descriptions. A graphic style using relevant imagery, fonts and colours brings structure and coherency to the user interface; it can help delineate one subsystem from another, and can distinguish one piece of software from others in the same market. MUSE does not explicitly address the needs of creative input, but it is clear that designers have to be involved early in the design process because their ideas may affect the structure of the user interface and the choice and grouping of widgets.

4.3.16 The need for 'right-sizing' MUSE

Many of the stages and design documents defined by MUSE are not mandatory or essential to the user interface design process. For any given project, the necessity of a stage will need to be assessed in order to decide if it is essential, and appropriate notations will need to be chosen for the deliverables of that stage according to their intended usage.

As we have found, many user interface analysis and design techniques can be used in parallel with

MUSE in order to strengthen and broaden the designs explored. We have also found that once the essence of the method is understood, various stages (mainly those in Phase 3) can be performed much faster using alternative notations.

The key stages of the MUSE method are essential to good user interface design:

- analysis of the task to be supported;
- analysis of existing systems which offer partial solutions;
- analysis of the target users and their work;
- statement of requirements/user needs;
- high-level design of the target system;
- iterative design of the user interface (interaction and visual design);
- specification of the user interface for development and testing.

Originally we saw MUSE as a user interface method to meet all needs, but we found it necessary to take the core concepts from the method and augment them with additional techniques. We also adopted notations which met the needs of the team. If MUSE is understood as a framework or skeleton of a user interface design method, and right-sized to meet the needs of the design task in hand, it is a valuable means for guiding and structuring the design process which supports communication between all involved and produces comprehensive documentation in order to support user interface development.

4.4 CONCLUSIONS AND RECOMMENDATIONS

In this chapter we have described the activities undertaken at EDS and Philips in our evaluation of the MUSE method for user interface design, and the key lessons learnt. Though we applied the method independently, and on different application domains, our findings are convergent. We are confident that our findings are generally applicable.

In summary our finding are that the MUSE method:

- helps improve communications within a project team;
- helps structure user interface analysis and design activities;
- provides a useful way to integrate the user interface and software development activities;
- can be used by software engineers.

However, it

- assumes that software requirements are available *a priori* and that they are fixed;
- has a rather strong focus on task-based design (at the expense of understanding users and to a lesser extent, the context-of-use);
- does not adequately support the latter stages of UI development – namely designing and visualising the dynamic behaviour or interaction;
- does not integrate prototyping within the method;
- does not integrate usability testing with the method;
- does not have any customized tool support;
- is poorly described and therefore its strengths only become visible when applying it on a project;
- does not provide assistance in overcoming the creative leap present in any design project.

Notwithstanding these shortcomings, we believe they are outweighed by the benefits and would recommend development teams to incorporate MUSE (as they see fit) into their development processes.

There is no doubt that MUSE has structured and improved our user interface design process. It has also helped us explicitly identify how and when it should be integrated with the software development process. However, these improvements are not for free; additional effort is required for the task analyses and subsequent design stages. We believe that this additional effort should *not* be dismissed as an overhead but as necessary in order to realize the benefits mentioned above. Readers considering introducing MUSE into their organizations should also note that the many design stages and documents are (a) not mandatory and (b) differ in the effort and resource required for their production. The practitioner is free to adopt and adapt MUSE and indeed must do so to maximize the overall benefit to his other particular product development process, application domain and organization.

We have learnt much and benefited enormously from our collaboration in this ESSI (European Software and Systems Initiative) project, funded in part by the Commission of the European Countries. MUSE offers a good starting framework on which to base improvements to user interface design and product usability. It can certainly be improved, both by the original developers and others moulding it to their particular environment. Above all, even in its present form, it makes a significant contribution both to software process improvement and to the design of more usable systems.

APPENDIX 4.1 THE MUSE METHOD FOR USABILITY ENGINEERING

The following is a simplified description of the original MUSE method as described in the textbook [Lim and Long, 1994].

MUSE is a structured method for usability engineering. The method was developed to address the problem of Human Factors (HF) contributions to the software design process being 'too-little-too-late'. Where an SE method is in use, the contribution of Human Factors may easily become limited to a late stage of design where the product developed by Software Engineers is available for usability assessment; unhappily, this stage of design is one at which changes to the product may be prohibitively expensive. MUSE addresses this problem by specifying the HF design process and the points at which HF and SE specifications should be checked against each other to ensure compatibility.

The design of the user interface is approached in a 'top-down' manner based on information derived 'bottom-up', and progresses in defined stages from specification of general features of the tasks to be performed (derived from analysis of the User Requirements and existing systems for performing the work) to specification of the specific details of the user interface to be implemented. Configuration of MUSE to a given SE method is performed by specifying the points at which certain features of the HF and SE design documents should be communicated between the design streams and checked to ensure that the functionality specified by the software engineering design team is compatible with that required by the Human Factors designers. Thus, the likelihood that the user interface under development will be implementable and provide the appropriate functionality to support the user's task is maximized.

The following paragraphs present a brief description of the method, outlining the three main phases of the method and providing a brief description of the main documents generated in each phase.

The *first* phase of the method is called the Information Elicitation and Analysis Phase. It involves collecting and analysing information intended to inform later design activities, and consists of two stages, the Extant Systems Analysis stage and the Generalized Task Model stage. During the former, background design information is collected that relates both to the system currently in use and to other systems that are related in some way, for example by having a similar task domain. The information concerns the users of the systems, the devices used and the tasks performed, and the objective is to identify those features of the systems that are problematic for users, or that may be suitable for reuse in the target system. During the Generalized Task Model stage, a device-independent task model of the *existing* systems is generated using the task descriptions from the previous stage, and this is used in conjunction with the Statement of Requirements to produce a Generalized Task Model for the *target* system to be designed.

The *second* phase of MUSE, the Design Synthesis phase, begins by establishing the human factors requirements of the design, in terms of performance criteria, likely user problems or required task support, and these are recorded in the Statement of User Needs. The semantics of the application domain as it relates to the worksystem are also analysed in this stage, and are recorded as a semantic network called the Domain of Design Discourse. The Composite Task Model expresses the conceptual design of the *target* system, and is produced using the two Generalized Task Models produced at the end of the first phase. The process of producing the Composite Task Model is informed by the information in the Statement of User Needs and the Domain of Design Discourse, to promote consideration of user problems and particular characteristics of the task domain that should be reflected in the user interface design. The resulting specification is checked against that of the software engineering stream to ensure that the correct functionality will be provided to support the user interface. The conceptual design addresses error-free task performance only in order to avoid obscuring the overall structure of the task; potential user errors are addressed in Phase 3 of the method, where the design is refined iteratively so that the potential for error is minimized.

During the System and User Task Model stage, the Composite Task Model is decomposed to separate the subtasks that are to be performed using the system under development from those that are performed using other devices. The subtasks performed using the 'target' system are represented in the System Task Model, while the remaining ('off-line') tasks are represented in the User Task Model. Within the System Task Model, allocation of function between user and computer is performed, and represented by designating actions as belonging to either 'H' (the user) or 'C' (the computer).

The *final* phase of MUSE is termed the Design Specification phase, and develops the conceptual design further to arrive at a device-specific implementable specification which includes error-recovery procedures. In the Interaction Task Model stage, the leaves of the System Task Model that represent user ('H') actions are further decomposed to produce a device-level specification of the interaction. This specification is mainly informed by the selected User Interface Environment, but the Statement of User Needs and Domain of Design Discourse may also be used to inform design decisions. The Interaction Task Model is annotated to indicate the locations of intended major screen transitions, which in practice are generally the boundaries of individual subtasks. Subsequently, the leaves of the System Task Model representing computer actions are decomposed to produce a set of Interface Models. These are detailed descriptions of the behaviours exhibited by screen objects in response to specified events. In the Display Design stage, a set of Pictorial Screen Layouts are defined to correspond with the screen boundaries identified in the Interaction Task Model. The interface objects that make up the screens are described in the Dictionary of Screen Objects. A further document called the Display and Inter-Task Screen Actuation Diagram is produced that details the conditions under which screen transitions may occur, together with the conditions that would trigger the presentation of an error message. The error messages and dialogues are listed in the Dialogue and Error Message Table.

The look and the feel having been designed, the specification may now be presented to the software engineers for implementation.

The analysis and design information that is developed is documented in a hierarchical structured diagram notation. Documents describing *existing* systems are suffixed with (*ext*) while those related to the *target* system are suffixed with (*y*) in order to differentiate them.

To summarize, MUSE consists of three phases divided into the following stages: Extant Systems Analysis, General Task Model, Composite Task Model, Statement of User Needs, System & User Task Model, Interaction Task Model, Interface Model and Display Design.

REFERENCES

Bass, L. and Coutaz, J. (1991) *Developing Software for the User Interface* (Addison-Wesley).

Bell, D., Gupta, A., Spencer, E. and Rozendaal, H. (1995) Building bridges between human factors and software engineering. *Proceedings of HCI'95*, August.

BIUSEM, Annex A, BIUSEM: Metrics Data, CEC ESSI Project 10290, Oct. 1995.

BIUSEM, Annex B, BIUSEM: Consortium-wide Metrics, CEC ESSI Project 10290, Oct. 1995.

BIUSEM, Annex C, BIUSEM Final Report – EDS Defence, CEC ESSI Project 10290, Oct. 1995.

BIUSEM, Annex D, BIUSEM Final Report – EWI-UK, CEC ESSI Project 10290, Oct. 1995.

BIUSEM, Annex E, BIUSEM Final Report – Philips, CEC ESSI Project 10290, Oct. 1995.

BIUSEM Final Report, Final Report, BIUSEM: Benefits of integrating Usability and Software Engineering Methods, CEC ESSI Project 10290, Oct. 1995.

Browne, D. (1994) *STUDIO Structured User-Interface Design for Interaction Optimisation* (Prentice Hall).

Catterall, B. (1991) Three approaches to the input of human factors in IT systems design: DIADEM, The HUFIT Toolset and the MOD/DTI Human Factors Guidelines, *Behaviour & Information Technology*, **10**(5): pp. 359–371.

Curtis, B and Hefley, B. (1994) A WIMP No More – The Maturing of User Interface Engineering, *ACM Interactions*, Jan., pp. 22–34.

Hix, D. and Hartson, H. R. (1993) *Developing User Interfaces: Ensuring Usability Through Product and Process* (New York: Wiley).

ISO 9241, *Ergonomic Requirements for office work with Visual Display Terminals*. ISO.

Jordan, P., Draper, S., MacFarlane, K. and McNulty, S. (1991) Guessability, learnability, and experienced user performance. *Proc. of BCS HCI'91 Conference on People and Computers VI*, pp. 237–245.

Lim, K. Y. and Long, J. (1994) *The MUSE Method for Usability Engineering* (Cambridge University Press).

Macaulay, L., Fowler, C., Kirby, J. and Hutt, A. (1990). USTM: a new approach to requirements specification. *Interacting with Computers*, **2**(1): pp. 92–118.

Paulk, M., Curtis, B., Chrissis, M. and Weber, C. (1993). *Capability maturity model for software, Version 1.1.* CMU/SEI-93-TR-24, ESC-TR-93-177. Software Engineering Institute, Carnegie Mellon University, Pittsburgh, Pennsylvania 15213.

Sutcliffe, A. G. and McDermott, M. (1991) Integrating methods of human-computer interface design with structured systems development, *Int. J. of Man-Machine Studies*, (34), pp. 631–655.

Wasserman, A., Pircher, P., Shewmake, D. and Kersten, M. (1986). Developing interactive information systems with the user software engineering methodology. In Baecker and Buxton (eds) *Readings in HCI* (Morgan Kaufman), pp. 508–527.

5

A Logic-Based Approach to the Specification and Design of the Control System of a Pondage Power Plant

M. Basso[a], **E. Ciapessoni**[b], **E. Crivelli**[c], **D. Mandrioli**[d], **A. Morzenti**[d], **E. Ratto**[b] **and P. San Pietro**[d]

[a]TXT Ingegneria Informatica, Milano, Italy
[b]CISE Tecnologie Innovative, Segrate, Italy
[c]ENEL/CRA, Cologno Monzese, Italy
[d]Dipartimento di Elettronica e Informazione, Politecnico di Milano, Milano, Italy

EXECUTIVE SUMMARY

We report on an experiment in applying a formal method to the specification and design of an industrial application: the control system of power plants of ENEL, the Italian Energy Board. The experiment was conducted within a project aimed at enabling end-users to apply, on a routine basis, a formal specification method based on a logical approach to the specification and design of automation and control systems. We describe the goals of the experiment, illustrate the specification, validation and verification activities, discuss the fundamental problem of training and teaching formal methods, and assess the encouraging results obtained in the project.

5.1 INTRODUCTION

We report here the results of an ESSI experiment, called ELSA (Experimentation of a Logical approach to the Specification and design of Automation control systems), in applying a formal method to the specification and design of an industrial application concerning the control system of pondage power plants of ENEL, the Italian Energy Board.

The chapter is structured as follows. In the present introductory section we illustrate the motivations, objectives and expected outcomes of the project; in Section 5.2 we briefly overview the TRIO language and tool environment that were applied in the experiment; in Section 5.3 we describe the activity performed, which consisted of education and training, requirements specification, validation of the specification, design, implementation and verification; in the final Section 5.4 we draw conclusions by evaluating, from the technical, business and organizational viewpoint, the results obtained and the lessons learned.

5.1.1 Motivations and Background

Power production, transport and distribution, and the managing of large utility networks (telecommunications, oil and gas transport, railways, underground, highways, etc.) are today largely automated processes, and huge investments are made by several agencies and companies to procure and update the automation systems designed to support these processes. In many cases these systems are committed to external industries on the basis of requirement specifications. This fact justifies a widespread strategic interest in techniques and tools supporting requirement specification guaranteeing a clearer separation from the subsequent design and implementation phases, and a high degree of maintainability of the specifications. Furthermore, such interest in formal requirement specification is fully justified by the need for rigorous techniques for developing *verified* and *validated* systems. In most cases the required apparatus has to be purchased in large quantity, and the inconveniences due to installation delays or to errors in its developed form are so important that it is justified to adopt almost any means to detect conflicting requirements, discrepancies between requirements and design specifications, etc. as early as possible.

A long-term objective of ENEL, and a main motivation of the ELSA project, was to improve the quality of the products managed by ENEL without subverting the life cycle applied in ENEL, which derives from experience matured over several decades. In this life cycle both functional and non-functional requirements must be clearly defined before beginning the development phase. Application requirements are described in natural language according to informal schemes. Then the domain experts produce the detailed system specification, by using informal expression or semi-formal languages (e.g. SADT, SART). Next, the supplier, selected through a public bid, designs and implements the system, supported by means of appropriate methods, languages and tools in accordance with global constraints coming from dependability requirements. Final code is debugged and tested following the testing plans defined during the design phase. Often feedback actions on design and implementation must be undertaken. After hardware and software integration, the final result is submitted to assessment, carried out by ENEL. Assessment mainly consists of reproducing by simulation the behaviour of the plant or of the most critical parts.

The main drawbacks of the life cycle outlined above are as follows.

- ENEL experts and the supplier must interact closely to clarify the user requirement specification and to give an initial validation of the design.
- Test plans are defined during the design and the implementation phases (not during the specification phase): this implies lack of thoroughness and high costs.
- Test plan production is a high-cost activity whose results mainly depend on expert ability to take into account all the requirements and their modifications identified at every step of the development process.

- ENEL experts are involved in many activities of the software life cycle and the required effort is spread over a long period of time.
- Most errors and inadequacies in the initial requirement specification and design are identified during the final validation of the system.

On the basis of these motivations, some years ago ENEL started research activities on formal specification methods, and in particular an activity aimed at developing a logical specification method and a set of tools, called TRIO (*Tempo Reale ImplicitO*) [GMM90, MMG92, M&S94]. The TRIO framework is based on a temporal logic language, devised to formally express temporal constraints, and extended with suitable object-oriented primitives to support the specification of complex industrial real-time systems. The development of TRIO has involved ENEL/CRA (ENEL's Automatic Research Centre), CISE (an applied research centre controlled by ENEL), and Politecnico di Milano.

In past years, several case studies were conducted to investigate the adequacy of TRIO as a specification, validation and verification method [CSt90, CSt92]. The ELSA project was the first application of the TRIO-based method to the full development life cycle of an industrially sized application. Participants in the project included ENEL and CISE, involved in the project as partners, and Politecnico di Milano and TXT Ingegneria Informatica (an Italian software house), involved as subcontractors. In ELSA ENEL played two roles: on the research side as one of the developers of the TRIO methodology, and on the industrial side, as the user interested in experimenting with the approach. CISE and Politecnico di Milano provided technical and didactic support on TRIO and collected the feedback derived from its use. TXT Ingegneria Informatica acted as a supplier for designing and implementing the Coordinator. TXT, having previously developed a similar control system, could contribute to a more precise evaluation of the impact of TRIO on design, coding and testing activities.

5.1.2 Objectives

The aim of the ELSA project was to prove the adequacy of TRIO by experimenting with it on a real automation project. The results should allow ENEL to extend the use of TRIO, on a routine basis, for requirement specification and validation of plant automation systems. Since the consequences deriving from the use of TRIO cannot be confined to the specification and acceptance phases, but have an impact also on the design phase usually performed by external suppliers, ELSA has considered the *full development* of a control system (from here on called the Coordinator) for pondage power plants and also involved external developers.

The experiment addressed two further objectives, namely to evaluate user and supplier reactions to the adoption of a formal specification method, and to give feedback to TRIO developers to enable further improvements of the specification languages, tools and methodology.

5.1.3 Expected Outcomes

With respect to this scenario, use of the TRIO framework was expected to lead to the following advantages.

1. In the *requirements specification* phase, TRIO was expected to improve the overall quality of the specification documents, because its formality implies clear, unambiguous and understandable descriptions; its object-oriented constructs support well-structured, modular specifications; its descriptive approach allows the specifier to focus on requirements, forgetting design and implementation aspects.

2. *Design and implementation activities* were also expected to benefit from the adoption of TRIO. The use of TRIO should facilitate interaction between the automation specialist team and the design and development teams. TRIO was expected to reduce recycles in design/development due to incorrect or ambiguous requirement specifications, to make more precise the contractual obligations of external companies involved in system development, to reduce risks on cost evaluation, thus making the project schedule and required budget more predictable, and to allow for validation of partial specifications so that error detection can take place very early at each step of the specification development.

3. *Product acceptance* should also be facilitated, as test cases extracted by TRIO specifications would make possible a faster and better check of the critical requirements of the system.

4. In conclusion, the use of formal specifications, while augmenting the effort needed for the requirements specification phase, was expected to lead to a significant reduction in the costs and time of the overall project and, most important, was expected to improve significantly the quality of the design documentation and the correctness of the developed product. As a consequence, the gains in process productivity and product quality should increase and become more and more apparent in the later phases (design, product acceptance, and maintenance) of the developed system.

On the other hand, ELSA was expected to suggest important feedback about user acceptance of the method, training and support, a very crucial step for introducing formal methods in an industrial context. Such feedback is expected to contribute to further improvement of TRIO, by suggesting modifications and extensions relevant to language constructs and the functionality of tools.

5.2 AN OVERVIEW OF THE TRIO LANGUAGE AND ITS ENVIRONMENT

The TRIO environment includes a basic logic language here called LTRIO for specifying in-the-small, an object-oriented extension, here called OOTRIO, that supports modular reusable specification of highly complex systems, and a set of editing and semantic tools. LTRIO, OOTRIO and the tools will be presented, respectively, in Sections 5.2.1, 5.2.2, and 5.2.3.

5.2.1 The Basic Logical Language LTRIO

LTRIO is a first-order logical language, augmented with temporal operators to describe the truth of propositions at time instants different from the current one, which is left implicit in the formula.

The alphabet of LTRIO is composed of variable, function and predicate names, plus the usual propositional connectors '$\neg$', '$\rightarrow$', '$\wedge$', '$\vee$', '$\leftrightarrow$', and the quantifiers '$\exists$' and '$\forall$'. To permit the representation of change in time, variables, functions and predicates are divided into *time-dependent* and *time-independent* ones. Time-dependent variables represent physical quantities or configurations that are subject to change in time, and time-independent ones represent values unrelated with time. Time dependent functions and predicates denote relations, properties or events that may or may not hold at a given time instant, while time-independent functions and predicates represent facts and properties which can be assumed not to change with time.

LTRIO is a typed language, and among the various domains there is a distinguished one, called the *Temporal Domain*, which is numerical in nature: it can be the set of integer, rational or real numbers,

Operator	Definition	Explanation
AlwF(A)	$\forall t\ (t > 0 \rightarrow Futr(A, t))$	A will always hold
AlwP(A)	$\forall t\ (t > 0 \rightarrow Past(A, t))$	A has always held
Alw(A)	$AlwP(A) \wedge A \wedge AlwF(A)$	A always holds
Som(A)	$\neg Alw\ (\neg A\ )$	Sometimes A holds
Lasts(A, d)	$\forall d'(0 < d' < d \rightarrow Futr(A, d'))$	A will hold over a period of length d
Lasted(A, d)	$\forall d'(0 < d' < d \rightarrow Past(A, d'))$	A held over a period of length d in the past
Until(A$_1$, A$_2$)	$\exists t\ (t > 0 \wedge Futr(A_2, t) \wedge Lasts(A_1, t)\ )$	A$_1$ will hold until A$_2$ starts to hold
Since (A$_1$, A$_2$)	$\exists t\ (t > 0 \wedge Past\ (A_2, t) \wedge Lasted\ (A_1, t)\ )$	A$_1$ held since A$_2$ became true
UpToNow (A)	$\exists \delta\ (\ \delta > 0 \wedge Past\ (A, \delta) \wedge Lasted\ (A, \delta)\ )$	A held for a non-empty left time interval
Becomes (A)	$A \wedge UpToNow\ (\neg A)$	A holds now but not up to now

or any interval thereof, with the usual arithmetic relations and operators.

LTRIO formulas are constructed in the classical inductive way, starting from terms and atomic formulas. Besides the usual propositional operators and the quantifiers, one may compose LTRIO formulas by using primitive and derived *temporal operators*. There are two temporal operators, *Futr* and *Past*, which allow the specifier to refer, respectively, to events occurring in the future or in the past with respect to the current, implicit time instant. If *A* is an LTRIO formula and *t* is a term of the temporal type, then *Futr(A, t)* and *Past(A, t)* are LTRIO formulas that are satisfied at the current time instant if and only if property *A* holds at the instant *t* time units ahead or behind the current one. On the basis of the primitive temporal operators *several* derived ones can be defined. For illustrative purposes we show some of them (which include most operators of classical temporal logic) above.

5.2.2 The Object-Oriented Language Extension OOTRIO

LTRIO has proved to be a useful specification tool, since it combines the rigour and precision of formal methods with the expressiveness and naturalness of first-order and modal logic. The use of LTRIO for the specification of large and complex systems, however, has shown its major flaw: as originally defined, the language does not support directly and effectively the activity of structuring a large and complex specification into a set of smaller modules, each one corresponding to a well-identified, autonomous subpart of the system that is being specified. This is because LTRIO specifications are very finely structured: the language does not provide powerful abstraction and classification mechanisms, and lacks an intuitive and expressive graphic notation.

To support specification of large systems, LTRIO has been enriched with concepts and constructs from object-oriented methodology, yielding a language here called OOTRIO. Among the most important features of OOTRIO are the ability to partition the universe of objects into classes, inheritance relations among classes, and mechanisms such as genericity to support the reuse of specification modules and their top-down, incremental development (for the sake of brevity we do not illustrate, in the following, genericity and inheritance: the interested reader is referred to [M&S94]). Structuring the specification into modules supports an incremental, top-down approach to the specification activity through successive refinements, but also allows one to build independent and reusable subsystem specifications that could be composed in a systematic way in different contexts. Also desirable is the possibility of describing the specified system at different levels of abstraction, and of focusing with greater attention and detail on some more relevant aspects, leaving unspecified, or less formalized, other parts that are considered less important or that are already well understood.

OOTRIO is also endowed with an expressive graphic representation of classes in terms of boxes, arrows and connections to depict class instances and their components, information exchange, and logical equivalencies among (parts of) objects. The ability to visualize constructs of the language and use their graphic representation to construct, update or browse specifications can make a great difference in the productivity of the specification process and in the final quality of the resulting product, especially when the graphic view is consistently supported by means of suitable tools, such as structure-directed editors, consistency checkers and report generators.

OOTRIO classes denote collections of objects that satisfy a set of axioms. They can be either simple or structured – the latter term denoting classes obtained by composing simpler ones in some way: the two categories are introduced in the next subsections.

```
class sluice_gate
    visible go, position
    temporal domain integer
    TD Items
        predicates go({up, down})
        vars position: {up, down, mvup, mvdown}
    TI Items
        consts Δ : integer
axioms
    vars t: integer
    go_down: position=upgo(down)∧Lasts (position=mvdown,Δ)→Futr(position=down,Δ)
    go_up: position=down ∧ go(up)→Lasts(position=mvup,Δ)∧Futr(position=up,Δ)
    move_up: position=mvup go (down)∧∃t NextTime(position=up,t)
                       →Futr(Lasts(position=mvdown,Δ) Futr(position=down,Δ),t)
    move_down: position=mvdown go(up)∧∃t NextTime(position=down,t)
    reliability: the Mean Time Between Failures of the engine must be greater than 5 years
end sluice_gate
```

5.2.2.1 Simple OOTRIO classes

Essentially, a simple class is defined through a set of LTRIO axioms premised by a declaration of all items that are referred to therein in much the same way as traditional Pascal-like programs consist of a declarative part followed by an executable part. The main syntactic features of such classes are explained in the example above, which refers to a sluice gate specification.

The example suggests a natural partition of the class definition into a header, a declaration of several elements, and a set of axioms. The class *header*, which gives the name of the class, is followed by the *visible* clause, which defines the class *interface*. In the example, *go* and *position* are the only available symbols when referring to modules of the class sluice_gate in the axioms of another class. The *temporal domain* clause determines the temporal domain of the specification. The domain is always numerical in nature: for instance, it can be the set of integer, real or rational numbers. Here, discrete time is considered. The keyword *TD Items* is followed by the declarations of the local time-dependent functions, predicates and variables; the keyword *TI Items* is followed by the local time-independent functions, predicates and constants. The declarations are based on predefined scalar types. In the example Δ is an integer constant, *go* is a unary time-dependent predicate on the set {up, down}, *position* is a time-dependent variable whose values may range on {up, down, mvup, mvdown}.

The *axioms* are LTRIO formulas or natural language sentences, thus allowing for the description of a system that mixes formal and informal specifications. The LTRIO formulas of the *axioms* are prefaced with an implicit universal temporal quantification, i.e. an *Always* temporal operator. A name can precede an axiom, to be used as a reference for axiom redefinition in inheritance. A *vars* clause between the keyword *axioms* and the axioms can be used to declare the time-independent variables occurring in the axioms. The items and the variables of a class (including the inherited ones) are the only symbols of variables, predicates and functions which can occur in class axioms.

The graphical representation of the above class sluice_gate is shown in Figure 5.1.

5.2.2.2 Structured OOTRIO classes

A class may have components of other classes, i.e. every instance of the class may contain parts that are instances of those classes. Classes which have components – called modules – of other classes are called *structured classes*. They permit the construction of OOTRIO modular specifications, especially suited to describe systems in which *parts*, i.e. *modules*, can be easily recognized. A first illustration of the notion of structured class is provided by the following example. A reservoir may have two actuators, one to control each sluice gate, and a transducer which measures the

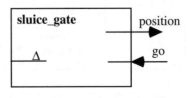

Figure 5.1 A graphical representation of class sluice_gate

```
class reservoir
    visible transducer.level, openInput, closeInput, openOutput, closeOutput
    temporal domain integer
    TD Items
        predicates openInput, closeInput, openOutput, closeOutput
    modules      inputGate, outputGate: sluice_gate
                 transducer: cl_transducer
                 actuator1, actuator2: actuator
    connections
        {       (openInput actuator1.open)
                (closeInput actuator1.close)
                (openOutput actuator2.open)
                (closeOutput actuator2.close)
                (actuator1.go inputGate.go)
                (actuator1.position outputGate.position)
                (actuator2.go outputGate.go)
                (actuator2.position outputGate.position)         }
    axioms
        Ax1: inputGate.position=down outputGate.position up
end reservoir
```

level of the reservoir. The external plant is able to send four commands to control the reservoir, to open or close each sluice gate. This can be described by defining the class *reservoir* as shown above.

Every instance of this class contains two instances of sluice_gate, one instance of *cl_transducer* and two instances of *cl_actuator*. We assume classes *cl_transducer* and *cl_actuator* as already defined. The interface of *cl_transducer* includes a time-dependent variable *level*, and the interface of *cl_actuator* contains the propositional time-dependent variables *open* and *close*, plus *go* and *position* with the same meaning as in *sluice_gate*.

Connections is a list of pairs, denoting equivalence or identity between two items in the current scope. In the example, the commands openInput, closeInput, openOutput, closeOutput and the instantaneous

value of reservoir level are all that the external world is allowed to know of a reservoir. The connections state that the commands are not sent directly to the gates, but to the actuators, which control the gates and decide when to move them up and down. Connections are a useful tool for the specification of a complex system: the user describes system components separately; then he/she identifies information flows between them.

Structured classes have an intuitive graphic representation: the modules of the class are just boxes, with a name and a line for every visible item. The graphic representation of class *reservoir* is shown in Figure 5.2.

Modules cannot be used directly in axioms, because they are not logical symbols such as predicate or function names: they represent a set of item and module definitions, with related axioms. For the same reason the visible interface cannot list entire modules, but only their visible items, such as *inputGate.go*. The visible items of a module can be accessed in the axioms of an enclosing class by using a dot notation.

OOTRIO supports some more facilities to specify complex real-world systems. We illustrate the array construct by elaborating the previous example: a class specifying a four-gate reservoir may be built as follows:

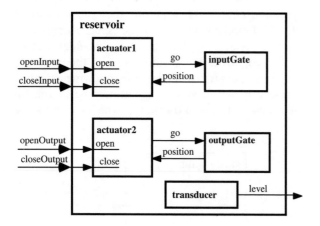

Figure 5.2 Graphic representation of the structured class reservoir

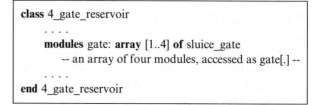

```
class 4_gate_reservoir
    . . . .
    modules gate: array [1..4] of sluice_gate
        -- an array of four modules, accessed as gate[.] --
    . . . .
end 4_gate_reservoir
```

As in traditional Pascal-like languages, the user can access elements of an array by indexing. So, *gate[2].position* is the component *position* of the second element of the array *gate*. Enumeration types, for instance (input, output, emergencyInput, emergencyOutput), can be used as array ranges.

5.2.3 The TRIO Environment

A major feature of the LTRIO language is its *executability*. This allows for the construction of semantic tools that help specification verification and implementation validation, e.g. through prototyping (specification simulation) and through test case generation, respectively.

Executability is achieved in LTRIO along the following lines. A model-theoretic semantics is defined for the language, i.e. an interpretation schema is given that, for any LTRIO formula, aims at building possible *models* of the formula. (We recall that a model of a logic formula is an assignment of values to variables and predicates occurring in the formula, such that the formula evaluates to TRUE. In the case of TRIO, an assignment to a time-dependent variable or predicate means assigning a value in the suitable domain for each instant in the time domain. For this reason a model of a TRIO formula is also called a *history* thereof.) In general, since LTRIO includes first-order arithmetic, the satisfiability of arbitrary formulas (i.e. stating whether or not there exists a model for a formula) is undecidable. Thus, the general interpretation algorithm mentioned above is not guaranteed to terminate with a definite answer. Partial executability is however obtained by exploiting the idea of *finite approximation of infinite domains*. Original interpretation domains, which are usually infinite, are replaced by finite approximations thereof. Of course, there is no *a priori* warranty that the result obtained in the finite domain coincides with the theoretical result that would be obtained on the infinite domain. In practice, however, we may often rely on this type of *specification testing* on the basis of the following considerations.

- Quite often our common sense and experience can tell us that if the system we are specifying and implementing has a dynamic behaviour with a time evolution of the order of magnitude of, say, seconds, then, after having tested it for several hours, all 'relevant facts' about it have been generated.

- We may try several executions with different time domains of increasing cardinality (domain T_{i+1} strictly includes domain T_i). If we detect that, from some T_k, the result of formula interpretation does not change, we may infer that it will not change forever in the future. In a similar way, several numerical algorithms are considered as sufficiently '*stable*' if their results do not change too much from one iteration to another one, even if no mathematical proof of convergence exists.

The TRIO environment includes both editing tools (for writing and documenting specification and related artifacts) and semantic tools (for analysing specifications and supporting validation and verification activities), which we outline below.

- An interactive, graphical editor for LTRIO and OOTRIO. The editor supports the incremental writing of TRIO-based specifications by checking them against syntactic incompleteness and inconsistency, but allowing the specifier to continue the editing activity even in erroneous states, after having output appropriate *warning* messages. In principle, it should support the editing of specifications both in textual and in graphical versions in a completely interchangeable manner. The present prototype, however, supports in a completely automatic way only the translation from graphical to textual versions and provides only a limited help in the opposite direction.

- A test case editor. This tool supports the production of *testing documentation* (test cases, testing results, comments of any type, etc.) associated with an OOTRIO specification. It is already integrated with the specification editor.

- A translator from OOTRIO to LTRIO.

- An LTRIO interpreter. This tool allows for prototyping of specifications and verification of their properties such as consistency. Different operating modes allow the designer to manage a trade-off between generality and complexity. For instance, in the 'history checking' [F&M94] mode the user supplies the specification and a possible behaviour of the specified system, and the tool checks whether the latter is compatible with the former. In the 'history generation' mode the user supplies only the specification and the tool generates all behaviours that are compatible with the given specification. Clearly, the former operating mode is far more efficient than the latter.

- A test case generator [MMM95]. This tool allows the semi-automatic – i.e. user-driven generation of functional test cases associated with a given LTRIO specification against which the designer can check implementation correctness. The core of the tool, again, is interpretation mechanisms that generate models compatible with the given specifications. The interpretation algorithms, however, are tailored to the specialized use of test case production.

5.3 ACTIVITY REPORT

The performed activity consisted of education and training, requirements specification, validation and verification planning, and design, implementation and verification. We report on these activities in the following sections 5.3.1 through 5.3.4.

5.3.1 Education and Training

TRIO, like any other formal method, requires appropriate training of users to avoid a negative impact. Thus, the ELSA project included an initial training activity whose trainees were ENEL experts in the application domain and TXT designers and developers. Several seminars, focusing on practical use of TRIO languages, methodology and tools, were organized by CISE and Politecnico di Milano during the first months of the experiment. The seminars were structured in four sections:

1. *basic propositional and predicate logic*, dealing with notions of logical connectives, quantifiers, predicates and functions;
2. *basic TRIO language*, covering the TRIO temporal logic with its operators, aimed at allowing the trainees to write and understand simple TRIO specifications;
3. *OOTRIO language and methodology*, focused on the object-oriented version of the language and the associated methodology (at the end of this phase, the trainees were able to produce structured specifications of complex system components);
4. *TRIO tools*, centred on the use of the graphic and textual editor and test case generator (some examples were developed by trainees with the assistance of the teachers).

The outcome of the training activity was satisfactory concerning the use of the language for system specification: the trainees learned to use the language in a real application with a reasonable effort. Special attention was needed to develop the necesssary basis of mathematical logic: this, in fact, turned out to be the major conceptual difficulty, mainly for older people without a fresh mathematical background.

5.3.2 Requirements Specification

The system under specification is a hydroelectric power generation plant, as schematically depicted in Figure 5.3, which includes its main physical components.

A pondage power plant is composed of a reservoir where the main water supply accumulates and whose level is regulated by means of a sluice gate. When the sluice gate is open the water flows through a channel into a tank. From the tank the water is forced into the power station, where its mechanical energy is converted into electrical energy. The power plant is monitored through a set of sensors and is regulated by means of a set of actuators governed by a central control system.

The formal specification activity did not start completely from scratch, but was preceded by a preliminary and preparatory activity whose purpose was to produce an overall description of the system structure and an informal specification of its requirements.

Owing to the complexity of the system this activity had demanded a significant amount of time and human resources. It had been conducted by skilled personnel who were particularly expert in the application domain, although not particularly fluent and experienced in the exploitation of formal methods. This activity resulted in the production of a document about 50 pages long, written mainly in an informal, unstructured way: natural language (Italian prose) for general descriptions mixed with simple mathematical and graphical notations for describing some quantitative aspects.

The actual formal specification activity was based on this informal specification document. It led to the production of two kinds of documents.

First, a set of notes was produced to update and correct (mainly to eliminate inconsistency and incompleteness) the initial informal specification. These notes, about 20 pages long, were written in the same style as the informal specification, and their

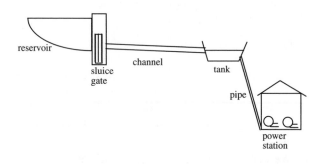

Figure 5.3 Physical components of the pondage power plant

purpose was to complement it in order to provide all the information that was actually necessary to perform the formal specification. These additional notes were prepared by a team of specifiers including some of the people involved in the preparation of the initial document: it must be supposed that the same persons, when faced with the task of writing the formal specification of the system requirements, feel compelled to be more precise and start to ask themselves more questions than they do when they need provide only an informal system description.

Secondly, an OOTRIO formal specification document was produced, which included TRIO logical formulas and declarations of classes describing the system components, their relations and the system structure, and their graphical representation according to the syntax and semantics of the OOTRIO language. The formal specification document was about 120 pages long; this however included several 'comments' added to the logical formulas as a supplement for the uninitiated (or hurried) reader.

Since OOTRIO adopts object-oriented concepts and methods, the formal specification is naturally centred around the physical components of the system. Thus it includes the declaration of classes such as *reservoir*, *sluiceGate*, *channel*, *powerStation*, *tank* and *operator*, which obviously correspond to the above-described components of the hydroelectric power plant. Following an orthogonal approach, the formal specification also focuses on the main *activities* performed by the described system, which are briefly listed below:

- *monitoring*, which consist of recording the most significant physical time varying quantities in the system, and controlling whether they satisfy some constraints related to the planning activity;

- *planning*, consisting of the choice of the objectives to be reached (by means of the regulating activity, see next point) according to the expected evolution of the environment (based on the monitoring activity) in a medium-term period (24 hrs);

- *regulating*, which consists of all the actions necessary to maintain the regular functioning of the plants when the environment evolves according to the assumptions made during the planning activity;

- *watching*, consisting of all the actions necessary to ensure the plant integrity and safety when unplanned extraordinary events occur.

The formal specification did not include requirements regarding some aspects of the operating environment (such as range of temperature, electromagnetic interferences etc.) and some overall system features regarding safety, availability and robustness. Although the specification language OOTRIO could easily have been employed to describe these requirements, it was decided not to include them in the final specification because they were to be ensured by the chosen platform (a well-established, carefully designed and thoroughly tested combination of hardware and system software that is commonly employed in all ENEL plants) over which the implemented software was expected to run.

It is worth pointing out once more that each of the above-listed components of the specification is conceived to be, as far as possible, self-contained and independent from the context, in order to be reusable, if necessary, as a module of the specification of a system that includes the corresponding device or physical object. Moreover, the specification is parametric with respect to all aspects that are more likely to change from one instance of the power plant to another, so that it can be adapted with negligible effort to virtually any power plant having the same structure as that shown in Figure 5.3.

5.3.2.1 Overview of the main specification component

Although the specification modelled the whole pondage power plant and the relevant parts of its surrounding environment, the system that was actually designed and implemented was the controller of the power station, whose principal purpose was to balance the power production load among the various power generation groups depending on the current values for water supply and energy demand, and according to a variety of policies aimed at minimizing the wear of each generation group by avoiding needless state changes. Figure 5.4 sketches the overall structure of the *powerStation* class.

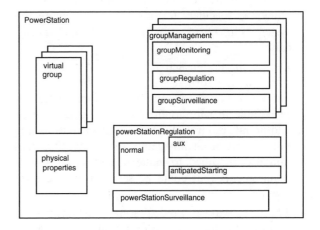

Figure 5.4 Modular structure of the powerStation class

For reasons of resolution the numerous existing connections among the modules and the exported items are not shown. Also notice that modules 'virtual group' and 'groupManagement', graphically depicted as a row of boxes in a line, are in fact arrays of modules, consisting of as many elements as there are power generation groups in the station (of course the powerStation class is generic with respect to such a number).

We do not illustrate the plant and power station specification further: the interested reader is referred to the project documentation.

5.3.3 Validation and Verification Planning

In the ELSA project, validation was performed by manual and automated analysis of the specification, while verification took the form (for the part involving the TRIO specifications: other more traditional verification activities were also carried out) of test planning. We describe these activities in the following Sections 5.3.3.1 and 5.3.3.2.

5.3.3.1 Validating the specification

The activities of writing the specification and using it to drive the design phase and test case production showed that the formal specification of the system is a continually evolving object that undergoes a great number of modifications. We cite in the following the main reasons why such adjustments may be necessary.

- During its revision, the specification needed corrections because of remaining incompleteness, or inconsistency. This validation activity was effectively supported by the use of semantic tools that allow the specifiers to animate and simulate the system behaviour starting from the formal specification.

- During the design activity some requirements, as stated in the formal specification, proved to be unfeasible or too onerous for the implementation to be able to support them. When acquisition of additional resources for their implementation was not possible or advantageous, the formal specification was modified to make it express the useful requirements that could be satisfied at a reasonable cost.

- The specification needed some adjustments to improve its structure, without really changing the functional requirements expressed in it, but with

the purpose of favouring important connected activities such as validation and verification.

- The specification needed to be changed because of adaptive maintenance, which could be necessary not only after the system implementation has been released, but even during development, for example because of some technological changes in the environment or in the devices employed which require the system behaviour to change slightly.

5.3.3.2 Test plan construction

The TRIO methodology supports *black-box testing*, a testing strategy that, unlike *white-box testing*, is not based on the code of the implemented system, but relies only on the system's functional specification. The reader can refer to [MMM95] for the main definitions of test case generation starting from TRIO specifications. We only briefly recall some basic definitions. A *test case* (TC) is a sequence of events (history) such that the specification is verified. Events are called *input events* when they represent values to be provided to the implementation at a given time instant, *output events* when they represent the results that the implementation must provide at a given time instant. A *test case in-the-large* for an OOTRIO module is a TC for the axioms of the module and of its components. A *bottom-up testing-in-the-large strategy* is a strategy of test case generation that builds test cases for a module starting from test cases for its components. A *top-down testing-in-the-large strategy* builds test cases for a component module C of a module M starting from test cases for M.

The test plan considered only the part of the specification to be implemented, namely the OOTRIO class *powerStation* and all its modules. The main strategy of the generation was bottom-up. This was motivated by the desire to anticipate the verification of the single axioms, in order to test them and to be able to correct the specification as early as possible. A certain number of TCs in-the-small were planned to test the specification of single modules and to enable the verification of the correctness of their implementation. The tests were planned so that they tested some particularly meaningful expected behaviours of the coordinator, such as an occurrence of a failure or of a change in some external condition while the system is working correctly.

Some modifications of the specification were necessary in order to generate TCs. For instance, the number of power units was reduced to three, while in principle it was unbounded, and various physical variables, such as the level of the reservoir or the position of a unit, were approximated with a finite, small set of values.

To test the whole system and not only its modules we planned the bottom-up generation of some TCs in-the-large. A bottom-up generation should reuse some of the TCs in-the-small to build one or more TCs in-the-large. For the results to be meaningful, the TCs in-the-small were built using homogeneous data.

The plan also included a coverage analysis of the resulting test cases, such as how many axioms or predicates have been covered by testing.

The TCs in-the-small that were generated almost respected the plan both for number and meaningfulness, but sometimes the generation followed unforeseen modalities, mainly because of bugs in the tool. For instance, some TCs had to be generated by hand and then verified with the history checker; in a few cases this was because of the unfeasibility of generation due to the size of the specification. Notice that, as far as testing of the implementation of the coordinator is concerned, it makes no difference whether the test cases are generated by hand or by a tool. However, most histories generated in this way could probably have been generated more efficiently in a semi-automated manner, if some bugs in the tool could have been fixed in time.

The bad state of the tools at the beginning of the activity, which forced us to carry out extensive debugging of the tools, and some problems in personnel allocation, make it difficult to estimate exactly the time needed for test generation, which took approximately 2 to 3 person-months. This time could probably be reduced with improvements in the tools and in the training itself.

In spite of these difficulties, the activity met its main objectives, that is, generating test cases in-the-small and testing the specification, and its results can be regarded as quite satisfactory. In fact, various errors in the specification, sometimes very subtle, were discovered. This happened when the histories generated with the tool were incompatible with the expected behaviour of the system, or when the tool was unable to generate a history corresponding to a particular correct behaviour, or when a correct history, generated by hand, did not verify one or more axioms. The results are somewhat poor with respect to generation in-the-large. In fact, this part of the activity was sacrificed in favour of the activities in-the-small, both for the short time devoted to it and for the organization of the testing activity itself with a bottom-up strategy. The bottom-up composition of test cases required a careful preparation of TCs in-the-small to be composed, which was possible only in

a few cases because of problems of time and resources, and the difficulty of managing this complexity by hand. The top-down composition had to be done completely by hand, since no tool is yet available, hence it was neither an easy nor a reliable activity.

In the current project, furthermore, more traditional work was required for system and integration testing, since the available TCs in-the-large are not enough to cover such phases adequately. However, the few results obtained have shown that the methods of generation in-the-large, especially the top-down method, can be very effective, but they must be supported by automated tools.

5.3.4 Design, Implementation and Verification

Starting from the formal specification of the requirements and the test cases, TXT performed the design, implementation and verification of the powerStation component. These activities were conducted using the software development technology already in use at ENEL, namely the MOOD and MME environments, which were a particularly suitable match for the TRIO paradigm, thanks to the common object-oriented approach.

The activities of designing, coding and testing the powerStation component were quite straightforward, because the formal specification was very well settled and structured by the time design and coding started, having been revised during the validation and test plan production phases.

The use of TRIO guaranteed the detection of most of the inconsistencies or inadequacies in the requirements specification in the early specification phase. The modular structure of the TRIO specification gave the development a significant advantage.

It can also be noticed that the implemented system has proved to satisfy by and large the *performance* requirements regarding the speed of system reaction to external stimuli. In fact the main difficulty in system specification and design did not derive from its requirements in terms of *pure speed* (the fastest required response times were of the order of milliseconds) but rather from the high complexity and variety in the system's behaviour and from the fact that the requirements are very *rigid*: a failure to meet them is unacceptable since it would imply disastrous losses in terms of property or human lives.

5.3.4.1 Design

The method adopted in ELSA for the design phase was MOOD (Mml Object Oriented Design), an object-oriented design method for developing real-time embedded applications, targeted to the MML programming language [Bas94, MR94].

MOOD, which shares its approach with the well-known methods Booch and HOOD, requires designers to concentrate first on concurrent objects (*sequences*) and then to decompose them recursively into lower-level objects (*complex components*), down to the lowest decomposition level entities (*modules*), which can be directly mapped onto compilation units. Aspects concerning exception and interrupt handling, which are of crucial importance for real-time applications, are dealt with very early in the design process. This method is supported by a proper tool set, providing graphical and textual facilities for building the design models, for consistency checking, and for code and documentation generation.

The design of the Coordinator was conducted in two main phases, the architectural and the detailed design. The first step taken by the designer in identifying the overall system architecture was to examine the requirements specification in detail in order to identify the concurrent activities or functionalities of the system. In fact the concurrency requirement influenced the system software architecture, in terms of concurrent entities (objects) and their relationships (synchronization).

The Coordinator was designed as a set of interacting sequences, whose dynamic behaviour was defined explicitly. Most sequences corresponded to the entities identified in the TRIO requirements specification; a few were added to implement the non-functional requirements typical of the ENEL automation systems, not specified in TRIO but essential in the real situation, such as fault-tolerance requirements.

This solution was identified by analysing three alternative implementation approaches that, starting from TRIO requirements, could address the design constraints, namely: (1) *functional decomposition*, where the focus is on the Coordinator's functionalities; (2) *completely concurrent OO decomposition*, focusing on the constituent objects; (3) *semi-concurrent OO decomposition*, a compromise between the above two approaches.

Choosing the last solution allowed us to obtain a certain level of concurrency in the system, although not totally granting the system concurrent behaviour as described in the TRIO specification. This restriction represents a good trade-off between run-time costs and system effectiveness, whereas the completely concurrent solution would have been too

expensive in terms of system load and the completely serial solution would have been too ineffective. Moreover, this solution also ensured a high correspondence with the entities defined within the TRIO specification, because of the common object-oriented approach.

During the design of the Coordinator, some minor problems in the system's TRIO requirement specification were emphasized, such as differences in the *vertical* structuring of a given specification or lack of a formal specification of the non-functional requirements. This convinced us of a strong need for a methodology guiding the adoption of TRIO for specific application domains.

5.3.4.2 Coding

Although the coding and testing phases of the ELSA project concerned only the Coordinator component, it was necessary to build a proper *simulation layer* to support the subsequent testing phase, reproducing the context in which the Power Station is supposed to work in the real situation. The actual testing experiment was made possible by providing:

- a complementary subsystem for *field simulation*;
- a complementary subsystem for *simulating the missing part of the Coordinator*;
- a proper *test-bed* supporting the test cases both in-the-small and in-the-large.

For these coding and testing activities, we adopted *MME*, an environment for developing real-time embedded distributed systems, based on the concurrent object-based language *MML* (Multiple Microprocessor Language). This environment, which supports the host-target approach and the target independence of the application under development, provides a powerful simulation tool allowing the designer to run the application on the host machine during its development.

For the Power Station execution simulation, we chose a proper target architecture (composed of two nodes), granting a total decoupling of the field simulation and the automation subsystems, by means of two different time bases.

5.3.4.3 Testing

The testing of the powerStation component was performed on the basis of the test cases derived from the TRIO specification in the early stages of the project. A test case specifies the system behaviour, within a temporal range and under a given working condition, both expressed in terms of values assumed by TRIO *items* related to the TRIO entity under testing (a *module* or an *axiom*). For each instant in the range, it imposes a given value on the input items and asserts the expected value of the output items.

This mechanism was reproduced in the test-bed, providing functionalities for stimulating the system as stated by the test case, as well as facilities for monitoring the system behaviour when computed with the given stimuli.

Comparing values expected in the test case with the actual values detected during the testing experiment, it was possible to identify any potentially erroneous system behaviour, and rapidly eliminate it.

This testing experience based on the adoption of TRIO test cases was extremely positive. In fact, by giving the test case a precise track on the expected behaviour of the system, it was possible to identify the inadequacy of the implemented system against the given requirements. System error detection and test results analysis were strongly facilitated.

Nevertheless, during the testing phase some problems related to the TRIO approach were met.

- Some of the test cases developed for simple component modules disregarded whether input values were previously calculated by some other module or came from the external environment. This derived from a bottom-up approach to the construction of test cases that considered modules in isolation, leading to unrelated or even inconsistent test cases for modules included in a unique system component. This problem was successfully overcome by defining a method for generating test cases from modular specifications that considers data dependencies and information flow among modules [MMS96].
- When TRIO specifies a nondeterministic behaviour, i.e. it allows for more than one system reaction to given stimuli, the measured output during the testing experiment could be different from that suggested by the test case. In those circumstances it was necessary to recheck the results of the testing against the specification using the TRIO interpreter, as described in [MMM95].
- To perform the testing experiment the designer was forced to take some unnatural implementation decisions, e.g. to declare some global variables to achieve visibility of some system components.
- A difficulty found in the set-up of the testing activity, but deriving from the nature of the test system and not necessarily related to the adopted specification formalism, derived from the different time

constants of the various system components, which range from milliseconds to minutes: this led to a very long duration for some testing experiments and to huge report files.

All the above-mentioned problems could easily be overcome by providing the developer with further explanations and hints on the formal method and on the verification methodology.

5.4 OVERALL EVALUATION AND ASSESSMENT

Based on the activity report outlined above, we are now ready to analyse the results obtained, point out the key lessons we have learned, draw conclusions and suggest future actions.

5.4.1 Analysis of Results

In analysing the results we mainly focus on technical, business and organizational aspects.

5.4.1.1 Technical aspects

The adoption of a formal specification technique together with the related tools to perform validation and verification has certainly increased the cost of the *specification*. This increase in specification cost is, however, largely justified and balanced by the better quality of the specification obtained and of the related documentation, and we experienced significant reduction in the overall costs of design, coding, verification (e.g. testing) and maintenance of the implemented system.

The experience showed that a specification language (as well as a design language) must support abstraction and modularity. In particular, for a logical language, if the number and length of formulas is increased beyond the acceptability level, which is unfortunately quite low, the specifier spends a significant amount of effort and time in purely syntactical activity. In this respect the graphic notation of OOTRIO, with its ability to convey information in a compact structured way, and the editing tools, provided a valid support to this cognitive effort.

Validation of the specification and verification planning required more resources than expected. In fact, the test case generation had to overcome several difficulties due to inadequate training on the TRIO tools (the training did not point out all situations

EFFORT	Specification	Validation	Design	Coding	Acceptance	TOTAL
Power Scheduler	42	11	28	41	133	255
Coordinator	72	57	14.5	30	37.5	211

that could arise during the actual test planning) and the still incomplete state of the test case generation tools at the beginning of the activity (some bugs still needed to be fixed, and support for test case generation from modular classes was insufficient).

In spite of these difficulties, the main objectives were achieved, and the results can be considered satisfactory. The quality of the specification was been improved and errors, sometimes very subtle, were discovered. Most errors were detected in the specification because of inability to generate a test case corresponding to a particular correct behaviour, or in the implementation by comparing the generated test cases with the behaviour of the system measured during testing. The results are less satisfactory for the specification in-the-large, because of the short time available and the bottom-up strategy followed in the testing activity. In fact, this part of the activity was reduced in favour of the activities in-the-small.

The *design* activity was substantially simpler than in current practice, because of the higher quality of the specification, and also because particular attention was devoted to maintaining a close correspondence between the specification objects and the design objects (this was facilitated by the object-oriented approach shared by the specification and design notations). As a consequence the involvement of the users (i.e. ENEL experts) in the development process was significantly reduced.

For similar reasons we also experienced a reduction in the resources involved in the *coding activities*. This outcome was rather important and somehow unexpected: previously, the TRIO-based approach had been considered useful mainly in specification and testing activities. The systematic code derivation from the specification, supported by suitable tools, can make the TRIO approach very effective for the entire life cycle of a system. In this light, the ELSA experience can be the starting point for the definition of an appropriate methodology leading to code generation from the formal specifications.

Testing permitted the discovery of code errors in a thorough way. Five errors were found in the MML program; only one of them was caused by a misinterpretation of the specification, and it was easily identified.

5.4.1.2 Business and organization aspects

We evaluated ELSA results qualitatively and quantitatively with respect to an earlier version of a control system of a pondage power plant, which had been previously developed according to current practice (we now call the previous version the *Power Scheduler* as opposed to the *Coordinator*, representing the present version). Costs incurred in the *Power Scheduler* and *Coordinator* developments were compared by identifying two subsets of the applications whose products (*design, code, documents*) have similar complexity and size. The table above summarizes the result of this analysis, in term of person-days' effort required for each task in the two developments compared.

The overall effort required for developing the *Coordinator* is equal to 82% of the overall effort devoted to the *Power Scheduler*: a cost reduction of 18%. It must also be considered that some effort was spent on understanding how to use TRIO in practice and how to overcome limitations and bugs in the tools. The impact of TRIO would be even more positive, if TRIO had been used on a routine basis supported with improved tools to obtain user-friendly interfaces, better performance, more selected outputs, and a good level of integration. A quantitative estimate of this investment component is very complex and cannot be based, at the present time, on objective data and rigorous criteria; we can, however, extrapolate from successive experiences in applications of TRIO [GLMZ96] that improved experience and more extensive training of the personnel employed can reduce the effort by a factor of 50%, while the availability of better engineered tools can increase productivity by 25%.

Comparing the costs incurred in the Coordinator and Power Scheduler projects with respect to each activity of the life cycle, the following results were obtained.

- ENEL resources required in the specification phase of the Coordinator development were increased by 71%. But we estimate that 20% of the increase in the required resources was because of the novel use of TRIO and the prototype state of the TRIO editor.

- Supplier resources involved in the design and coding activities were reduced by 35%, due to the above-described favourable combination of factors.

- The effort spent on assessing (i.e. validating and accepting) the Coordinator was equal to 66% of the effort spent on assessing the Power Scheduler: a cost reduction of 34%. Notice that this reduction in assessment costs is obtained thanks to a dramatic 418% increase in validation effort. This additional validation activity is, however, more than balanced by a 72% reduction in acceptance costs.

Summarizing, in the Coordinator project, increased effort in the initial specification and validation activities, supported by an extensive adoption of formal methods, facilitated all successive phases and reduced the overall costs with respect to the Power Scheduler project. These results are graphically summarized in Figures 5.5 and 5.6 (in the pie charts the slices represent, clockwise from the top, the percentage of effort devoted to specification, validation, design, coding and acceptance).

The organizational impact deriving from the adoption of TRIO was very limited, since TRIO easily adjusted to the pre-existing development cycle and

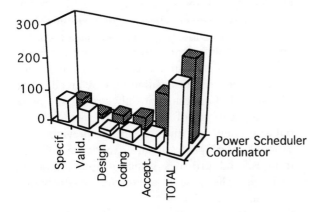

Figure 5.5 Comparative charts for the development efforts required by the Power Scheduler and the Coordinator

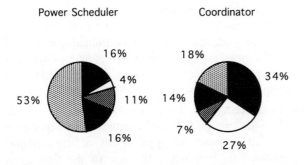

Figure 5.6 Comparative pie charts for effort distribution among the various development phases

did not dramatically change the role of the personnel involved. In addition, the TRIO-based approach was appreciated by people involved in the project because it made it possible to better separate the responsibilities of the customer and the supplier, and any flaw in definition, interpretation or implementation of the specifications could easily be attributed to the right source.

5.4.2 Lessons Learned

From the software engineering viewpoint, ELSA shows that the object-oriented approach for developing requirements allows one to structure the specification into several components that can be described at several abstraction levels. This kind of specification can be detailed at the right level, allowing the specifier to describe all important aspects of the system to be developed; to verify the requirements by following a step-wise approach and to make them easier to understand for the other application developers (designers, implementation developers). Moreover, starting from a modular and structured specification, other developers are also helped to build well-structured and reusable products.

Another main lesson we learned refers to the tools: their role both in the specification process and in test case generation is essential for practical use of TRIO; bugs and inadequacies identified during ELSA experimentation in some cases required some manual operations (e.g. transformation of temporal domains for test cases) and in some cases produced outputs of uncertain quality.

From a business viewpoint, ELSA shows that a formal approach to the requirement specification, supporting adequacy and consistency checking, improves the quality of the specification itself and of all the other artefacts of the system life cycle (design, documentation, implementation, etc.). These results require additional effort in specification development. However, ELSA shows that the resources employed are symmetrically reduced in the other phases of the development life cycle. Although our results are extremely encouraging, our quantitative evaluation of the advantages obtained cannot be generalized because the success of a project depends on a number of key factors; similarly it is difficult to give a correct evaluation of the additional costs needed in general to specify a time- and safety-critical system using formal methods.

Despite the above remarks on the difficulty of generalizing our results to other projects, products and organizations, we would like to comment on two crucial questions influencing the practical application of formal methods in an industrial setting, namely (a) how much time and effort is needed by the practitioner to become a proficient user of formal methods, and (b) what kind of computer-based applications would receive the highest benefit from the application of formal methods. Regarding point (a), again, a general estimate can hardly be provided: it depends significantly on the educational background of the user; thus a few hours of practice would suffice for a person with a deep knowledge of logic and discrete mathematics, while a programmer with a very limited mathematical background could be completely unsuited to any formal method. Regarding point (b), we believe that the employment of a formal method like TRIO, which provides a substantial and thorough support to specification, validation and verification, is most fruitful for non-trivial and non-standard applications, where the requirements may be complex and involved or may be initially formulated by non-computer scientists or by users with limited technical skills, and when the development of such applications is committed to an external supplier on the basis of the requirements specification.

In the development of a complex system, when the budget or workplan cannot be intended to cover all the formal specification effort, an intermediate solution can be proposed: application of the formal method can be limited to the system architecture and to the most critical components.

ELSA also demonstrates that the good quality of TRIO specifications supports more precise evaluation of the effort needed in the design, implementation and validation phases and a more accurate scheduling of the activities. This gives project management personnel a significant advantage in terms of visibility, both of the customers and of the suppliers. Moreover, the modularity and reusability of the specifications allow one to reduce the effort required to maintain them and to write specifications of new systems components using modules derived from previous projects.

5.4.3 Conclusions and Future Actions

Overall, the results of ELSA experimentation confirm the expected outcomes. Even if these results have been influenced by particular conditions met in the experiment, their projection onto other typical ENEL application developments seem fully to justify the ENEL's interest in the industrial exploitation of TRIO.

The expected high quality of specification has been verified on the Coordinator developed in ELSA. In addition to the properties (modularity, consistency,

adequacy) achieved in the experiment, ELSA has shown that the specification can adopt the same functional structure currently used by ENEL experts, who should consider the novel TRIO method as an *enrichment* of their current practice rather than a *change*. The reaction of specifiers involved in ELSA was very positive, because the concrete results of the project in the verification and validation activities convinced them that the additional effort required to write specifications in TRIO is well invested.

On the basis of the results obtained by the experiment the following future actions are being planned.

- Definition of guidelines to introduce TRIO methodology in ENEL life cycles. As already stressed, this would be based on a greater emphasis on the initial phases of specification and validation, coupled with rigorous final verification procedures, using formal methods; to facilitate the application of such methods some 'common domain knowledge' on typical features of ENEL plants could be embedded into some reusable OOTRIO specification classes which would describe some recurring high-level concepts.

- Definition of a training plan to educate ENEL domain experts and developers of ENEL systems to use TRIO in an effective way and within a short time. As we previously pointed out, success in the application of formal methods depends critically on the confidence and acceptance of its users; these, in turn, can be ensured only by an adequate educational effort that not only stresses the practical implications of the adopted methodology, but also takes into due account the previous educational and professional experience of the trainees, and provides sufficient foundations in basic disciplines such as discrete mathematics and mathematical logic.

- Use of TRIO in other projects to prove its adequacy for specifying systems where the data processing functions are prevalent (e.g. supervision systems). In fact, we are confident that the employment of formal methods (not only or not exclusively TRIO: the use of several distinct complementary formal methods could be combined to address the various aspects of the systems under construction) could be highly beneficial in a great variety of application fields.

- Engineering the tools to make them more user friendly, integrated and complete. The experience gained in practical applications of our method showed us that when the size of the developed system increases beyond a certain threshold, a significant part or even most of the engineer's time and effort is spent in purely mechanical activities, like checking the name and type of entities, or consistency between the use and definition of an object; in this case the availability of language-dependent tools – such as syntax-directed editors, graphic editors, automatic consistency checkers – provides support to precisely those parts of the specification activity that are not conceptually relevant or difficult, but become painfully intricate and time-consuming when specifications increase in size. The use of such automatic tools allows the designer to concentrate his/her efforts on the conceptually relevant and challenging aspects of the modelled system.

REFERENCES

[Bas94]   Basso, M. (1994) MML Object Oriented Design Methodology Reference, TXT (Ingegneria Informatica).

[CSt 90]   *Specification environments for real time systems based on a logic language,* Technical annex to research contract 27/90, December 1990, Case studies (in Italian) on a regulator in a pondage power plant and on high-voltage substations.

[CSt 92]   *Specification environments for real time systems based on a logic language,* Technical annex to research contract 49/92, December 1992, Case studies (in Italian) on programmable digital energy and power meters and on data collection and elaboration for dam security.

[F&M94]   Felder, M. and Morzenti, A. (1994) Validating real-time systems by history-checking TRIO specifications. *ACM TOSEM – Transactions On Software Engineering and Methodologies,* 3(4), October.

[GLMZ96]   Gargantini, A., Liberati, L., Morzenti, A. and Zacchetti, C. (1996) Specifying, validating, and testing a semaphore system in the TRIO environment. *Proc. of COMPASS, 11th Annual Conference on Computer Assurance,* June, Gaitersburg, Ma.

[GMM90]   Ghezzi, C., Mandrioli, D. and Morzenti, A. (1990) TRIO, a logic language for executable specifications of real-time systems. *The Journal of Systems and Software,* Elsevier Science Publishing, 12(2), May.

[M&S94]   Morzenti, A. and San Pietro, P. (1994) Object-oriented logic specifications of time critical systems. *ACM TOSEM – Transactions on Software Engineering and Methodologies,* 3(1), January, pp. 56–98.

[MMG92]   Morzenti, A., Mandrioli, D. and Ghezzi, C. (1995) A model-parametric real-time logic. *ACM TOPLAS – Transactions on Programming Languages and Systems,* 14(4), October, pp. 521–573.

[MMM95]   Mandrioli, D., Morasca, S. and Morzenti, A. (1995) Generating test cases for real-time systems from logic specifications. *ACM TOCS – Transactions On Computer Systems,* Nov.

[MMS96]   Morasca, S., Morzenti, A. and San Pietro, P. (1996) Generating functional test cases in-the-large for time-critical systems from logic-based specifications. *Proc. of ISSTA 1996, ACM-SIGSOFT International Symposium on Software Testing and Analysis,* January, San Diego, Ca.

[MR94]   Architetture e componenti software riusabili ad alta tolleranza ai guasti, Research Report, Milano Ricerche 1994.

6

A Structured Approach to Software Quality Management

Stefano De Panfilis and Nicola Morfuni

ENGINEERING – Ingegneria Informatica S.p.A. Roma, Italy

EXECUTIVE SUMMARY

The ENG-SODEPRO Case Study (ESSI 10476) demonstrates a very significant improvement in project manpower estimates and control through better requirements capture and reuse of corporate experience. By structuring that experience the company is able to modify appropriately the adopted software development process to address clients' specific requirements. Both functional and *non-functional* requirements are fully managed.

The experimental approach is based on the use of a Quality Metamodel and a related Software Quality Specification Process.

The Quality Metamodel can be tailored to support different software life cycles and organizations. Based on the formalization of and capitalization on the knowledge on «what» and «how» the organization can deliver in terms of quality properties within the software products developed, it makes quality requirements tangible and traces them through software development. In addition, Project Quality Plans are coherently generated and monitored.

Owing to its beneficial effects, Engineering Ingegneria Informatica S.p.A. (subsequently referred to simply as "Engineering") is incorporating the experimental results into its Quality System.

The chapter is structured as follows.

In the Introduction the proposed approach is sketched and its main novelties presented with regard to other approaches. The need for a structured approach which deals with software quality 'specification' is motivated.

Section 6.2 is devoted to describing the software development process (organization, methodology and technology) adopted by Engineering, describing its strengths and weaknesses. Hence the goals of the Application Experiment are derived.

Section 6.3 details the proposed approach to Software Quality Management. The Quality Metamodel and the Software Quality Specification Process are discussed.

Section 6.4 introduces and discusses the notion of a Company Quality Database. This is a database built according to the schema of the Quality Metamodel and containing the company's consolidated quality-related knowledge. Such source information acts as a reference during the specification process (as well as possibly being updated to take into account newly acquired general-purpose information). The experience in feeding and using such a database is also discussed.

The experiment carried out is discussed in Section 6.5, while Section 6.6 is intended to report the major lessons (successes and problems) learned from the experiment and to sketch possible further evolution of the approach.

6.1 INTRODUCTION

In spite of advances in Software Engineering methods and tools, major aspects of the so-called 'software crisis':

- low productivity,
- poor software product quality,

- overrun of schedules and budgets assigned to the development process,
- poor reusability of software products, and
- high difficulty in software product maintenance,

have not yet found definitive solutions, especially in the development of medium–large software systems.

A significant consensus has been achieved on the incorrectness for the software process, possibly even more than in other development environments, of the presumed opposition of Quality and Productivity. The low productivity in the development and maintenance of software products is strictly related to the poor quality of software artefacts and of products themselves.

Strongly interested in combining into its daily development activities high productivity levels and certified quality products[1], Engineering has carried out, supported by the EC ESSI initiative, an experiment devoted to improving its own software development process, with special attention to software quality requirements specification, project estimation, planning and control. This chapter is mainly devoted to reporting on the innovation explored in software quality requirements specification.

Achieving quality in software system development is a widely shared desire. Unfortunately, 'quality' is, in the current state of the art, implicitly a nonrigorous topic, negatively influenced by a subjective point of view, by lack of effective and unanimously accepted methodological approaches and by weak or undefined connections with development procedures and techniques.

It is interesting to recall here the results of a recent survey conducted by *IEEE Software* [7] by means of a questionnaire distributed to selected readers. The questions concentrated on their views of quality and quality issues. With regard to quality issues, the respondents were requested to rank, in terms of importance, a list of issues. The results were: (1) specifying quality requirements objectively (28 points); (2) setting up a quality-management system (20 points); (3) achieving operational quality that meets requirements (18 points); followed by (4) measuring quality achievements (17 points); and (5) agreeing with the customer on what quality means (15 points).

These results confirm the core motivation of the ENG-SODEPRO experiment. Above the 'quantification' of software quality achievement, which is based on metrics and numerically oriented measures, we are strongly convinced of the need for a structured approach to dealing with software quality 'specification'.

Typical approaches to modelling quality concentrate on defining and measuring product quality. McCall's quality model [2] and ISO/IEC 9126 [6] are representative of them[2]. In such models, the emphasis is on products and the related quality measurement. Integration with the development process and support for designing for quality are absent. On the other hand, from a practical and managerial point of view, between the definition of the software product qualities and the measurement of them, there is a crucial and mandatory step: the design and realization of a product with the requested quality characteristics.

Commonly, despite several efforts (e.g. [4], [5], [6], [9]) fragmented across defining metrics, measuring final products, organizing the quality assurance team, providing and enforcing standards, and using software engineering tools, a consistently global approach to the problem of 'defining and controlling quality across the development life cycle in order to gain satisfactory confidence of achieving the required level of quality in the final software product' is not yet available. In facing this main problem, solutions to a number of 'propaedeutic' aspects should be given; these are:

- a correct and unambiguous definition of quality concepts such as the distinction between dynamic quality attributes and static quality attributes, product quality and process quality, together with the definition and classification of quality factors and software engineering techniques and their mutual relationships;
- definition and classification of valuable, testable, recognizable suggestions to achieve the required level of quality suitable for every kind of project, together with their relationships to the activities of the software life cycle;
- tailoring and systematic utilization of a methodology to define quality requirements for software products;
- estimation of quality requirements, taking into account budget, resources and schedule constraints;
- outlining of critical activities and milestones belonging to the process model chosen for the project to assess the required level of quality, i.e. the definition of the quality plan: what to control, when to control, where to control, how to control;
- implementation of automated tools to support quality requirements specification, quality assurance, quality control, and, in general, the implementation of a quality-driven software engineering environment.

Such specifications should drive and make possible:

- obtaining 'tangible' results from quality requirements, which usually are 'not functional';
- 'tracing' quality requirements within the development process so that they can be recognized in the software products.

This is in the context of an approach which allows:

1. a more precise project estimate in terms of budget, time, resources and risk;
2. the definition of the company standard quality levels and the corresponding structure of the production process (skills, methods, techniques, tools). This should guarantee that all software products delivered by the company satisfy at least these quality levels;
3. the definition of criteria for the evaluation of 'additional' quality levels, their reachability, implications for skills, time and costs, and the required calibration of the process activities.

6.2 COMPANY SOFTWARE DEVELOPMENT PROCESS

6.2.1 Initial Assessment

The initial activity of the ENG-SODEPRO project was a thorough assessment of the development process of the company, in order to gain a complete understanding of internal problems and deficiencies.

The main business of the company is in the development of custom software products. Engineering has internally developed METHIS©, the company's software development methodology and associated set of methods. METHIS© is usually adopted in the company's projects, unless different choices are imposed (e.g. by compliance to customer's life cycle and methods, by contractual obligations, ...).

METHIS© identifies 10 Macrophases in the software life cycle, grouped into three categories.

1. Business and Organization
   - Enterprise Business Analysis
   - Information Systems Planning
   - Feasibility Study
2. Information Systems Development
   - Conceptual Design
   - Technical Design
   - Realization
   - System Test and Delivery

3. Information Systems Operation
   - Guarantee
   - Maintenance
   - Organizational Changes

Specific control activities are performed during all these macrophases.

- Project Management and Control
- Estimation and Planning
- Quality Assurance
- Configuration Management

Each Macrophase is subdivided into Phases, comprising, in their turn, Activities. Estimation, Planning and Control work at the activity level, taking into account that an activity can have single or multiple instances. Indeed, an activity aimed at producing more samples of a given product type (e.g. Coding) is considered as being composed of several elementary activities, each aimed at producing a specific sample (e.g. Coding of Program X). Thus, the elementary unit is always an activity:

- that produces a tangible output (deliverable);
- for which the elapsed time estimated for its completion by a resource is well defined.

The methods for Conceptual and Technical Design are based on Structured Analysis (Yourdon–DeMarco's Data Flow) and Data Modelling (Entity Relationship). At present, a version of the Conceptual Design based on the Object-Oriented Approach (OMT by Rumbaugh) is available too.

For project control and quality assurance purposes, checklists are defined for each Macrophase; furthermore, such checklists are divided into two sets, the first to check adherence to the development process stated in the company's quality system, the second to check correct usage of the methods adopted within the process.

CASE tools are largely used; in particular, if the project/customer does not require the use of other tools, analysis and design are performed using the company standard analyst workbench, System Architect© by Popkin.

Among other duties, the assessment conducted a deep analysis of 10 projects carried out by the company in 1992 and 1993. The assessment was performed according to a three-step procedure:

- data collection from available information sources (SAL – Stato Avanzamento Lavori/Monthly Progress Reports, reporting on both economic and technical aspects; reports from the QA Dept on checks made on the projects; reports from

Project Leaders to the company's management on specific problems);

- interviews with the Project Leaders involved;
- analysis, evaluation and generalization of the results with the company's management (Production Dept, Methodology Dept, Quality Assurance Dept).

This analysis produced the following evidence[3].

1. There was no systematic way to approach the non-functional (quality) requirements. METHIS© provided a step in the Conceptual Design phase, called 'Complementary systems analysis' which was judged unsatisfactory by project leaders.
2. There was no systematic way to tailor METHIS© in order to take into account project peculiarities.
3. There were insufficient capabilities to prevent instead of solve problems. Problems included:
   - management problems (e.g. inadequacy or insufficiency of the allocated resources; inadequacy or incompleteness of any development activity; inadequacy of methods and tools; etc.);
   - problems with the customer (e.g. unstable or unclear requirements, high number of requests for change, etc.);
   - time/cost problems (e.g. delay in the delivery, increased costs, etc.).
4. The average execution time for each process phase seemed to depend not only on the target environment, but also on time constraints.
5. The average error in the estimated effort was evident and both middle and operative management suffered from the lack of updated and correct figures for costs, both at analytical and consolidated levels.
6. There were no explicit data to analyse the average end-user acceptance time, in addition to low traceability of the achievement of user requirements during all the phases of the project. Such traceability was quite absent with respect to quality requirements.

6.2.2 Application Experiment Goals

On the basis of the assessment of the company software process, the main goals of the ENG-SODEPRO experiment were to have:

- a more complete methodology, with new features covering: (a) the definition–design–realization–test

of quality requirements, and (b) project estimation and planning;

- the capabilities to tailor in a controlled way the use of the company methodology within a specific project. The main factors to be taken into account in such customization were: quality requirements stated by the customer, project size, technological environment, and use of development support tools;
- the capabilities to control projects in great detail and on a fixed basis. The aim was the early identification of problems and adequate corrective actions;
- an enhancement of the qualitative level of the technical staff.

We think that this scenario is quite common in the software community, and that the intended objectives can also be of interest to a large audience. Indeed,

- the necessity of a large number of repetitions of development and implementation steps due to the difficulty of defining specifications in a complete and rigorous way,
- consideration only of the functional requirements of the software product under development, without any attention to the quality (or non-functional) requirements of the product itself[4], and
- the lack of estimation models which take into account specific development processes, specific adopted methodologies, historical company indicators, and quality requirements,

are problems which all software practitioners daily experience in their work.

The rest of the chapter is devoted to illustrating the innovations tried out in the company software development process with regard to software quality issues.

6.3 ENGINEERING'S APPROACH TO SOFTWARE QUALITY MANAGEMENT

The experimental approach is based on the design and development of a 'Quality Metamodel' serving as the anchor and common object:

- for the figures involved in 'quality' activities;
- to which activities, provided in the quality life cycle, refer;
- from which quality assurance and quality control representatives derive consistent information to perform their duties;

- in which it is possible to record the experience of projects carried out.

In the following, we describe the Quality MetaModel and its usage in software quality specification.

6.3.1 The Quality Metamodel

Figure 6.1 shows a high-level representation, through an Entity-Relationship schema, of the defined 'Quality Metamodel'. A «crow-foot» notation is used for relationships; each relationship is labelled with two names, separated by oblique strokes. The first is the name of the «direct» relationship, the second the name of the «inverse» relationship. The arrow on the edge shows the flow of the direct relationship.

The schema can be subdivided into three portions.

- *The static portion*, concerning quality attributes, introduces classical concepts as quality Characteristics and SubCharacteristics, providing a reference Characteristic/SubCharacteristic matrix. Furthermore, the Specification entity allows the identification of any concrete result in which the quality attributes of software products and artefacts materializes. The static portion represents the knowledge an organization has concerning software quality and acts as the framework within which each project works. In this sense, it is *static*, even if it is continuously enriched as the organization's knowledge increases.

- *The dynamic portion*, concerning the relationships between quality attributes and the project's needs, introduces the 'project' concept Requirement, and relates this to the suitable SubCharacteristics and

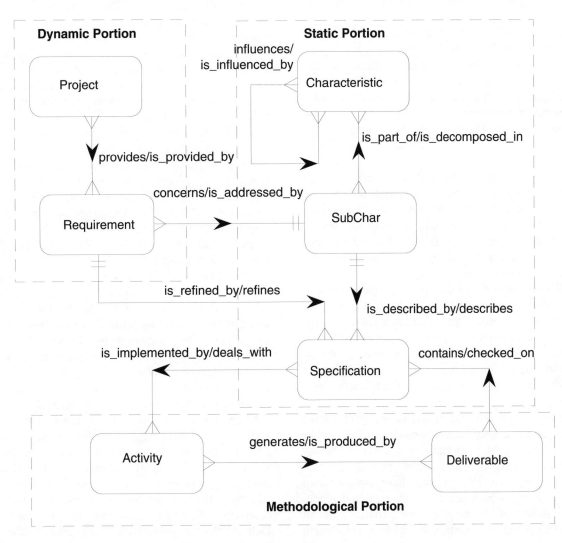

Figure 6.1

Specifications. Since it reflects the peculiarities of each project under consideration, it varies from project to project (i.e. it is *dynamic*).

- *The methodological portion*, concerning the relationships between quality attributes and the development process adopted (represented by Activities), relates Specifications to the development process: i.e. it relates Specifications to life-cycle Activities and Deliverables. This portion shows how Activities deal with Specifications and how Specifications can be checked against the Deliverables to assess the desired level of Quality. It is a *methodological* portion, since it relates the «what» to the «how».

Characteristics and SubCharacteristics are well-known concepts (e.g. ISO/IEC Std 9126), while the 'Specification' concept needs a more detailed description both because of our original interpretation and use of it, and because of the great importance residing in the relationship that Specifications have with other objects.

Specifications are detailed descriptions of 'real and tangible results' to be obtained by a production activity in order to satisfy a quality requirement that can be formally and/or effectively verified in the final product. They are the 'product-oriented' view of Quality SubCharacteristics. Thus, specifications are analogous to the 'functional specifications' of the process of Analysis and Design of a software system.

It should be noted that not all Specifications imply additional software to be written. Indeed, some of them tell 'how' to write software (e.g. complexity constraints), possibly requiring additional testing effort. Others imply additional software to be written (e.g. help management), requiring additional effort in each development phase.

The relevance of the concept 'Specification' as a 'knowledge accumulation point' should be clear for a software organization. The evolution of the Specifications population, possibly split into different populations for different business scenarios, should follow the evolution of the organization in terms of the software life cycle adopted, methods, techniques, experience, etc.

We stress again the tangibility property that must characterize the Specification objects in order to be really useful. So, for instance, our current Quality Metamodel database has been populated with Specifications like 'DC modules isolation' or 'used terms glossary' which constitute realistic and recognizable results of SW development activities and can be implemented and controlled just like any system functionality.

In the Quality Metamodel, Specifications are classified according to the following three levels.

- *Level 1* is for Specifications whose achievement is assured by the standard execution of the activities foreseen in the company's development process.
- *Level 2* is for Specifications that require some degree of sophistication in the execution of the development activities.
- *Level 3* is for Specifications whose achievement requires skills and/or activities not usually present in the company's development process.

The availability and determination of such 'levels' is crucial for the estimation procedures in which effort is evaluated taking into account project quality requirements.

The Dynamic portion enriches the Quality Metamodel, introducing the 'Project-oriented' perception of Quality Characteristics. In it we have two entities: Project and Requirement. The former represents projects for which the quality specification process is/was running. The latter, Requirement, defines the features to be assigned to the software product to satisfy the quality needs of the specific project under development. This object has mainly been introduced to allow traceability of the quality requirements within the software development process. As a matter of fact, Quality Requirements are related both to SubCharacteristics and to Specifications, the latter being their 'tangible translation'. Thus, the quality specification process can be, broadly speaking, depicted as selecting (and, possibly, defining new) Specifications that refine Requirements. The relationship between Characteristics and SubCharacteristics helps in evaluating possible conflicts which may exist among different Requirements.

The Methodological portion of the Quality MetaModel has been designed to support achievement of Quality, detailed by Quality Requirements and Specifications, along the Software Development Life Cycle. Our approach to Quality Metamodel adaptability with respect to both life cycles and software development methodologies is to represent them explicitly in the database [1]. This goal is reached by means of the two objects, 'Activity' and 'Deliverable'. Activity represents the macro-phases, phases and activities provided in the development model adopted. Deliverable contains a list of all the deliverables, such as documents, schemata, code and whatever else is provided by the production process, thereby also comprising artefacts, i.e. not just products effectively delivered to the customer. Deliverables and Activities are related to each other, each deliverable being implicitly built through the execution of precise activities and, conversely, each activity generating, or sometimes refining, one or more deliverables.

The linkage of the static portion to the methodological one is obtained through two relationships between Specification and Activity or Deliverable respectively. The first relationship allows us to establish which activity/ies of the development process is/are in charge of handling each Specification. Important attributes are associated with this relationship[5].

- *Type of treatment* specifies the type of treatment (e.g. Identification, Plan, Design, Implement, Control) an activity performs on a Specification.
- *Effort* indicates the effort required for the achievement of the Specification. It should be noted that such effort can be, in some cases, an absolute value, while, in others, it can be given as a multiplier of some software product dimension.
- *Skills* indicates the know-how and expertise needed for the fulfilment of the Specification.

The second relationship links each Specification to the Deliverable/s that implement/s it; an attribute of this relationship specifies the type of control to be performed on the deliverable (e.g. Formal, Inspection, Measure, etc.).

Through these two relationships, project managers and quality assurance staff have at their disposal precise indications on what, when, where and how to act or verify. So, significant support is furnished in the compilation of the Quality Plan document.

6.3.2. The Software Quality Specification Process

The Quality MetaModel static and dynamic portions are the basis for the Software Quality Specification Process. This process is very similar to the functional specification process, whose goal is to proceed from requirement definition to requirement specification following step-by-step refinements. In the proposed process, these refinements allow quality specifications and their required level of fulfilment to be defined.

This process is composed of (see the data flow diagram in Figure 6.2, where the grey bubbles indicate the METHIS© macro-phases):

- P1 – user needs analysis;
- P2 – quality requirements definition;

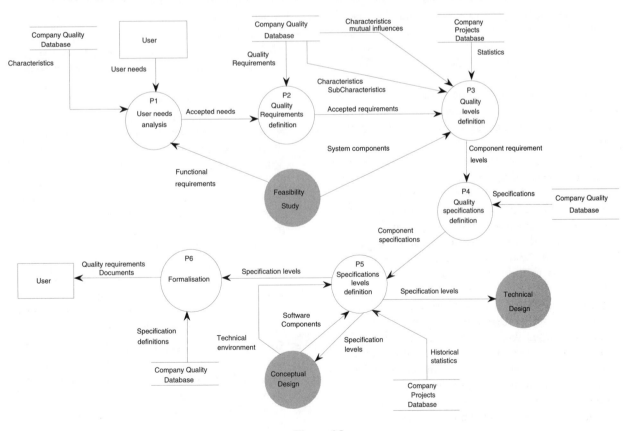

Figure 6.2

- P3 – quality levels definition;
- P4 – quality specifications definition;
- P5 – quality specifications required level definition;
- P6 – formalization (software quality document production).

The proposed process is based on the use of the Company Quality Database, a database built according to the schema of the Quality Metamodel and containing the company's consolidated quality-related knowledge. Such an information source acts as a reference during the specification process (as well as possibly being updated to take into account newly acquired general-purpose information). In addition, the Project Quality Database is the database relating to the specific project under development, progressively built during the process.

In addition to the use of the Quality Metamodel, the aspect concerning the definition of the required level of fulfilment for each Specification to be implemented is of great importance.

- *User needs analysis*   The aim of the first activity is to define quality user needs. These needs are similar to functional user needs and can be gathered by interviews, reading documents and so on. These needs should be balanced with the functional user needs in order to take technical constraints into account from the very beginning. The user is helped to identify the priorities and needs for each quality characteristic/subcharacteristic. By illustrating, by means of the Company Quality Database, the standard model (typical levels for characteristics, usual requirements, potential specifications), the user is guided in the elicitation of quality needs and in the definition of their priorities.

- *Quality requirements definition*   On the basis of the user's quality needs, the Project Quality Database is filled with the quality requirements and their relationships to Subcharacteristics, extracted as much as possible from the Company Quality Database. If it is not possible to do that for all needs, some new requirements have to be introduced and possibly added to the Company Quality Database. Typical examples of quality requirements are: 'Advice on the use of the system' associated with 'Usability/Operability'; 'Ease of use' associated with 'Usability/Understandability; 'Low code complexity' associated with 'Maintainability/Analysability' and 'Maintainability/Testability'; 'Optimization of response time for on-line functionalities' associated with 'Efficiency/Time behaviour'; 'Self-documented code' associated with 'Maintainability/Analysability'.

- *Quality levels definition*   After the planning phase it is possible to assign requirements to the macro-component of the system being built together with their level of importance (so, for example, 'Ease of use' is crucial for subsystem A, devoted to a set of naive users, while 'Optimization of response time for on-line functionalities' is of great importance for subsystem B, which has a large set of clerical users). Another important issue to be dealt with is the resolution of potential conflicts among the defined requirements.

- *Quality specifications definition*   The relationships Requirement/SubCharacteristic and Subcharacteristic/Specification make it possible to find the 'candidate' Specifications for each Requirement (so, for example, for 'Ease of use', we identify, through the 'Understandability' SubCharacteristic, a set of potential Specifications including, among others, 'Message standardization', 'Help at dialogue screen level', 'Help at error message level', 'Help at field level'). Some of them are not suitable for the project and so are discarded. In the Company Quality Database the Specifications are partitioned by the minimum level of quality they can fulfil. Taking into account the required level of importance of each requirement for each macro-component, the selection of suitable Specifications is performed.

- *Quality specifications required level definition*   Some of the Specifications selected need only to be implemented in the system under development; others need to be further detailed in order to establish their required level of fulfilment. For example, once the analysis phase has further subdivided each macro-component into components, some of the Specifications can be assigned to these suitable (e.g. 'Help at field level' for components X and Y; 'Help at dialogue screen level' for component Z). Another possible case concerns those Specifications that can be numerically defined (e.g. 'Cyclomatic number < 12' for each module of component W; 'Response time < 2' for inquiries in component Z; and, analogously, for specifications on nesting levels, number of field present in screens, etc.). This activity should be performed taking into account the target technical environment and the statistics about former projects.

- *Software quality document production*   The project quality requirements, specifications and their required level of fulfilment are collected in a document which emphasizes the quality aspects of the project. The definitions needed are drawn from the Company Quality Database. For example, this document can be arranged using the DOD-STD-2167 standard.

6.4 ENGINEERING'S INSTANTIATION OF THE QUALITY METAMODEL

6.4.1 The Company Quality Database: Content

The population of the Engineering Quality Database was conducted according to the following guidelines and limitations.

- The methodological portion of the database was built according to METHIS©. At the moment, the Engineering Quality Database does not take into account the more recent evolution of the methodology (e.g. the version for object-oriented analysis by the adoption of the OMT approach). Even though METHIS© covers the whole software life cycle (including strategic information systems planning, business analysis and feasibility study), the database obviously explicitly represents only the activities and deliverables of the stages directly involved in software production (conceptual analysis, technical design, implementation, system test, and delivery).

- We adopted ISO/IEC Std 9126 as the product quality model.

- The specifications included (more than 420) were derived from both company experience and know-how and from the adoption of proposals present in the relevant literature (e.g. [8]). The inclusion of each specification required a thorough evaluation of its significance in the company environment and of its relationship with the development process.

- In several cases we found that it was impossible to fully generalize results but it was necessary to specify alternatives or to suggest applicability depending on several factors, the main ones being the

target environment and the availability of support tools.

The following table lists the breakdown of the 420 Specifications according to the Characteristics/SubCharacteristics addressed by them[6].

Characteristic	SubCharacteristic	# Specs
Functionality	Suitability	29
	Accuracy	23
	Interoperability	29
	Compliance	103
	Security	15
Reliability	Maturity	14
	Fault Tolerance	14
	Recoverability	25
Usability	Understandability	24
	Learnability	24
	Operability	35
Efficiency	Time behaviour	25
	Resource behaviour	25
Maintainability	Analysability	182
	Changeability	149
	Stability	17
	Testability	64
Portability	Adaptability	43
	Installability	8
	Conformance	2
	Replaceability	13

As a simple example, the following example shows a fragment extracted from the current version of our Quality Metamodel database, relative to some specifications addressing the Learnability subcharacteristic and the corresponding activities involved in their achievement. The scenario depicted refers to a mainframe-based target environment with two different options: presence or absence of support for automatic generation of help transactions. The two options imply different effort estimates; so, two values, separated by oblique strokes, are reported for the Effort attribute in the relationship between Specifications and Activities.

Characteristics:
   Functionality, Reliability, Usability, Efficiency, Maintainability, Portability

SubCharacteristics
*(those that are 'part_of' **Usability**):*
   Understandability, Learnability, Operability

Specifications
*(a subset of those 'describing' **Understandability**, with the indication of the level):*
   Message standardization (Level 1)
   Help at dialogue screen level (Level 1)
   Help at error message level (Level 1)
   Help at field level (level 2)

(Continued overleaf)

Activities

*(a subset of those 'implementing' **Message standardization**, with an indication of the values of some attributes of the link between the specification and the activities: the type of treatment and the requested effort)*:

Conceptual Design – Preliminary Analysis – Standards Definition C-01-2
(Treatment: Identification; Effort: 1/1 mandays)
Conceptual Design – Complementary Systems Definition – Complementary Systems Analysis C-08-2
(Treatment: Design; Effort: 0.75/0 mandays)
Conceptual Design – Complementary Systems Definition – System/Complementary Systems Links C-08-3
(Treatment: Design; Effort: 0.25/0 mandays)
Technical Design – Skeleton and Library Modules Definition – Application Modules T-03-3
(Treatment: Design; Effort: 3/0 mandays)
Technical Design – Skeleton and Library Modules Coding – Code and Unit Test of Library Modules T-11-2
(Treatment: Implement; Effort: 2/0 mandays)

Activities

*(a subset of those 'implementing' **Help at dialogue screen level**, with an indication of the values of some attributes of the link between the specification and the activities: the type of treatment and the requested effort)*:

Conceptual Design – Preliminary Analysis – Standards Definition C-01-2
(Treatment: Identification; Effort: 2/2 mandays)
Conceptual Design – Complementary Systems Definition – Complementary Systems Analysis C-08-2
(Treatment: Design; Effort: 0.75/0 mandays)
Conceptual Design – Complementary Systems Definition – System/Complementary Systems Links C-08-3
(Treatment: Design; Effort: 0.25/0 mandays)
Technical Design – Skeleton and Library Modules Definition – Application Modules T-03-3
(Treatment: Design; Effort: 1/0 mandays)
Technical Design – Skeleton and Library Modules Coding – Code and Unit Test of Library Modules T-11-2
(Treatment: Implement; Effort: 1/0 mandays)
Construction – Software Construction – Code and Unit Test of Programs R-02-1
(Treatment: Implement; Effort: 1/1 manhours for each managed screen)

6.4.2 The Company Quality Database: Practical Usage

In Section 6.3.2, the Software Quality Specification Process was introduced. As explained, it is based on the use of the Company Quality Database and one of its outputs is the Project Quality Database.

The experimentation during the ENG-SODEPRO projects was carried out without the support of a computer-based tool. The experience demonstrated clearly the need of such support for an effective usage. So, an ambitious objective, which the company is interested in reaching in the near future, is the development of an advice tool, based on the Quality Metamodel, supporting the quality requirements specification process together with the automatic compilation of the Quality Assurance Software Plan document.

In particular, effective computer-based support to the Quality Metamodel should include, at least, the following main functionalities.

- A Data Storage functionality in charge of storing the organization's project data.

- Each project must be associated with a specific life cycle. So, functionality for Tool Calibration is required. Since no single software development methodology is the best in all circumstances, the envisaged functionality should allow for configuring various life cycles and methodologies.

- Finally, a Quality Requirement Specification functionality should constitute the core of the computer support. It should be a functionality typical of a decision support system, rather than of a design tool. The decisions should involve questions such as:

  ◇ definition, specification and prioritization of the requirements which represent quality needs;
  ◇ identification of the best quality level to be reached in comparison with effort, duration, resources and budget constraints specific to the project;
  ◇ identification of suitable activities needed to reach the prescribed quality levels;
  ◇ identification of the product technical characteristics which guarantee the desired quality;
  ◇ compilation of the Quality Plan;

◇ depending on the specifications' quality level, suggestions on the quality verification and possible validation action types (formal, inspection, measure,...), and an indication of the deliverables to examine according to suitable checklists.

So far, a first prototype (SQUAD, Software Quality Analyser and Designer), with a minimal set of functionalities, has been developed[7]. In the following, a sketch of its capabilities is furnished along with a description of a practical usage of the Quality Metamodel.

In Figure 6.3 are shown the capabilities offered for loading some or all of the Company Quality Database into a specific Project Quality Database.

Figure 6.4 shows the graphical interface chosen for the interaction. The schema of the Quality Metamodel acts as a reference[8]; by selecting an object in the schema, the user is presented with the functionalities available for such an object. So, for example, by clicking on Requirement, the user is allowed to insert new requirements, to list those already defined, to associate a requirement with a set of specifications, and so on.

In particular, Figure 6.5 shows how the tool supports the identification of the specifications relevant for the achievement of a requirement. The user is presented with the specifications associated with the quality subcharacteristics with which the requirement is concerned. By analysing such a set, and possibly by further analysing the description of specific items, the user is helped in the complete and correct selection of the relevant specifications.

6.5 THE APPLICATION EXPERIMENT

6.5.1 The Baseline Project

A large project – well suited because of its representativeness and characteristics (technological environment, user's requirements and constraints, etc.) to be used as pilot project in which to experiment with the new process and the innovation described above – acted as the baseline project for the Application Experiment. Owing to the size of project, and associated technical and economic risks, the experiment was carried out on a subproject.

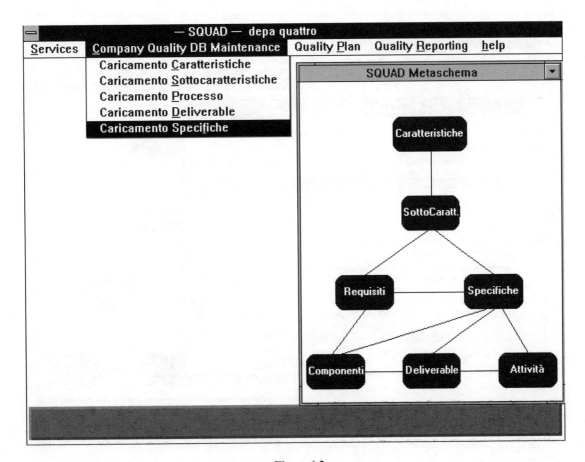

Figure 6.3

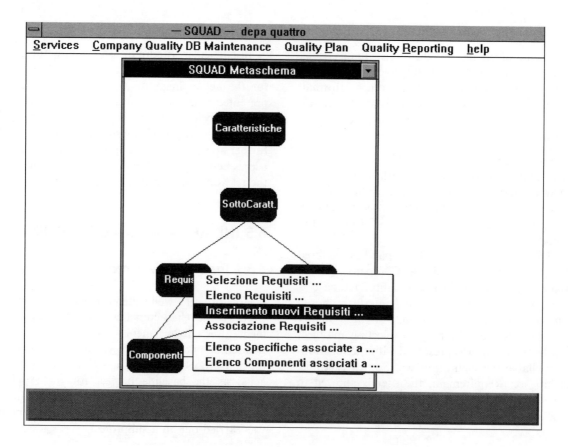

Figure 6.4

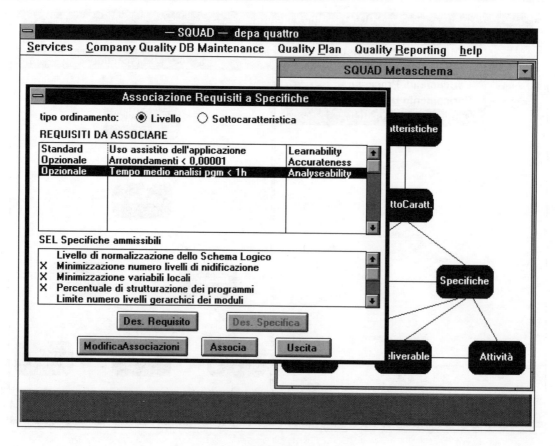

Figure 6.5

The project objective was to provide advanced networking services able to support all the heterogeneous hardware/software platforms used by the Italian banks.

The quality (*non-functional*) requirements for the new system were categorized according to the Quality Characteristics and to the suggested Sub-Characteristics as stated by the ISO/IEC 9126 standard. Thus, according to the specifications sketched above, and ISO/IEC 9126, the main quality (*non-functional*) requirements for the system are summarized as follows.

- **Functionality – Compliance**: *the system needs to be compliant with communications protocols standards due to its specific functionalities.*
- **Functionality – Interoperability**: *the system needs to be able to interact with banking applications on the one hand, and with transfer machines on the other.*
- **Functionality – Accuracy**: *data integrity of moving objects has to be assured.*
- **Portability – Adaptability**: *the system has to be adaptable with as few as possible modifications to several hw/sw platforms (MVS/CICS, MVS/IMS, UNIX, DPS/7, DPS/8, BS2000).*
- **Reliability**: *each primitive action has to detect errors and, depending on the error level, overcome the error or close the operation without any data corruption or loss of data.*
- **Efficiency**: *the system has to have minimal interference, in terms of resources and time, with the other Banking applications.*

6.5.2. The Experiment

The case study demonstrated the effectiveness of the proposed innovation in targeting the goals defined in Section 6.2.2.

The experiment required the training of project leaders and analysts on the new methodology defined for the specification/design/construction/test of quality requirements, on the new methods for project estimation, planning and management, and the appropriate customization and use of associated tools (Popkin's System Architect, the adopted CASE tool; Endelon[9], an in-house developed tool for project estimating; and Microsoft Win-Project).

The major experimental enhancements fall into three areas.

1. Development process, with increased software quality identification, design and construction capabilities. The adoption of a structured approach to quality requirements, with a quality specification process similar to the functional specification process, allowed such a result.
2. Project and quality control, with increased prevention capabilities. A set of project and quality control documents have been defined and introduced: Project Technical Characteristics; Initial Project Estimation: resources, costs, time and risk (produced by using Endelon); Project Quality Requirements; Report from the Quality Assurance Department, stating the starting condition of the project; Project Monthly Reports (produced by the project leader using Microsoft Project); Periodic Synthesis Reports (produced by the Quality Assurance Department); Periodic Control Reports (produced by the Quality Assurance Department); Software Quality Report (produced by performing automatic quality control on code samples).
3. Estimation procedures, with their calibration to take into account software quality requirements and quality control aspects. The ENDELON knowledge bases have been tuned and enriched to take into account in the effort estimation the quality requirements as well, with increased confidence in the result (average discrepancy between estimated and actual values less than 10%).

Two main organisational results have to be underlined:

1. the awareness by the technical staff of the software quality-related issues and the implications on the development process;
2. a precise definition of the role of the Quality Assurance function and its effective integration within the company's business mainstream.

Supporting and monitoring the work performed in the project have furnished significant inputs for improving and calibrating methods and procedures. Among others are the following.

- Set-up of the Company Quality Database. According to the Quality MetaModel, the Company Quality Database has been populated with more than 420 quality specifications and its usage detailed in the methodology handbooks.
- Definition of advice policies with regard to quality requirements identification, implementation and assessment. Such policies define the company standard quality levels and the corresponding structure of the production process (skills, methods, techniques, tools) and the criteria for the evaluation of 'additional' quality levels, their

reachability, implication on activities, skills, time and costs.

- Calibration of the estimation procedures with a particular regard to project managers' effort; indeed, the causes of growth in project managers' effort relates both to software quality, and to the quality control aspects. The former is due to the introduction of new activities in the software development process; the latter to the implications inherent in ISO 9000 certification. Such calibration produced a new version of the knowledge bases of Endelon.

- Revision of the operational procedures to be followed in project management by the project leader and of the corresponding control procedures to be applied by the Quality Assurance Department.

- Alignment of the innovation with the current evolution of the company's quality system.

6.6 CONCLUSIONS

The major lessons learned from the application experiment can be summarized as follows.

- The experiment confirms that a well-founded approach is needed to tackle the complexities of managing software application quality requirements. The experimental methodology has enforced consciousness of producing quality software in the technical staff involved in the experiment, and what is necessary to develop quality software. Nonetheless, there were reports of reluctance by project leaders and analysts to use it unless an efficient tool support was provided, due to the implied overhead in effort, in particular with respect to project leaders' duties. Two aspects have to be underlined.

  1. There are not yet commercially available tools that succeed in integrating product quality and process quality aspects and support auditability to ISO 9001 and ISO/IEC 9126.
  2. Measurement cannot be defined in a totally context-independent manner. Measurements must be defined locally within an organization to ensure that analysis models are automatically calibrated to the environment within which the measurements were made.

  So, we are convinced that the achievement of the final goal of high quality software at an affordable price will require the availability of a computer-supported toolset, configurable to meet different requirements.

- The methodology implies a minimum worthwhile project size and it is not always possible to apply it.

  Any structured approach implies an extra effort. The approach targets medium–large projects, for which it seems to guarantee a cost/benefit ratio less than 1. At the moment we think it is worthwhile for projects with a value of at least 250,000 ECU.

- In real commercial situations, it is not always practicable to obtain the information necessary to make a detailed activity plan. In such a case, it becomes difficult to apply the methodology fully in the initial phases.

END NOTES

1 Engineering was, among the major Italian software companies, the first to obtain, in January 1994, the certification of the compliance of its company quality system to ISO 9001.
2 For a detailed discussion on quality models, see [7].
3 More details, including analysis of quantitative data (like life-cycle effort subdivision, program average effort, LOC per person/day, estimated versus actual effort, etc.) on the assessment, can be requested from the authors, subject to a non-disclosure agreement.
4 It is only in recent years that the first international standards appeared, which try to establish the principles to follow. A correlation between a software quality product and the related software development process is totally lacking in the traditional context.
5 It is interesting to note how this relationship, with its associated attributes, details the 'first-cut' indication given by the 'Level' attribute of the Specification entity. The relevance of such data for estimation purposes is obvious.
6 Since a Specification can be associated with more than one SubCharacteristic, the sum of the values in the #Specs column is greater than 420.
7 The authors apologize for the presence of several Italian terms, owing to the work-in-progress status of the prototype, in the hardcopies of some screens presented in the following.
8 It should be noted that a new object has been inserted in the Quality Metamodel: a Component identifies a product portion (e.g. a subsystem within a global system) to which a requirement is applicable.
9 Endelon is a decision support system for estimating and planning software development. It incorporates logic which simulates the reasoning of experts; this implies that input data may be approximate rather than exact. This way, Endelon can be used as an assistant during the organization phase of a software development project, because it supports the simulation of different scenarios to balance cost, risk, time and quality levels. To this end, it produces two different kinds of deliverables: *global indi-*

cators (staffdays required for project completion; estimated delivery time for the project; optimum staff size and composition for each project phase; GANTT schedule for project activities with automatic resource levelling; economic risk of the project; total effort of the project; quality levels associated with each quality characteristic) and *detailed results* (effort estimate for each planned activity; confidence level in effort estimation; effort estimate for project management activities; necessary project skills; major risk component). Based on expert system techniques, Endelon makes a clear distinction between the estimation engine and the relevant knowledge bases (activities, skills, costs, ...), allowing for good flexibility and precise calibration of the estimation.

REFERENCES

[1] Armenise, P. and De Panfilis, S. (1991) Conceptual modelling for software development methodologies. *Proceedings of 3rd International Conference on Software Engineering and Knowledge Engineering*, Skokie, Illinois, June, pp. 271–278.

[2] Cavano, J. P. and McCall, J. A. (1978) A framework for measurement of software quality. *Proc. ACM Software Quality Assurance Workshop*, November, pp. 133–139.

[3] Deutsch, M. S. and Willis, R. R. (1988) *Software Quality Engineering: A Total Technical and Management Approach* (Englewood Cliffs: Prentice-Hall).

[4] Evans, M. W. and Marciniak, J. J. (1987) *Software Quality Assurance and Management* (Wiley-Interscience).

[5] Hollocker, C. P. (1990) *Software Reviews and Audits Handbook* (Wiley-Interscience).

[6] ISO/IEC 9126 (1992) *Information Technology – Software product evaluation – Quality characteristics and guide-lines for their use* (International Organization for Standardization).

[7] Kitchenham, B. and Pfleeger S. L. (1996) Software quality: the elusive target. *IEEE Software*, January, pp. 12–21.

[8] Kitchenham, B. and Walker, J. An Information Model for software quality management, *TSQM deliverable A24*.

[9] Smith, D. J. and Wood, K. B. (1989) *Engineering Quality Software* (Elsevier Science Publishing Ltd).

7

FAME: Framework for Management and Design of Multimedia Applications in Education and Training

Theoni Pitoura

First Informatics, SA, Patras, Greece

7.1 INTRODUCTION

Multimedia applications have rapidly emerged in recent years as a major type of software system, and constitute a considerable part of the software market, especially in areas such as education and training, with extremely promising expectations for the future. As a software product, a multimedia application is produced by applying practices and methods driven by traditional software techniques. However, there are specific requirements and unique problems that are met during the development of an educational multimedia application and should be considered, such as (see also [GAR93]):

- coordination of a development team which consists of people with different skills can be a problem;
- cooperation between members with different expertise can sometimes be difficult;
- design involves understanding and organizing the structure of a complex domain, and making it clear, accessible, comprehensive and educational to users;
- the quality of this kind of application involves not only the quality of the traditional software (which is complicated in itself) but also quality characteristics which come from their multimedia nature and their educational goal;
- integration of multimedia material often provokes technical problems which delay the production.

Therefore, improving the development process of an educational multimedia application is a difficult task but necessary to satisfy customers and users and promote business objectives.

This was the main objective of the FAME (Framework for Management and Design of Multimedia Applications in Education and Training) application experiment, an EC-funded project under the ESSI Programme. More specifically, its main objective was to improve the process of educational multimedia applications development by adapting and integrating state-of-the-art methodologies and tools in most phases of the development of a real multimedia application. First Informatics S.A. participated as the project coordinator. Other partners were the Lambrakis Research Foundation and the Benaki Museum.

First Informatics S.A. is an R&D software engineering company, specializing in advanced software development and informatics consulting. Among its special competence areas is the development of multi-platform multimedia applications and hypermedia networks, multi-database systems and telematics applications. First Informatics specializes in educational and training multimedia applications. Among its activities in this area was the production of a complete encyclopaedia of Byzantine history and art on CD-ROM, an interactive multimedia course for students and instructors in the area of neuroscience, multiple commercial demonstrations and presentations, and training courses for qualified engineers on the production of multimedia titles. Therefore, development of multimedia educational software has been a main activity and interest in First Informatics and the request for software best practices in this area was the main motivation for the FAME application experiment.

In this chapter we describe the FAME application experiment, and the experiences and results that First Informatics gained during it. Particular emphasis was given to the early phases of development and to project management activities, but also to quality assurance activities, measurements, review and evaluation. We describe the framework consisting of these methodologies and tools and the way they were adapted and integrated in the process. The framework consists of a development paradigm, design methodologies and techniques, evaluation and measurement processes, size, productivity and quality metrics, quality assurance processes, participation of consultants, and an authoring tool and a multimedia database. The most important results obtained, significant lessons learnt and some problems encountered during the application experiment are also described in this chapter. Finally, we discuss how these experiences and results are going to be used and incorporated into future plans at First Informatics.

7.2 THE APPLICATION EXPERIMENT

7.2.1 Overview

The FAME application experiment aimed at improving specific areas of the development process of an educational multimedia application, giving more emphasis to the early phases. It proposed a framework consisting of state-of-the-art methodologies and tools which were adapted and integrated in most phases of the software process. The framework was applied in the development of a real educational multimedia application, a multimedia title on Byzantine Art serving as an electronic library for English-speaking users. A small-scale experiment was also executed to adapt selected parts of the application experiment to a different environment, a museum. For dissemination and transferability the application experiment also established a small special interest group, whose members included cultural and educational organizations and multimedia technology professionals.

First Informatics' role in the experiment was to explore, select and integrate state-of-the-art methodologies and tools for most phases of the development process of an educational multimedia application, viewed both from a software engineering and a project management perspective. Specifically, the company's main interest was in requirement analysis and specification, design, evaluation, estimation, measurement and metrics, and quality assurance.

7.2.2 Software Engineering Practices at the Beginning of the Experiment

First Informatics was extensively involved in the development of multi-platform multimedia applications, especially in the areas of education and training, with its participation in the development of interactive multimedia courses for students and instructors in neuroscience, the development of training courses for qualified engineers on the production of multimedia titles, and the production of a complete encyclopaedia of Byzantine history on a CD-ROM, 'SOPHIA', with the collaboration of the Lambrakis Research Foundation. During these projects, First Informatics became aware of several problems, and deficiencies appeared during the software life cycle of educational multimedia applications.

In the requirements analysis and specification phases, significant concern and effort were given to the definition of users' objectives and the description of their needs. However, problems were encountered in analysing requirements efficiently, mainly because there was no formal way to introduce customers to multimedia technology.

During design, customers' participation was limited, which was the main reason why misunderstandings between them and developers remained unnoticed and were discovered later in the development.

Moreover, the final cost of a multimedia application usually exceeded the initial cost estimation, and the activities undertaken exceeded time limitations because of the complexity of a multimedia project and the particularities concerning the divergent expertise of people involved.

The metrics used were not efficient enough, and quality assurance activities should consider the specific requirements of an educational multimedia application.

Although everything worked out satisfactorily in the end, the software development process of this particular kind of application needed to be improved. The experience obtained from the above projects was the motivation to initiate the application experiment and proved an extremely useful guide during its implementation.

7.2.3 The Objectives

The main objective of the FAME application experiment was the adaptation and integration of state-of-the art methodologies and tools for software engineering practice for the purpose of improving the current process of software development in the area of educational and training multimedia applications. FAME was interested in integrating state-of-the-art methodologies and tools for most phases of software design and development. It emphasized requirement analysis and specification, design, quality assurance, metrics, review and evaluation. Dissemination and transferability of experience and results were also included in its objectives.

7.2.4 The Experiment

The experiment had five key phases.

- A preparation phase, called *Current Status Assessment and Analysis Preparation for the experiment*, where an assessment of current software engineering practices and state-of-the-art tools and methodologies took place, followed by selection, acquisition and training in the most appropriate methodologies and tools.

- The main phase of *the Application Experiment*, where new software practices were adapted, integrated and monitored in the baseline project.

- The *Transfer* phase, where the formation and transfer actions of a Special Interest Group (SIG) took place, as well as preparation and monitoring of a small-scale application experiment (an experiment with a main objective to adapt selected parts of the application experiment to a different environment, a museum).

- *Dissemination* of results.

- A final phase, called *Measurement and Evaluation*, where measurements and evaluation procedures were determined and the results of the application experiment were evaluated.

Specifically, the role of First Informatics in the different phases of the experiment can be described as follows.

During Current Status Assessment and Analysis Preparation for the experiment, the following activities took place.

1. *A current status assessment* consisted of the detailed assessment of the current status of multimedia development. The initial platform for this activity was knowledge and experiences accumulated during the development of the multimedia application 'SOPHIA'.

2. *Assessment of new tools and methodologies*, the results of a survey conducted based on the acknowledged deficiencies of the current status and covering existing software engineering tools and methodologies as well as tool providers and consultant firms.

3. *Tools and methodologies selection and acquisition*, based on the assessment made during the previous activity. First Informatics purchased communication and collaboration tools associated with improving project management, the necessary software tools for improvement in the requirement analysis, specification and design phases (user interface prototyping tools, authoring tools, analysis tools etc.) as well as the necessary hardware tools for upgrading its existing workstation to support the introduction of these tools. Consultant firms and prestigious individuals from the academic area formed a group of experts to assist in the adaptation of new tools and methodologies and the formulation of the new software engineering practices. Additionally, this group provided the necessary training on the newly introduced techniques.

4. *Preparation for the application experiment*, when the plan for the integration and adaptation of new tools and methodologies in the application experiment was created.

5. *Training*, during which a group of experts provided the necessary training to participants and the personnel involved in the baseline project. Training covered the implementation and adaptation of new tools and methodologies. There was a general training which covered the new practices in general and more specific training according to the area of interest of each participant.

The Application Experiment phase mainly covered adaptation and integration of new software practices in the requirements generation and specification phases, the design phase, project management, quality assurance and estimation life-cycle phases of the baseline project.

The Dissemination of results phase involved many dissemination actions, such as presentation to conferences and workshops, participation in European and international events, cooperation with ESSI Dissemination Actions, organization of and participation in a European workshop that took place in Athens at the completion of the experiment (November 1995), and promotion and use of the same methodologies and tools in similar projects within First Informatics.

During Measurement and Evaluation, the following activities took place.

1. *Determination of measurements and evaluation procedures*. A main purpose for this activity was the creation of the exact measurements and evaluation procedures for the application experiment. During this activity, a measurement process plan was defined, which was applied to all the activities of the development process. The main goal was to evaluate the results of the experiment by addressing the main deficiencies of the software engineering process, as identified at the beginning of the experiment. The measurement methodology was a top-down one, based on the Goal Question Metric (GQM) approach, and measures were collected using measurement forms completed by the manager and members of the development team on a regular basis.

2. *Evaluation of results*, which started at the completion of the application experiment and was based on determination of measurements and evaluation procedures. One of its main purposes was to evaluate the results of the application experiment.

7.2.5 The Baseline Project

The baseline project was the development of a multimedia title on the Byzantine civilization for cultural and educational purposes, called *Portraits Of Byzantium: Faces and Facets of the Byzantine Culture*. This multimedia title is a synthesis of text, images, graphics and sound, enriched with original sources of Byzantine literature and art, which attempts to raise the awareness of particular aspects of Byzantium and motivate the interest of the end-user in Byzantine Culture (further details in annex 6 in [PIT96]).

The members of the development team of the baseline experiment consisted of the production manager, the multimedia designer, Byzantine experts, history scientists, graphic designers, and software engineers composing the authoring team.

During the baseline project, the state-of-the-art methodologies and tools were introduced, their integration was monitored and evaluated, and, finally, their implications for the development process were measured.

7.3 RESULTS AND DISCUSSION

7.3.1 The Framework

The application experiment adapted and integrated state-of-the-art methodologies and tools in

the production of a real application of this special kind of software. In the following sections we describe these methodologies and tools and the way they are adapted and integrated in the process. They involve a development paradigm, design methodologies and techniques, evaluation processes, measurement processes and metrics, the participation of education consultants, quality assurance activities, an authoring tool and a multimedia database.

These methodologies and tools constitute a framework for project management and most phases of the development process of an educational multimedia application.

7.3.1.1 Methodologies

a) A development paradigm   In an educational multimedia application development, as in any traditional software development project, it is necessary to structure and define the development process in terms of a life-cycle model. However, the development process for an educational multimedia application should consider the factors that differentiate this particular software from traditional software. Such factors may be that the objectives of an educational multimedia application are application domain oriented and users' requirements are not clear and specific at the beginning of the development, educational multimedia application design concerns aesthetics in conjunction with cognitive aspects and didactic features, and many others.

Therefore, an efficient process model for multimedia development should encompass prototyping as well as intensive testing and repetitive evaluation by users. A prototype could be either a separate multimedia application developed using an authoring tool different from the tool used in the development of the final application, or a part of the final application developed using the same authoring tool. Results obtained by testing and evaluating the prototype are used in the development of the final application.

The software development process model selected to be used in the experiment was a combination of the traditional life-cycle model (i.e. waterfall) with a prototype application, developed using the same authoring tool. The life-cycle phases include the phases of the waterfall, i.e. requirements analysis and specification, design, implementation and testing and evaluation, except that a prototype application was produced in the early phases. The prototype application was evaluated and refined and the results of the evaluation were used in the remaining phases of the waterfall model (see Figures 7.1(a) and 7.1(b)).

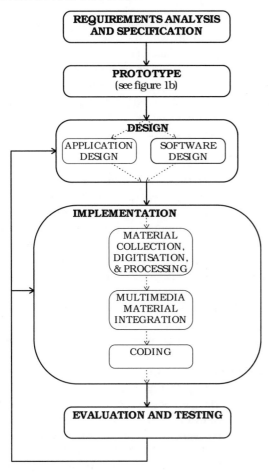

7.1(a) Process model

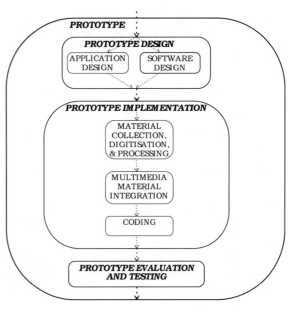

7.1(b) Prototype life-cycle phases

Specifically, the life-cycle phases are as follows.

1. Requirements analysis and specification
2. Prototype
3. Design
4. Implementation
5. Evaluation and testing

The design phase (of both the prototype and the final application) considered both application and software design phases, which are described below. The implementation phase included the following activities: collection and organization of the material (i.e. the multimedia resources), digitization of the material, processing of the digitized material and authoring.

The process model is shown in more detail in Figures 7.1(a) and 7.1(b).

Prototyping was selected as an efficient life-cycle model for a number of reasons, including: misunderstandings between developers and experts can be identified while the application functions are demonstrated; missing user services can be detected early

and services which are difficult to operate or understand can be identified early; incomplete requirements are detected and treated; and design issues are refined and determined at an early phase of the development process. Prototyping also enables the project manager to make a fairly reliable estimate of cost, time and resource allocation.

b) Design methodologies and practices The design process used for the application experiment included application design and software design.

Application design This concerned the creation of the conceptual structure, the navigation structure and the presentation of the application, corresponding to the three basic components of a multimedia application, which are content, structure and presentation.

The conceptual structure is the organization of the content, with content meaning the pieces of information included in the application. The navigation structure is the global structure represented by a graph, where its nodes are the screens and arrows are the transition links between screens, which also describe the navigational paths. The presentation of the application concerns the user interface design and the style, i.e. how the content and functions of the application are shown to users.

The conceptual and navigational structure was based on an educational model, with two goals: to organize application domain knowledge and to monitor and evaluate user–application interaction. According to [DUM92], there are four components of the model that should be considered:

- domain (the material to be transmitted to the user);
- learner (monitoring and evaluating the user's knowledge, usually in order to adapt the system);
- didactic (predefined – static – learning navigation paths);
- communication (a step-by-step user–system dialogue).

The above model was consulted during application design, but special emphasis was given to the domain and didactic components (i.e. using hyperlinks to restrict the user to predefined navigation paths, descriptors to provide additional information about objects, connections to different aspects of the application content, etc.).

During application design, storyboard prototyping techniques were applied.

Storyboards were used as screen design documents, produced during application design. A storyboard is a graphical outline of the screen, which also contains all the required information to create the final screen and identifies its creators, sources and dates of their creation. Examples of information contained in a storyboard are: all multimedia elements of the screen (i.e. text, images, sound, animation, video), their position and dynamics; position of the screen in the navigation structure (i.e. identification of the other screens to which transition could occur under specific conditions); special details concerning presentation, such as background colour, text size and fonts, type of graphics, etc. A storyboard is identified by a number (or name) and it is dated and preserved as a reference for future design. Storyboards may require additional time and effort to be created but they become extremely valuable during implementation and especially when changes and modifications are made.

Storyboard prototyping is an iterative process of design and evaluation of storyboards through a series of small-scale demos to users and experts, organized at appropriate intervals. This iterative process of users' and experts' evaluation and refinement of storyboards leads to correctly representing users' needs and requirements.

Software design   This concerns traditional software design.

Object-oriented techniques and object-oriented software design tools appear to be the most efficient for this phase of the development. Object-oriented software design was effectively used in describing various graphical elements, i.e. object classes (such as buttons, pop-up windows, screen or background templates, etc.). Parameters were controlled by object classes and corresponded to appearance and behaviour (such as size, target position, colour, etc.). Methods were used to perform operations (such as selecting a template picture, colouring some region, inserting applicable text, playing a sound file, etc.).

c) Evaluation process   Although evaluation is a complex process, in general there are two different types of evaluation that can be followed: summative and formative. Summative evaluation takes place after the project has been completed and its purpose is to evaluate the final product. Formative evaluation is a continuous process throughout the development cycle, and examines a variety of issues such as specification, design, documentation, organization and management. Its purpose is to collect information that can be used to make decisions about improving aspects of the design and implementation of multimedia applications. In other words, its results are used as feedback for other phases of the application development process [KOU94, MAR95].

Formative evaluation was selected to be followed during the experiment. The main objective of the evaluation procedure was to measure and improve the quality of the application. Formative evaluation during the application experiment was planned to combine two separate methodologies: product reviews by experts consisted of reviews by experts and usability evaluation tests; experts' reviews involved content, design and technical reviews.

During the early stages of the development, content experts checked the material relative to the application domain and its conformance to the intended users' profile. During storyboard prototyping, iterative evaluations were performed by design experts, checking navigation and interface issues, and by content experts, testing the organization of the content. At specific time intervals during the development process, technical reviews on all application aspects were held with the participation of managers, members of the development team, and design experts. On completion of the prototype, content, design and technical reviews were held. During development, a limited-scope usability laboratory test was planned to be performed. The best time to perform a usability laboratory test is at the end of the development of the prototype and near completion of the application. This test involves a minimal set of end-users with a common background (familiar with the application domain and with similar computer skills), gathered to use the application in an environment simulating the intended application operating environment. Questionnaires checking user interface and content structure are usually the data collection tool. The results of the test were meant to be used in later versions and modifications of the application and in similar future projects.

d) Measurement processes and metrics A measurement process plan was applied during all the activities of the development process. The goals of the chosen plan were twofold: first, to establish a baseline upon which results of the experiment could be evaluated according to its objectives, and second, to establish a metrics/performance baseline by collecting and storing data to be used for comparing and estimating future projects. To achieve its first goal, the plan used a top-down process, based on the Goal Question Metric (GQM) approach [BAS84], and to achieve its second goal, it used a bottom-up process, which mainly aimed at collecting as many data as possible, especially data used to measure productivity and the quality of the product.

d.1 Top-down Process The main policy of a top-down process is that the objectives of a project should drive the choice and definition of measures. In the application experiment, the main objective was to improve the process of educational multimedia applications development. More specifically, the project aimed at eliminating deficiencies identified in the assessment of the current status of software practice. As an example, among its goals were to improve the analysis of users' requirements, to improve the communication between members of the development team, to obtain more accurate and reliable estimation of time, effort and cost, and to improve productivity and the quality of the product. For measurable goals, the Goal Question Metric (GQM) approach was followed; for goals which could not define quantitative measures, results were obtained by interviewing the persons involved in the experiment or by completing specific questionnaires

during or at the end of each activity (this is described in more detail in a following section).

Specifically, the main objective of the experiment was to improve educational multimedia development. More specifically, the results expected to be gained by the experiment can be summarized as: (a) increase product quality, (b) reduce production duration and cost, (c) improve monitoring and management, (d) improve quality assurance mechanisms.

By further decomposing these goals, we can arrive at 17 detailed goals which correspond to the deficiencies of the current status of software practice which the experiment aims at eliminating. Table 7.1 shows the correspondence between the four top-level goals and the 17 detailed goals, which are as follows.

Requirements Analysis and Specification
1. More efficient analysis of requirements.
2. More efficient communication between users and developers.

Design
3. Better quality of the user interface design.
4. Better organization and use of the collected multimedia material.
5. More efficient communication between members of the design team.

Project Planning and Scheduling
6. Explicit and clear definition of the multimedia application development phases and activities.
7. Better time and cost estimation.
8. Clear and complete risk identification and avoidance.

Coordination and Control
9. Better understanding of project objectives among the members of the development team.
10. Agreement on methods of work among the members of the development team.
11. More efficient communication between subject matter experts and software engineers.

Measures and Metrics
12. Definition of metrics for productivity and quality of the development process.

Table 7.1 Correspondence between top-level and detailed goals

	1	2	3	4	5	6	7	8	9	10	11	12	13	14	15	16	17
a	✓	✓	✓						✓				✓	✓			✓
b		✓		✓	✓	✓	✓	✓		✓	✓	✓				✓	✓
c		✓				✓	✓	✓	✓	✓	✓						
d															✓	✓	✓

13. Definition of metrics for the quality of the product (i.e. application).
14. Application of usability evaluation and testing methods for multimedia products.

Quality Assurance
15. Application of quality assurance activities, appropriate for the development of multimedia applications.
16. Improvement in productivity.
17. Improvement in quality of the product and the process.

Many of the above goals cannot define quantitative measures, such as the improvement of the co-ordination and control process. An improvement will be estimated only, based on the experience of the persons involved (by interviews). On the other hand, for measurable goals, the Goal Question Metric (GQM) approach is followed [BAS84].

i) Measurable goals The GQM starts with an identification of goals to be satisfied, i.e. the goals an organization wishes to achieve, uses these to generate questions of interest for each of the defined goals, i.e. answers to which will determine whether the goal has been met, and identifies measurements that will answer the questions.

- *Goal definition.* The measurable goals specified above are goals 1, 3, 7, 16 and 17.
- *Questions of Interest.* For each one of these goals, some questions of interest are generated. As an example (see Figure 7.2), the following questions can be generated for goal 7:

Q7.1 What is the deviation of time schedule for an activity?

Q7.2 What is the deviation of cost schedule?

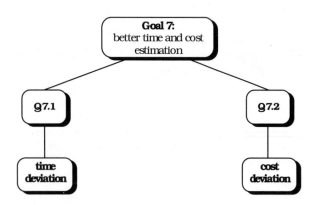

Figure 7.2 Goal question metrics approach – an example

- *Measures and Metrics.* For each one of the above questions, metrics are defined. In our example:

For question Q7.1:

$$\text{time deviation} = (T_2 - T_1)/T_2 * 100\%$$

where

T_1 : estimated time

T_2 : actual time

and for question Q7.2:

$$\text{cost deviation} = (C_2 - C_1)/C_2 * 100\%$$

where

C_1 : estimated cost

C_2 : actual cost

ii) Non-measurable goals To evaluate progress in goals 2, 5, 9, 10, 11 (i.e. mainly in communication and control activities between members of the development team), interviews with the members of the development team and managers were held. The other non-measurable goals were directly achieved by the application of new state-of-the-art methodologies and tools.

d.2 Bottom-up process The bottom-up process used in parallel with the above approach aimed at creating a historical metrics database for comparing and estimating future projects. This approach included data collection, computation and interpretation. Measures were collected and organized, most of them stored in a database, computed based on metrics definitions, and interpreted in order to discover the underlying reasons for the results computed. Among the defined metrics were size metrics (ones designed especially for multimedia applications since traditional ones, such as lines of code and function points, were not efficiently applicable), productivity metrics and quality metrics.

The bottom-up process was decomposed into process-oriented and product-oriented methods.

Process-oriented method The goal of the method was to collect process and resources measures. The method consisted of data collection, computation and interpretation.

1. Data collection. As many data as possible were collected, in conjunction with the ones collected by GQM.
   Metrics were collected for each of the phases and sub-phases of the development process.

Therefore, before defining the corresponding metrics, the phases and sub-phases of the development process were defined.

Specifically, the following main phases were defined (according to the process model defined earlier).

requirements analysis and specification
prototype
    prototype design
    prototype implementation
    prototype evaluation and testing
design
implementation
evaluation and testing

The following sub-phases were defined

[design]
    application design
    software design
[implementation]
    collection, digitization, processing and organization of the material
    integration
    coding

Traditional metrics for sizing software, i.e. metrics that count source code, such as Delivered Source Instructions or Lines Of Code, and metrics that count functionality, such as Function Points, were either inefficient or not easily applicable for multimedia applications. New size metrics were defined and used, such as (a) during design, number of Storyboards (S) or number of Objects in a Storyboard (OS), and (b) during the implementation phase, number of Pages (P) or number of Objects in a Page (OP). Objects in a storyboard or page of a multimedia application can be text fields, images, graphics, sound clips or video clips.

Some examples of metrics for productivity, quality and cost defined using traditional definitions are as follows.

$$\text{productivity} = S/\text{personmonth}$$

$$\text{quality\_of\_phase}_i = \text{no\_of\_defects during phase}_i$$

$$\text{cost} = GDR^3/S$$

2. Data computation. During the application experiment, data were collected and stored in a database.
3. Data interpretation. This focused on the underlying reasons for the results obtained. Standard evaluation methods may be considered, in order to interpret more results than those obtained by GQM, but the shortage of historical data, i.e. data collected by previous projects which have used a similar software metrics baseline, constrained the completeness of this interpretation.

Product-oriented method The goal of the method was to collect product measures. This was mainly achieved during experts' reviews and users' evaluations. Quality metrics were the most significant of them.

As a first approach to defining and measuring quality, quality characteristics were defined. These characteristics combined both traditional software quality characteristics [PRE92] and characteristics specific to educational multimedia applications, combining characteristics of interactive multimedia [NIE90] with characteristics of educational applications.

Among traditional software quality characteristics were the following.

- **Correctness**: The application should operate correctly (i.e. no failure of the application with an unpredicted user behaviour). Correctness can be measured by the number of defects per application size unit.
- **Maintainability:** Maintainability refers to the ease with which the application can be corrected when an error is encountered. Maintainability can be measured by the Mean Time To Change (MTTC).

The above quality characteristics were measured and corrected by testing during development.

Among quality characteristics specific to educational multimedia application were the following.

- **Usability:** Usability is a measure of the ease with which an application can be learned and used, its effectiveness and efficiency, and the attitude of its users towards it. It is associated with five usability parameters:

(a) Learnability (easy to learn): Users should quickly have some work done using the application, i.e. be able to understand the most basic functions and the navigation structure of the application (i.e. the organization of the information provided), and use them to get to the information they want. It can be measured by the time and effort required to reach a specified level of performance. *Specifically for educational applications this means that:* users should be able to learn and educate themselves without having to familiarize themselves with the entire structure of the application. Therefore, the content of the information provided should be clear and easy to understand.

(b) Throughput (easy to use): A high level of productivity should be reached when users learn the application. It can be measured by measuring the speed and the number of errors while experienced users perform specific tasks. *Specifically for educational applications this means that:* users should learn concepts most relevant for their purposes without having to learn or go through non-relevant or already familiar material more than necessary.

(c) Easy to remember: Users should be able to use the application effectively (such as, remember how to use its main functions and remember its structure) after a period of not having used it, without having to learn everything from the beginning. It can be measured by the rate of errors users make when they return to using the application after some period of not having used it. *Specifically for educational applications this means that:* users should remember sufficient information relevant to the content of the application as well as where and how they can find the information they want in the application, after a period of not having used it.

(d) Few errors: The application should minimize the possibility of user errors, with in-built facilities for detecting and handling errors. Users should be able to check their inputs, and correct errors or potential error situations, i.e. they should be able to return to a previous state in the application when they discover that they have followed a wrong link.

(e) Pleasant to use: This describes users' attitude, positive or negative, towards the application. It can be measured by subjective user satisfaction. *Specifically for educational applications this means that:* users should find it more entertaining to use the application to get the information they want rather than using traditional methods (such as reading a book).

- **Consistency:** The application should look and work consistently with the real world as experienced within and among other applications. Several attributes are relevant to consistency and should be considered, such as: concepts and metaphors familiar to users, consistent sequences of actions for similar situations, identical terminology for operations, prompts, etc., consistent appearance, colour and behaviour of identical objects. *Specifically for educational applications this means that:* concepts and metaphors should be drawn from the subject area to which users belong.

- **Reliability:** The application should provide reliable information. *Specifically for educational applications this means that:* reliable information is of significant importance in the case of educational applications. The content of the scientific information provided and its conceptual structure should be correct (e.g. historically accurate information). Usability can be measured by organizing usability evaluation laboratories. Usability and other factors are usually estimated by experts using review checklists.

e) Participation of education consultants
Multimedia applications, more than any traditional software, demand that the development team has knowledge of both the specific application domain and software. Application domain experts, those who are responsible for providing the application with its content, and multimedia designers and developers must cooperate in order to capture users' requirements and fully determine the objectives of the application.

To this end, the participation of experienced education consultants was required. Their role was to introduce the development team to pedagogical methods and to advise them on the objectives of a computer-based educational tool. Moreover, they helped the development team to capture users requirements efficiently and to design the most appropriate educational model (particularly content and navigation structure) for the particular application.

It was necessary to introduce consultants to different types of existing educational multimedia applications (i.e. through a series of demonstrations), such as educational multimedia courses, computer-based training applications, electronic libraries, training simulators, etc., in order for them to be familiar with the capabilities and limitations of multimedia technology in education and to be able to communicate with developers using a common 'language'. This approach is essential, especially when consultants are not familiar with multimedia applications, and almost always leads to the specification of complete, clear and reliable specifications for the application that are as close as possible to users' requirements and needs. Consultants participated in the evaluation of the prototype and the final application, evaluating content, content organization and the application's educational role.

f) Quality assurance activities A quality assurance plan was followed during the development of the application experiment, based upon the guidelines of the ISO 9000 series [ISO] for the development of software. It encompassed the following activities:

- analysis, design, implementation and evaluation and testing methods and tools,
- a measurement process plan,
- evaluation procedures,
- experts' reviews during development,
- a procedure to assure compliance with software development standards (ISO 9000), when applicable,
- reporting mechanisms.

Methods for capturing and analysing users' requirements, methods and tools used during design and implementation, a measurement process plan, and evaluation procedures including reviews (formal and informal) are described in other sections of this chapter.

Reporting mechanisms included internal dissemination of activities' records and documents, distributed to the development staff on a need-to-know basis. Internal dissemination was mainly focused on transferring experiences to all personnel involved in the application experiment as well as to all personnel in First Informatics. Specifically, internal meetings were held in the multimedia department of First Informatics in order to disseminate the results of the application experiment to both technical and administrative personnel; project reports (both reports of experience and technical reports) were and are available to all personnel in the company, and measurements forms produced during the application experiment were distributed to all personnel for evaluation and refinement.

A procedure to assure compliance with ISO 9000 standards included monitoring and periodic reviews by members of staff independent of the particular project (usually developers from other similar projects), and by consultants responsible for ensuring the application and successful integration of new methodologies and tools during the experiment.

7.3.1.2 Tools

a) An authoring tool A market survey covering all the state-of-the-art tools and methodologies which support design for multimedia applications under the MS Windows environment was conducted at the beginning of the experiment. The selection of the authoring tool (Multimedia ToolBook 3.0, Asymetrix) was based on the specific application design requirements, with a preference for MS Windows as the operating system environment. Among the requirements were the coexistence of both interactive and programming interfaces, an event-driven system that exploits the highly interactive nature of the MS Windows environment, device independence, and the use of an object-oriented language, which offers efficiency, flexibility and extensibility.

b) A multimedia database A multimedia database to collect, digitize and organize the material (i.e. text, images, animation, sound and video) used in the application was a very useful and valuable tool during design and implementation. It gave application domain experts and designers the capability of searching and retrieving material quickly and easily. The use of a multimedia database saved time and effort during the design and implementation phases, and it also organized the material for future use (i.e. enhancement or modification of the application).

7.3.2 Process to Measure Results

As we described above, a measurement process plan was applied during all the activities of the multimedia application development process, which combined two methodologies: a top-down methodology based on the Goal Question Metric (GQM) approach, and a bottom-up methodology for creating a historical metrics repository to be used as a performance baseline for comparing and estimating future projects. Measures were collected during development by the production manager and members of the development team on a regular basis and when a work activity was finished.

The top-down process was the one which was used to measure and evaluate results according to the objectives of the application experiment described above.

7.3.2.1 Results according to objectives

Following the top-down measurement process, the first step is to define the main goals expected from the experiment, which were: increasing product quality, reducing duration and cost of production, efficient monitoring and managing and improving quality assurance mechanisms, as presented in a previous section. These goals were further decomposed according to specific deficiencies identified in the status of software engineering practice of the participating organizations, carried out before the experiment began. These goals can be distinguished as: (a) measurable goals, for which corresponding questions were formed and metrics were defined as answers to these questions (following the next two steps of the GQM approach), and (b) non-measurable goals, for which improvement was estimated by interviewing the persons involved in the experiment. The most important results obtained by following this process, corresponding to measurable and non-measurable goals, are described in the following paragraphs (see also [PIT96]).

a) Results corresponding to measurable goals
Among the measurable goals of the experiment were: overall time and cost reduction, improvement in productivity, better estimation of time and cost (measured by time and cost deviation), and improvement in product quality (considering the measurable characteristics of quality, such as the number of defects encountered).

Production *duration* (meaning time needed for design, implementation, evaluation and prototyping) was reduced, compared with previous projects (where prototyping was not a separate phase of the process model). This was mainly because, during prototyping, the main deficiencies were identified early, and therefore any correction or improvement in design was made at an early stage without significant delays in production.

Time deviation in the baseline project (the difference between actual and estimated production time) was measured to be 15%. Some inefficiencies of the production management scheme, which is described in Figure 7.3, and, particularly, problems related to the coordination of the working groups, caused some delays in the completion of specific tasks. However, these problems were detected and overcome early.

There was a significant improvement in *productivity*[5]. Comparisons with previous similar projects cannot be made, since exact past measures had not been stored. However, a rough estimation of the

productivity of the design and authoring teams showed that productivity was increased by 20%. The use of state-of-the-art tools, better design techniques and more efficient coordination were the main reasons for this improvement.

Because of the extended time needed in the early phases of the prototype and delays, especially these due to organizing the activities of the development team, the final cost exceeded the initial budget. The initial budget increased not only because of delays in the workplan, but also because of underestimation of the effort allocated to the project.

There was a significant increase in *product quality*, compared with previous similar productions. This was mostly because of the formative evaluation which was adopted during the development process. Defects were detected and corrected early, either in application design or in code production. Most of the defects in design were encountered and corrected during reviews after the completion of the prototype.

b) Results corresponding to non-measurable goals Among the non-measurable goals were efficient monitoring and management and improvement of quality assurance mechanisms. These goals were achieved by the adaptation of the framework of new methodologies and tools, as described above. More specifically:

More efficient *monitoring and management* were achieved by structuring the development process according to an efficient life-cycle model and by adapting and following a management structure from the beginning of the development, as described in Figure 7.3. Briefly, the structure is composed of: the *Production Manager,* responsible for the coordination of the multimedia application production activities and the work undertaken by the working teams; the *Multimedia Designer,* responsible for the user-interface design of the multimedia application as well as for the structure of the multimedia database; the *Application-domain Experts* who participate during requirements analysis, content collection and application design to advise the multimedia designer and the material collection/digitization/processing team on the quality, quantity and availability of material and to guarantee the academic credibility of the multimedia application; the *Material Collection/digitization/processing team*, responsible for collection, digitization and processing of the material; the *Authoring team*, responsible for the electronic production of storyboards and implementation (coding) of the multimedia application; the *Advisory Committee*, consisting of the multimedia designer, the leader of the authoring team, the application-domain

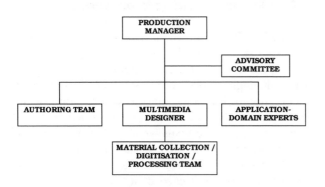

7.3 Production management scheme

experts and the production manager, responsible for issues concerning the development and for suggesting alternative solutions when needed.

The life-cycle model, whose main characteristics were the prototype creation at the beginning of the development and the evolutionary electronic story-board prototypes during design, led to an explicit and clear definition of the development activities. Moreover, a management structure was adopted from the beginning of the development, which clarified each individual's responsibility and helped the coordination and monitoring of all the activities of the development process. However, some inefficiencies and delays could not be avoided, but they were not fatal.

Quality assurance activities based on the ISO-9000 standards were followed. Some difficulties were met in trying to incorporate characteristics specific to an educational multimedia application into these standards (such as, the different definition of quality of a multimedia product compared with traditional software).

Moreover, *definition of metrics* for the quality of the product was achieved by recognizing quality characteristics and defining metrics for each of them. Quality characteristics incorporated characteristics of traditional software as well as characteristics specific to an educational multimedia application. Clearer and more detailed risk identification and avoidance was also achieved by identifying risks, and especially risks specific to this kind of development (such as misunderstandings between experts and developers, delays from content providers due to unavailability of resources, etc.). By collecting specific measures during the development process (such as the number of changes in design specifications, time needed to collect material, etc.), most undesired situations were avoided.

Better *organization of the multimedia material* was also achieved by using the multimedia database; organization of material has been significantly improved from its previous 'chaotic' state, and it will be further improved in future by improving the structure and functions of the database.

7.3.3 Successes

7.3.3.1 Business

Among the results that First Informatics obtained was that it dedicated special concern and great effort to creating a historical metrics database, useful for comparing and estimating future projects. A metrics database is useful for management to control the

development process, avoid difficult situations and be ready to take corrective action in case of problems. The metrics database will be improved and used in similar projects.

Moreover, experiences and methodologies will also be exploited in other business areas in First Informatics, since quality management is one of its major concerns. First Informatics' concern for standardized methodologies and especially adaptation of quality assurance mechanisms has helped and will continue to help the company to increase its credibility and competitiveness in the Greek, and also the European, industry.

Other benefits gained were individual promotion and increased credibility, which were achieved to a substantial degree by the project dissemination actions, such as: participation in and presentations to European events on software best practices, organization of a European meeting on Multimedia and Hypermedia in Education and Culture, collaboration with ESSI Dissemination Actions, etc.

Through the dissemination actions in which First Informatics participated, it had the opportunity to exchange experiences and views with European organizations with similar concerns and expectations. It also established good relationships with some of them, which have already led to new partnerships.

7.3.3.2 Organizational

Better cooperation and understanding between members of all teams and individuals involved during the experiment was one of the major results. The adoption of an effective production management scheme and standardized procedures were the main reasons for that. People involved with the experiment had to become aware of the state-of-the-art tools and methodologies in multimedia technology and practices. Additionally, they also had to obtain knowledge of total quality management, assessment methods, measurement methodologies and evaluation procedures for educational multimedia applications.

7.3.4 Problems

All personnel involved in the experiment were happy to use state-of-the-art tools and methodologies in the development process. However, some negative responses were registered against the more rigorous procedures that they were asked to follow (such as completing forms and reporting on a regular basis, keeping all records of storyboards, even when there were minor changes in them, etc.). This was because they considered these procedures non-productive and an overhead to their actual work. Perhaps, some of them were also afraid that management was trying to measure and evaluate their productivity. In order to overcome these problems, management tried to explain the importance of formal procedures during production and to clarify that there was no intention to measure individuals' productivity. Additionally, management simplified the forms and the procedures.

One significant limitation to our goal of measuring improvement was the insufficiency of reliable measures collected from previous applications. Information had been based only on individuals' experience gained from similar past projects and not on existing documents or data stored in metrics databases. Therefore, any comparison with the previous status of software engineering practice would be unreliable. Another obstacle in measuring and interpreting the results was the fact that new methodologies and tools had been applied together, making it very difficult to estimate their roles in a possible improvement independently.

At the completion of the experiment we realized that it would have been better if the experiment had planned a formal assessment at the beginning (e.g. under a specific framework, such as SPICE, CMM, etc.). This would help the company and the other partners to organize the overall steps aiming at process improvement and the final results would include comparisons with previous process status in the organizations; the last would make results from the experiment more meaningful and valuable.

7.3.5 Lessons Learnt

The most important lessons learnt from a technological point of view can be summarized in the following.

- Traditional methodologies and techniques do not apply directly to an educational multimedia application development. The best practice is to use them as a baseline but also consider the specific needs that make it different, such as: integration of code with multimedia material, more complex relationship between developers and user/customer, quality aspects that consider the educational role of the product, etc.

- Prototyping, both by producing a prototype application in the early phases of the development and by designing evolutionary storyboard prototypes, is essential in order to capture users' requirements and needs at an early stage, detect and correct defects, and improve application quality.

- The use of a multimedia database to store and organize the digitized multimedia material saves time and effort during design and authoring. A multimedia database can also be useful for later modifications of the application.

The most important lessons learnt from a business point of view can be summarized in the following.

- The participation of education consultants in all phases of the development process of educational applications is very critical.

- Training developers in new technologies is necessary; it may cost or require more time spent in non-productive activities, but, in the end, it increases productivity (since it saves time during development), and also improves the quality of the product.

- Market research on the status of multimedia technology at the beginning of any multimedia project is very important, since multimedia technology is evolving rapidly and tools (software and hardware) rapidly become obsolete. The selection of development platforms should consider and foresee the future trend worldwide.

- Management should be especially concerned about quality aspects (especially the adoption of international quality standards).

7.4 FUTURE PLANS

First Informatics intends to improve and finalize the metrics database which was designed in parallel with the experiment, to expand it to an experience database, storing more information during development, and to use it as a baseline for comparing and estimating future projects and documenting process improvement. Moreover, the use of electronic storyboards will help developers to store and compute measures concerning the application (size and complexity) automatically.

The research to define and apply more appropriate size metrics has not yet been completed. It will proceed in two directions: new metrics will be defined according to the complexity of the page, and function points will be modified in order to be applied in multimedia applications.

Moreover, application of the ISO 9000 standards is planned to continue and extend to other activities in First Informatics. The company also plans to continue the experiment to other phases of a multimedia application life cycle.

7.5 CONCLUSION

The main conclusion obtained from the experiment was that the adaptation and integration of state-of-the-art methodologies and tools during educational multimedia application development should be a continuous process, since software process improvement is a continuous process. Therefore, the experiment should be repeated in other similar projects and be extended to involve all phases of multimedia application development.

Moreover, we concluded that standardized methodologies may exist but only up to a certain point. Multimedia technology is continuously evolving and practices and tools must always be updated. However, standards driven by traditional software practices, such as quality assurance standards and standards in project management practices, can and should be adapted. Then, the best possible quality and the most efficient and fruitful cooperation between members of the production teams could be achieved.

ACKNOWLEDGEMENTS

Part of this work was supported by the European Commission, under the ESSI programme FAME (Framework for management and design of multimedia applications in education and training, project no. 10760).

END NOTES

[1] In the HDM model [GAR93] *objects* are referred to as *slots*.
[2] Page is the same as a Screen or View or Window.
[3] GDR: Greek currency.
[4] An *error* here means any undesired task performed by users, such as when users move to a page different from the one expected.
[5] Productivity here does not refer to individuals' productivity but to the productivity of the team responsible for a specific task, such as: design team, authoring team, etc.

REFERENCES

[BAS84]   Basili, V. B. and Weiss, M. W. (1984) A methodology for collecting valid software engineering data. *IEEE Transactions on Software Engineering*, **10**(6), pp. 728–738, November.

[BAS91]   Basili, V. and Selby, R. (1991) *Paradigms for Experimentation and Empirical Studies in Software Engineering, Reliability Engineering and System Safety*, (England: Elsevier Science Publishers Ltd), pp. 171–191.

[DUM92]   Dumslaff, U. and Ebert, J. (1992) Structuring the subject matter. In Tomek, I. (ed.) *Computer Assisted Learning*, Lecture Notes in Computer Science 602 (Berlin-Heidelberg: Springer-Verlag), pp. 174–186.

[FEN91]   Fenton, N. (1991) *Software Metrics – A Rigorous Approach* (Chapman and Hall).

[GAR93]   Garzotto, F., Paolini, P. and Schwabe, D. (1993) HDM: A model-based approach to hypertext application design. *ACM Trans. Off. Inf. Syst.*, **11**(1), pp. 1–26, January.

[ISO]   ISO 9001:1994. Quality systems – Model for quality assurance in design, development, production, installation and servicing. ISO 9000:1991. Part 3: Guidelines for the application of ISO 9001 to the development, supply and maintenance of software.

[KOU94]   Kouroupetroglou, G. and Viglas, C. (1994) Evaluation in the development process of multimedia applications. *Proc. of the 2nd Conference on Educational Informatics*, Athens, Greece, pp. 43–52.

[MAR95]   Marino, M. (1995) Evaluating Interactive Multimedia. *ED-MEDIA 95 Workshop*, Graz, Austria.

[NIE90]   Nielsen, J. (1990) *Hypertext and Hypermedia* (San Diego, Ca: Academic Press).

[PIT95]   Pitoura, T. and Karambelas, L. (1995) Improving the process of educational multimedia development. *Proc. of the European Conference on Software Process Improvement (SPI'95)*, Barcelona, Spain, pp. 382–394.

[PIT96]   Pitoura, T., Tsakarissianos, G. and Karambelas, L. (1996) Final Report, The FAME Project, ESSI Project no 10760, Version 2, March.

[PRE92]   Pressman, R. (1992) *Software engineering: A practitioner's approach* (Singapore: McGraw-Hill).

[SAN94]   Sanders, J. and Curran, E. (1994) *Software Quality: A Framework for Success in Software Development and Support* (Addison-Wesley).

8

System and Software Project Management and Management Accounting Methodology

Mikel Emaldi[a] **and Geoff Marlow**[b]

[a]*Departamentos de Tecnologias de la Informacion y Calidad/Competitvidad, Bilbao, Spain*
[b]*Cambridge Consultants Ltd, Cambridge, UK*

EXECUTIVE SUMMARY

This document summarizes the lessons learned in the ESSI Application Experiment 10836, PRAMIS, which relates to the development and evaluation of a system and software project management and management accounting methodology.

The project set out to evaluate existing practices in the partner companies, LABEIN and CCL, and to identify improvements and associated computer-based support tools. The project included a nine-month pilot experiment to evaluate the impact of the selected techniques and tools on project performance.

The lessons learned so far mainly relate to the development and deployment of a Project Management Manual, changing established work practices and the challenges associated with specifying, acquiring and commissioning support tools. The issues of corporate culture which such changes imply are a key aspect of such improvements and will be important factors in the success of similar initiatives throughout the EU.

8.1 INTRODUCTION

8.1.1 Objectives and Justification

The objective of the PRAMIS Application Experiment is to demonstrate the benefits of an integrated Project Management and Management Accounting process particularly in terms of software productivity and quality, through application to live pilot projects.

Management Accounting should make possible the global management of the company with respect to its projects; it should be fast and accurate enough to support management decisions, as opposed to Financial Accounting which has to produce auditable accounts, and which can be slower.

The primary benefit sought is an enhancement of the quality of the development processes of a particular company and, consequently, its products and services in order to guarantee their conformity with the customer's requirements. Such development processes would also take into account the ISO 9001 Standard.

The reason for the collaboration between LABEIN and CCL is to experiment with two different organizations which face similar problems, even though they have different histories and cultures. The justification of the experiment is that if solutions are applicable to both of them, they should be applicable to a large number of organizations throughout Europe.

The application experiment includes a clear definition and assessment of the existing practices in both companies, the development of the existing procedures into an integrated Methodology for the complete life cycle of software projects, training of the personnel involved in the experiment and, finally, a new assessment to measure the results of the experiment.

8.1.2 Importance of Project Management

Even though every author is probably expected to claim that his/her topic is the most important topic in the book, we would make the point that, while project management would probably not guarantee that a project succeeds without sound technical expertise, it will be very difficult for a project to succeed in the face of bad project management.

It is significant that, of the famous 20 clauses in the ISO 9001 standard, many of them refer to project management issues, and the same applies to many of the key practices in the Software Engineering Institute's Capability Maturity Model for software development organizations, or to any other model for quality or process maturity.

It is therefore clear that if an organization's business is project-oriented then it must master project management in order to be successful in the marketplace. It is also clear that project management is not unique to software developers, since any other engineering-oriented organization will face similar problems.

8.1.3 Expected Benefits

A number of benefits are expected from the project in both partner organizations. Some of them are listed below.

The main expected benefit of the experiment is the availability of a methodology which provides support in the accurate dimensioning and management of systems and software development projects, thereby reducing the errors and losses due to mistakes in the early stages of the projects and to inadequate management based on reaction to unexpected events (the firefighter approach). Such events are common in project development since projects usually differ and experience is, therefore, hard to generalize.

Worthwhile improvements in quality and efficiency can be realized by LABEIN, CCL and other EU-based organizations through integrated Project Management and Management Accounting tools based on the *Open Systems* philosophy for computing systems.

Better control of project development activities, such as specifications, design, implementation and testing, and anticipation of possible problem areas will help in project management, facilitate better communication with the customer and achieve general customer satisfaction.

A common management framework in terms of data, support tools, common procedures and so on, should allow the integration of a vertical or horizontal group of projects at different levels (e.g. department manager, division manager, company manager) to obtain different data of interest (e.g. expenses, technical results, human resources allocation). A global view of the state of the company should be available. This global vision facilitates the reusability of the results of the projects, the collaboration between groups and the flexibility of staff utilization within and between projects.

Personnel productivity is also expected to increase through decreased rework and earlier problem detection.

At the same time, an increase in the quality of the products will produce important savings in the maintenance phase, which will mean important savings for the customers and an improved commercial image for the developer. Customer satisfaction should lead to increased sales.

ISO 9001 and ISO 9000-3 certification, partially enabled by the experiment, will also provide an important competitive advantage, both from the objective (increased quality) and from the marketing points of view.

The companies potentially interested in the results of this application experiment would include all organizations that work in a project-oriented fashion. This is the case for all R&D organizations, as well as for engineering and consultancy firms in general.

Well-known references in the literature talk of large savings generated by improved project control and management information visibility within project-oriented organizations. Some of the benefits are very difficult to evaluate quantitatively, such as the more robust decision-making process based on better data, or the reduced stress of project personnel towards the end of the projects, but should this application experiment make possible a very conservative 1% saving in the general project development costs, it would mean an annual saving in LABEIN (as an example) of around 75 kECU leading to a payback period of 3.3 years. The actual savings and non-quantified benefits are expected to be significantly higher, though.

CCL would expect to achieve at least 20% reduction in project overspends, itself about 2.5% of annual turnover (15 MECU); the objective is to reduce both actual spend and spend underestimates. This would give a direct quantifiable saving of 75 kECU per annum, plus hidden benefits in improved efficiency, morale, teamworking and better organizational learning. At project level the problem is spend underestimates, while at company level small reductions in the total company expenditures would amount to large amounts of money.

Arising from all these justifications the partners had high expectations for this project.

8.1.4 The Participants

LABEIN is an independent, non-profit and multi-disciplinary organization dedicated to Contract R&D, Consultancy, Testing & Certification and Dissemination services for the industrial and services sectors in several technological areas. Approximately one-third of LABEIN's income comes from systems and software development activities.

In 1994 LABEIN had a total of 176 employees, 30% of whom were dedicated to R&D in software, had an annual turnover of around 11 Million ECU and was based in Bilbao (Spain).

Cambridge Consultants Ltd (CCL) is a contract design and development company specializing in project-based development, and consultancy in technology and technology management. The majority of CCL's development projects have some software element, and many major projects have a significant software content.

In 1994 CCL had around 250 employees, 50% of whom are dedicated to software-related R&D, had an annual turnover of around 20 Million ECU and was based in Cambridge (UK).

Both are contract-research organizations, therefore projects are often unique and seldom repetitive. In this regard both organizations face more difficult problems than traditional software houses, since these companies often have standardized products which they customize as little as possible for different customers; therefore the amount of repetitive work is large and estimating is fairly easy.

8.1.5 Work programme of PRAMIS

PRAMIS was divided into several tasks (see Figure 8.1).

1. Assessment. Process audit and development.
   Following an independent assessment of the current processes, these were reviewed and/or redesigned.
2. Metrics.
   Since metrics are important in all improvement efforts, effort was invested in analysis and metrics identification, not to evaluate the success of the application experiment itself but to enable future improvements by the partners.
3. Tools selection.
   A large part of the tasks involved in the redesigned processes need the support of tools, which were selected, customized and deployed for the pilot experimentation at each of the partner's premises. The basic tools' requirements are those of project accounting, i.e. management of timesheets and all

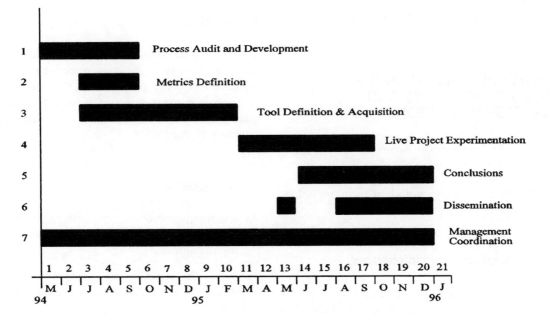

Figure 8.1 PRAMIS tasks

other kinds of costs and invoices, as well as project progress. It is also essential to track planned versus actual figures, and propagate these costs and progress figures throughout the organization to create global enterprise figures useful for Management Accounting (as distinct from Financial Accounting). Also, the application is a commercial product, supporting the main principles of Open Systems.

4. Pilot project experimentation.

The new processes and tools were tested by use in live projects.

In this application experiment (AE), in contrast to most of the other AEs, the pilot comprised not only one project, but a group of projects within a functional unit in each of the partners. This is core to the nature of PRAMIS, since some of the facilities required apply to groups of projects rather than isolated projects.

5. Conclusions.

Another assessment was conducted in order to make a comparison with the results of the initial one, and so to ascertain progress.

6. Dissemination.

A number of dissemination actions have taken place in order to disseminate the results of PRAMIS, among them this book.

7. Management and coordination.

It might be surprising that a project dealing with best practice in project management and scheduled for 18 months slipped by four months. This was due to a single problem, mid-project, and arose from tool customization taking much longer than anticipated. The delay was discussed with the officials of the EC and accepted. No further delays have taken place.

8.2 PROBLEMS DETECTED IN THE EXISTING PROCESSES AND SUGGESTED SOLUTIONS

The initial process assessment was very useful in the detection of both suspected and unsuspected problems at both partners. The main problems are summarized below, even though not all of them apply to both partners.

8.2.1 Structural and organisational

It was clear that in some cases the Project Manager's role and responsibilities were not clearly defined, leading to a range of symptoms since the Project Manager is the single most important person in any project management-related process.

Another problem was related to lack of company-wide procedures, which in this case led to isolated estimating, planning and follow-up processes in different business centres or units.

For the same reason, the integration of newcomers was difficult since there was no procedure to bring them up to speed with common practice across the company.

8.2.2 Human

It was confirmed that, as suspected, there was poor communication among projects, which was the main cause of poor sharing of experiences. This again led to problems with the integration of newcomers, and to repeated errors.

8.2.3 Technical

Even though the partners make use of tools for software development, these tools are generally lower case tools, lag the leading edge, and tend to lack the use of latest practice of Software Engineering methods.

It was found that different people often used different tools in order to solve the same problem. This was due to the lack of a common framework of project planning and follow-up tools.

8.2.4 Process

There were confirmed overruns in time and costs. Reducing these was the main objective of both companies through this project and other initiatives.

There is much to improve in project management, quality assurance, configuration management, and retention of experience.

8.2.5 Suggestions

As a consequence of the aforementioned problems, the assessor's suggestions for improvement included the following areas.

- Modify the organization structure and clarify the Project Management functions and responsibilities.
- Facilitate communication.

- Integration of Project Management and Management Accounting in a common framework, a prime area for improvement.
- Improve tracking of progress against plan as a key area to achieve rapid returns from PRAMIS.
- Offer better on-line access to encourage project managers to keep plans up to date.

In order to reach these goals, the Project Management Methodology needed improvements in the following areas.

- Project management, risk analysis, estimation, planning, follow-up.
- Quality assurance; increased use of metrics.
- Project management integration and reduced variability across the company.

It is interesting to note that most of these problems relate to the issue of 'repeatability', which would be basic for the transition from CMM level 1 to level 2.

8.3 PRODUCTS OF THE PROJECT: METHODOLOGY AND TOOLS

There are two main outcomes from PRAMIS, namely:
- a Project Management Methodology,
- supported by a computer-based tool.

Due to the contract-research nature of both partner organizations, we use a variety of methodologies to suit the client's need. Sometimes it is something similar to the classical V model, but frequently it is something more akin to the spiral model. Increasingly we have to do prototyping to reduce risks, such as:

- technical risks – e.g. performance capacity evaluation;
- functionality and usage risks – e.g. several iterations of a user interface by simulation before finalizing the design of a mass-produced LCD;
- timescale risks – e.g. interface definition and confirmation to allow maximum development concurrency.

The diversity of the work we undertake means we need this flexibility, but also means we must demonstrate the capabilities and competences of those doing the work (via training and experience records). This will not be the case for many of the software companies who might read the book.

The Project Management Methodology is documented in a Project Management Manual and Procedures which describe in detail what must be done in order to manage a project successfully. Two Manuals have been written, one for each partner, which differ, although they have basically the same contents. They are different for a number of reasons.

- One of them is written in English, the other in Spanish.
- The companies have different histories and cultures, which had to be accommodated.

The Manuals include: Project Manager's Handbook, Software Procedures, Project Documentation – all are approximately one hundred pages and include guidance, mandatory procedures and onward references. Procedures are defined so that people know what is mandatory and what is optional, also how they justify deviations from default procedures. It is always clear that these procedures are designed to support the project manager, but the project's success is his/her responsibility and therefore a number of issues are optional.

In any case, the Manual includes:

- procedure for Quotes/Contracts;
- procedure for Project Startup (Estimating/ Planning);
- procedure for Project Follow-up;
- procedure for Project Closure.

For all phases, they include descriptions of:

- objectives of the phase;
- participants and responsibilities;
- tasks to fulfil and sequence of actions;
- forms;
- examples and typical contents of documentation;
- other guidelines.

All these documents are designed in conformance with the ISO 9001 standard.

Most of the metrics we use for the moment are time and resource metrics, basically related to schedule, cost and progress evaluation. It is surprising that most companies manage projects based on cost progression (how much have we spent?) instead of progress progression (how much have we attained?). They seem to assume that progress follows cost, therefore leading to the infamous 99% complete syndrome. We feel that it is very important to track progress separately from cost and also from invoicing, since it provides management with an estimation of work-in-progress which is fundamental for the management of the company. How progress estimates are done is another subject, suitable for debate.

There were requirements for the computer-based support tools over and above those generated within the Project Management process redesign. The main tool sought was basically oriented to project tracking, also allowing tracking estimates and resource management. These further requirements include:

- support for worksheet processing and expense tracking;

- support for project cost, progress and income tracking, and the matching of these (often projects are tracked only on the basis of cost, leading to the infamous 99% complete syndrome at a time when it is too late to take action);

- support for performance tracking at cost centre and company levels;

- support for Resource Management;

- Business Plan tracking;

- links to Financial Accounting systems;

- robustness from a commercial product, with multi-user support, security, openness for improvement, UNIX and standard database management system (DBMS) and/or fourth generation language (4GL) based, and generally based on the Open Systems philosophy.

The market for this breadth of tool is surprisingly sparse, in spite of almost every company having a tool which supports some subset of this functionality. In most cases these tools are internally developed.

The selected tool, named 'Project and Research Manager', was developed by CHA Computer Solutions plc (UK), and is built on top of a commercial 4GL (COGNOS' PowerHouse) which supports the main RDBMS in the market as well as flat C-ISAM files. The platform is UNIX even though it could also be VMS. This is a fairly well-known tool with a number of installations in engineering and especially academic institutions in the UK and Australia.

8.4 LESSONS LEARNED

A number of important lessons emerged during the work, which deal mainly with the changes in the culture of an organization, and the development and deployment of new working methods, including the specification, installation, commissioning and training of staff on the system selected.

Our approach to procedure generation and uptake (which also seems to be the most successful way our clients have found for developing and implementing their procedures) is as follows.

1. Identify (or proactively create) key influencers in the development area who recognize the need.

2. Agree the scope and content with them.
3. Draft the procedure (ideally get them to do this but they're usually the busiest of people).
4. Review the procedure with them and other experienced people.
5. Apply the procedure on a pilot project.
6. Review and revise.
7. Roll out across all relevant projects.

Often in reality this process is conducted in retrospect – i.e. a procedure that has evolved and worked well on past projects is adopted as the de facto standard.

Since such procedures demonstrably work and have the patronage of respected developers, uptake is usually high.

These lessons are summarized below.

8.4.1 Do Not Confuse Methodologies with Tools

The deployment of new tools for project management might lead to the erroneous belief that a database could be a substitute for sound project management practices. This could certainly arise in an environment with little experience of project management and given the early focus of training on tools. Furthermore, it is easier to learn and adopt tools than to learn and adopt good project management.

The deployment of sound procedures is much more important than the tools that support them because the procedures provide the framework which will support project management itself. However, some practices become almost unfeasible without tool support.

8.4.2 Recognise the Impact on Working Practices

Any company involved in such a project must recognize that people who have already bought into the new system may opt out again when they realize its impact on their existing working practices. The new system results in changes in practice, roles and responsibilities, as well as changes in job boundaries (particularly, but not limited to, the Accounts Department). As the impact of changes is gradually appreciated by those affected, the willingness to cooperate is significantly increased if senior management handle the changes with tact and sensitivity. Whether this lesson has been fully learned will become apparent as the AE progresses.

Beware being too definitive with the new system. Some flexibility in early use of the system should be allowed, since all the new opportunities cannot be predicted in advance and people need an opportunity to learn and disseminate good practice.

Some of the project managers have useful skills and good practices, built up over the years, which should not be lost in the new system. Integration of previous good practice within the new system and procedures must be explicitly managed.

Be sure to pursue and explore any vaguely expressed concerns.

Demonstrate some tangible results quickly which show people how the new approaches and tools help them personally; this is the best way to get personal and public acceptance of new methods and tools.

8.4.3 Manage Change

The installation of a new management system offers a superb opportunity to achieve lasting change, but this change must be managed so that its users have time to familiarize themselves with it, accommodate it and embrace it.

Actively manage the changes to maintain momentum. Beware the effects of too many changes at once; in particular beware of people responding to more personal changes (e.g. structure and job role) and therefore not responding to the procedural changes (e.g. project management systems).

Do not underestimate the time it takes to build and maintain consensus and commitment to the new management system and the changes it will involve. The partners held many working meetings with users of the system, involving them in the evolution of specifications of requirements. There was a significant amount of time spent on this in order to help ensure that the AE would be supported by a committed user base.

Develop and communicate a clear message about where all effort is leading and why. Keep reinforcing the message. A new management system sends many messages, some of which might not be those intended by its supporters.

- What is measured is valued.
- What is not measured can be safely ignored!

8.4.4 Allow for Plenty of Training

A new project management accounting system must be backed up by, and integrated with, training in project management and clear messages about its

significance for the business. Particularly for this topic, because it influences so much of the company, there are many underlying assumptions which need to be explained to the staff.

8.4.5 Manage the Deployment of the Tools

Be very clear which functions and features are:

- feasible but not included;
- included but not yet implemented;
- fully implemented.

Differences in perceptions will cause conflict between stakeholders, perceptions that the system is incomplete, general uncertainty and lack of confidence.

Minor bugs and errors in a system can create a major loss of confidence, especially among the less technically qualified. This was observed in this AE when, at the very beginning of the pilot experience, the system would crash half a dozen times a day, generating a number of corrupted files which needed to be restored from backup. Although the problem lasted only for a few days, months later the directors were still demanding robustness of the system.

8.5 FULFILMENT OF PRAMIS OBJECTIVES

PRAMIS' objectives at the proposal stage have been described in Section 8.1.3, and a global evaluation of how well the AE satisfies them is included in Section 8.6 on conclusions. Yet in order to be more detailed, we could classify the lessons learnt as follows.

Benefits and lessons		Unplanned	Planned
	Realized	Outcomes realized but unplanned	Outcomes planned and realized
	Not realized	Disbenefits and warnings	Outcomes planned but not realized
		Unplanned	**Planned**
		Benefits sought	

8.5.1 Outcomes Planned and Realized

Among the outcomes expected at the beginning of the project, those realized include the following.

- A common management framework provides customized information for different levels of management and for different functional concerns throughout the company. As one single framework, everyone in the company uses the same tools.

- The system provides insight for senior management into the health of the company by collecting and integrating results from many projects. This was one of the prime objectives of the project.
- The process by which projects are planned, initiated, monitored and controlled is now streamlined and integrated, as the result of the process redesign.
- A common methodology for estimating and dimensioning projects, together with resource planning and allocation, has been established. It was often the case that estimating and planning were strongly dependent upon local circumstance and the individuals involved.
- Better control of resource expenditure and earlier detection of problems have been seen in practice.

8.5.2 Outcomes Realized but Unplanned

Some outcomes and observations, though valuable, were relatively unexpected. These include the following.

- The installation of project management and accounting tools provides a clear message across the organization about the importance of good project management for the health of the organization.
- The very fact of measuring some parameters resulted in significant improvement in business performance. This reflects the earlier observation that what is measured is valued but what is not measured can be safely ignored. It remains to be seen whether this improvement is sustained.
- Starting data collection resulted in the closure of 10% of the projects open at the time, which was useful in itself in helping the companies to remove administrative garbage and an illustration of the result mentioned above.
- The primary effect of methods and tools is to raise the average performance by helping the less able to become more effective. Competent project managers are not helped as much, but may achieve an increase in efficiency.
- New ways of collecting and combining data highlighted problems with previous approaches, which allowed modification to the management processes.

8.5.3 Outcomes Planned but Unrealized

Some areas did not meet expectations or highlighted deeper issues.

- Implementation of the project management and accounting tools turned out to require longer than planned.
- To make use of accumulated data and experience from past projects to support future estimating activities requires:
  - a characterization of project types;
  - a change of culture to overcome the tendency to see each project as unique;
  - a formal post-project audit to highlight useful experience in a constructive way.

Meeting these requirements was difficult, but not impossible, for the partners in PRAMIS because both are contract-research companies and projects are therefore very seldom repetitive. It would be potentially easier for the typical software house, often working from internal products against more common requirements.

- The system provides little support (except accounting) for unpredictable workloads of shorter and more intense activities, such as consultancy and testing and certification services.

8.5.4 Drawbacks and Warnings

Some outcomes highlight specific warnings.

- The deployment of such a system will require realignment of job roles and boundaries, which should be recognized early and managed.
- Custom reports are essential to gaining user acceptance, specially if users are already familiar with a previous system. Problems arise when users are offered greater flexibility but fail to analyse their fundamental requirements, since they tend to respond by adding unnecessary complexity, or sticking to old habits out of unquestioning familiarity. One of the partners started the pilot experience with twelve reports, which were designed to be able to cope with all needs in the system; the experience was that six months later there were over sixty reports on-line.
- Because less competent project managers are seldom alert to the benefits offered by tools and procedures, active promotion is required to ensure the adoption of best practice.

- Some of the objections to change have nothing to do with the new system. Very often, people use the opportunity presented by the introduction of a new system to surface old complaints about almost anything, from 'the printer is very old' to salary issues.
- Minor bugs and errors early in the implementation can create a major loss of confidence in the system; bad news is quickly relayed and impressions last much longer than the errors.
- Beware the implications of failing to respond to each of the lessons mentioned in Section 8.4 (differences between methodologies and tools, managing change, working practices, training, and managing the rate of change).

8.5.5 Other lessons

The final assessment was performed just like the initial one. The same independent consultant was hired and made the same assessment, checking out a number of the projects in the pilot experiment, as well as assessing the department housing the pilot experiment itself. The results of this assessment were then compared to the initial results in a checklist, with qualitative evaluations such as yes/no/frequently/seldom. Since the evaluation was not quantitative, the global evaluation had to be qualitative again. Yet it might be significant that a recent (July 1996) SPICE[2] assessment of LABEIN implemented by a third party showed us at level 3 in our Project Management practices.

The final assessment detected that, after a year, the deployment of the system had resulted in big improvements in project planning and tracking, and even in communication within the project teams.

There is a clear danger related to any attempt to achieve precise resource management in pursuit of better utilization of staff time. Often people try to go from nothing to the perfect solution, whereas in this case it is often much better and certainly more feasible to stay with approximate and simple solutions.

A comment, very widely repeated among the partners, related to the need for high availability of experts in order to help the users. In fact, the experience shows that the existing internal audit programme is very useful as a vehicle for support and training, rather than merely to police the application of procedures.

A common complaint was that the administrative 'load' was perceived to be disproportionate for small projects. This has prompted refinement of procedures in some areas.

Finally, a completely unexpected comment from the project managers themselves was that common methods and tools improve the feeling of 'a team' throughout the company.

8.6 CONCLUSIONS

During the course of this project a number of lessons have become clear, such as the following.

- New methods upset existing power structures and established practices.
- Introducing new methods and tools presents particular challenges in terms of culture and management.
- Even 'mature' tools may require significant on-site debugging.
- Changes must be actively managed in order to gain support from staff.

If we look at the original basic objective of the partners, namely the improvement in productivity, it is not easy at this moment to assess whether it has been achieved, although the feeling at both companies is that the methodologies, procedures and tools have helped. Both will need some extra time in order to measure the benefits, since projects are long and need to be finished in order to assess overall profitability.

Although CCL was already ISO 9001 certified beforehand, LABEIN gained ISO 9001 certification for the pilot department within the time scope of PRAMIS, and this attainment has been partially made possible by PRAMIS itself.

Beyond the scope of PRAMIS, both companies are actively disseminating the results throughout the companies themselves, which should achieve standardization of all that PRAMIS represents within the companies by mid-1996, therefore it is clear that both consider the project worth the effort and expense involved.

Both companies consider PRAMIS a success.

REFERENCES

1. [SEI 93] Capability Maturity Model for Software, version 1.CMU/SEI-93-TR-24, Software Engineering Institute, Carnegie-Mellon University (USA), 1993.
2. [SPICE] Software Process Improvement and Capability dEtermination, draft ISO standard, European Software Institute (ESI), Tel: +34 4 420 95 19, http://www.esi.es/

9

Introducing Systematic Reuse in an SME

Jose Manuel Villalba Quesada

ELIOP SA, Madrid, Spain

EXECUTIVE SUMMARY

The ISORUS project aimed to develop and evaluate a methodology to introduce reuse into the software process at ELIOP. Its objectives were to reduce costs and time-to-market, and improve software reliability, by means of the introduction of systematic reuse practices. The project was undertaken by ELIOP as the single contractor, with some support from external subcontractors, and was financially supported by the European Commission in the framework of the European Systems and Software Initiative (ESSI).

ELIOP SA is a Spanish company with one hundred employees, thirty of them directly involved in software engineering. Its main activity is the delivery of industrial control systems, including software for standard computers and embedded into microprocessor-based in-house manufactured equipment. Such systems require real-time continuous operation, and often they are controlling critical industrial processes. Software is a very important part of the added value of ELIOP products.

The work performed started with the identification of an adequate reuse approach, a review of the current practices and definition of the specific improvements to be made. After that, appropriate metrics were identified, the necessary tools were selected and installed, and required training activities were done. The experiment itself included the identification, development and use of the reusable assets. Final stages of the project included a review of the procedures and an evaluation of the results of the experiment and the human and organizational aspects of software reuse practices. As a result, plan-

ning for the introduction of the improvements as a regular practice in ELIOP was done.

Key lessons learnt from the project are the following.

- Reuse of other assets apart from code is very important.
- Introduce domain analysis to allow systematic reuse of software within a specific domain of application.
- It is necessary to have strong configuration management practices in place for all software assets in order to carry out reuse successfully.
- To reduce risks, allow the software assets to be modified when reused, if necessary. This decreases costs and has lower organizational impact.
- An appropriate level of process and product quality is a prerequisite to introducing reuse. Productivity benefits will appear only after introducing the necessary quality improvements.
- Consider human and organizational barriers when introducing reuse. To overcome them, define your process and all organizational roles explicitly. Keep managers and developers informed as closely as possible.
- In order to facilitate reuse, the organization must define a business strategy looking beyond the current projects, anticipate needs and define product lines.
- To reduce risks, do improvements based on an evolutionary, step-by-step approach, rather than a 'revolutionary' approach.

As a result of the experiment, ELIOP is introducing the methodology tested as a regular practice.

9.1 BACKGROUND INFORMATION

9.1.1 Objectives

From the technical point of view, the objective was to 'develop and evaluate a methodology to introduce reuse in the ELIOP software process.' As can be appreciated, this is an objective focused on the process itself.

From the business point of view, the defined objectives were as follows.

- Reduce costs (this objective was stated quantitatively as a 30% reduction).
- Decrease time-to-market of products including software.
- Improve software reliability (that is, decrease the number of failures in the delivered software).

9.1.2 Companies Involved and Their Roles

ELIOP was the single contractor for this application experiment. Some specific tasks were done by consultants under subcontracts (see section 9.2.4).

ELIOP SA is a relatively small company with one hundred employees, thirty of them directly involved in software engineering. Its main activity is the delivery of industrial control systems.

The systems offered by ELIOP normally include both in-house manufactured equipment and standard computers with in-house developed software, together with other equipment (for instance, communications and sensors).

ELIOP manufactures a range of microprocessor-based equipment for different industrial applications, including Remote Telecontrol Stations, Process Automation and Energy Management, among others. Both software and hardware of this microprocessor-based embedded equipment are developed internally.

9.1.3 Starting Scenario

As can be seen from the information given, software is a very important part of the added value of ELIOP products. Specific characteristics of generated software are real-time, continuous operation, and often critical industrial applications. Another concern is the variety of environments.

At the beginning of the experiment, the engineering practice at ELIOP was oriented to the classic life-cycle steps: requirement analysis, design, coding, testing and maintenance. ELIOP developed a simplified methodology that establishes specific documentation for each phase.

Many new projects are considered as upgrades to previous software. These projects are developed by adding new software or modifying existing software to cover a wider range of cases. Another trend was to make flexible software by means of user parameters that allow the user to adapt it to a specific application.

Regarding the organizational aspects, there are several software development teams. There are one or more teams for each different software environment.

Another issue is that ELIOP was committed to getting ISO 9001 certification for all its processes at the same time the ISORUS project was undertaken, although this was not a specific goal of the project. Actually, certification was granted by the end of the project.

9.1.4 Workplan

Following is an overview of the activities carried out during the project, in chronological order.

- Setting up of the project organisation.
- Identification of a reuse approach. This was an activity to learn from the available knowledge about reuse, including other experiences, in order to focus the work to be done in the remainder of the project.
- Process assessment and review. This task was done to review the current practices and define the specific improvements to be made.
- Identification and setting up of the appropriate metrics.
- Selection and installation of tools to support the experiment.
- Training for the people involved, in both tools and methods.
- The experimentation itself had two different activities:
  1. identification and development of the reusable assets;
  2. use of these software assets.
- Final stages of the project included a review of the procedures and an evaluation of the results of the experiment and the human and organizational aspects of software reuse practices. As a result, planning for the introduction of the improvements as a regular practice in ELIOP was done.

In order to clarify the terminology, the word 'experiment' will be used to identify the experimental activities that are the essential part of the 'project'. (The two are not the same thing, because the project also includes some preparation activities, intended to create the appropriate conditions for the experiment, evaluation tasks, and management activities.)

The experimental phase of the project was planned to affect all software development activities at ELIOP. Any software activity was a candidate to use some kind of 'reusable asset' from the software library. In practice, the greater amount of reuse was performed within one specific project. This project was the development of a new family of microprocessor-based products with embedded software.

9.1.5 Expected Outcomes

A first benefit that was expected was to encourage best software practices. In fact, reusable modules should have higher quality attributes than application-specific software, and this should demand better methods and tools in their development process. It was planned, in the context of the experiment, to design and evaluate some improvements to our standard practices, affecting both methodologies and tools, in the different steps of the software production process.

An important expected benefit was to decrease software development time, especially in the coding and testing phases, when using reusable modules.

Another anticipated important benefit was to achieve more reliability of new software, derived from the use of well-tested reusable modules.

A benefit in cost was also expected. Although it was realized that the effort needed to produce reusable modules is higher than for normal modules, the use of these modules saves further development costs. Resulting from both facts, a decrease in costs was expected, estimated at 30% savings in the development phases, with some further savings in the maintenance phase, derived from the higher quality associated with the approach addressed by the experiment. This 30% figure was the estimate at the time the project was planned. The degree of analysis of the software reuse issues was not very deep at that time. This figure did not include the investment costs incurred to introduce new practices, and should be considered only as a measure of the expectations that this project aroused in the company.

As a consequence of the above, a remarkable improvement in customer satisfaction was envisaged. No measurements for customer satisfaction improvement were identified. Customer satisfaction depends upon many factors, and the degree of detail of a practical survey does not allow the very specific causes of the changes in the degree of satisfaction to be established.

In fact, a survey that was introduced by the company just after the project only evaluates the 'quality' of the product, but the quality depends upon many factors, other than software. So, the expectations of better customer satisfaction are supposed to be a natural consequence of quality improvement, and no quantitative objectives were stated.

9.2 WORK PERFORMED

9.2.1 Organization

The project was organized around the following elements.

- The project manager, who took overall responsibility for the project.
- The work group, with participation by the project manager, two team heads and two senior engineers. People from the work group did the high-level technical work and control and supervision of the experimentation tasks.
- A number of other software engineers participated in the experimentation tasks and other activities, such as tool evaluation and installation.

9.2.2. Technical Environment

Several tools were selected, installed and evaluated in order to support the different activities related to the experiment. Tools can be classified into two classes.

- Specific tools intended to support reuse. A Reusable Software Library was installed.
- Non-specific tools were also needed in order to fulfil some requirements for the reusable software, regarding testing, portability, metrics, and other general issues. Also, a networked environment was necessary to share the needed information.

9.2.3 Training

Training activities were focused in several directions.

- Provide a wider vision of the different environments to engineers who normally work only in one specific environment.

- Learn the essential information about reuse concepts and the proposed methodology.
- Learn about the tools to be used.
- Gain wider acceptance for the changes implied in this process improvement project.

By the mid-term of the project, we held a presentation of the progress of the project to all software engineers and management, emphasizing process improvement proposals and specific reuse issues.

After the end of the project a detailed presentation and training about the methodology to be introduced was held.

9.2.4 Role of the Consultants

Two different subcontractors participated in the experiment as consultants.

- The University of Madrid (Faculty of Informatics of the Universidad Politécnica) participated in two different specific works.
  1. Study of specific reuse practises for Windows environments using object-oriented languages.
  2. Requirement analysis and data design for a Reusable Software Library based on a standard database management system.
- COYPSA, a Spanish consultant company, collaborated in the definition of the new internal procedures, and assessed and reviewed them, in order to verify the accomplishment of ISO 9001 quality standards.

9.2.5 Phases of the Experiment

9.2.5.1 General approach study

In this phase, the organization of the project was set up, as described in Section 9.2.1. A lot of information was read and discussed by the work group to learn from other experiences and gain a general knowledge of the complex issues related to the project. Some references are given at the end of the chapter. From the practitioner's point of view, we have found that there are many books, papers and articles, but few practical guides focused to the introduction of software process improvements based on reuse. Additionally, existing information is normally not addressed to small–medium companies, or is addressed to specific sectors of activity (military, space, etc.).

A very first conclusion was that reuse was already done at our company but not in a systematic and organized way. So, we redefined our objective to be the introduction of 'systematic' or 'planned' reuse.

Further analysing reuse issues, we realized that, at the time the experiment was planned, only 'horizontal' reuse was considered. The concern of horizontal reuse is on general-purpose, portable pieces of software ('software assets') that can be applied to very different software products and domains of applications. During the general approach study, we identified the concept of 'vertical reuse', as the reuse of software assets in several products within the same domain of application. As these software assets deal with objects and functions specific to the domain, they can be applied to many products within the domain. Reusability is restricted to the domain, but considering that our company delivers products that belong to a small number of application domains, this restriction is not as important as we might suppose at first sight. Additionally, this approach allows us to reuse higher-level and large-volume application-specific software, while horizontal reuse is normally restricted to lower layers of the software products.

From a different point of view, we considered two opposite approaches to reuse. In the black-box reuse approach, assets must be used without modification. White-box reuse allows the reuse of components by modification and adaptation. The white-box approach was considered more interesting because it has lower costs and organizational requirements, because no specific people are assigned to the development and maintenance of reusable software assets. Black-box reuse is more expensive because software assets must be more generic, more complex and very well tested in all possible circumstances. White-box reuse allows us to reuse existing or newly developed components with minimum cost. The basic idea supporting white-box reuse is that, if a software component can be easily understood, it also has good maintainability and should be easily reusable. The white-box approach has lower risks, because the investment in reuse is lower, and so it is maybe the only practical choice for SMEs.

A summary of the conclusions from this stage of the project follows.

- Both horizontal and vertical reuse must be considered (they are complementary approaches).
- We decided to adopt the white-box reuse approach, and discard the black-box reuse model for the reasons stated above.
- We decided to try reusing all types of software assets, other than source code: specifications,

designs, test procedures and other documents are very interesting reusable assets.

- We identified a need for written procedures and guidelines to define the reuse methodology.
- Measurement is needed in order to get some feedback on the practical results of the improvements.
- software assets must be standardized, based on the application of coding rules for source code, and templates for documents.
- Some important non-technical issues were identified.
  1. Long-term management support is needed, because a process improvement focused on reuse is an investment that gives its benefits in the mid and long term.
  2. Software engineers' acceptance is essential. A software reuse programme must give benefits to the software engineers.

9.2.5.2 Revision of internal procedures

The next stage of the project was a process assessment and review, with two main objectives.

- Identify the specific improvements to be introduced.
- Define and put onto paper the new methodology.

This was done by means of a self-assessment conducted by the work group, with some subcontractor support. The followed method was based on several activities.

- Review independently every phase of the life cycle: requirement analysis, design, coding, integration and testing, and maintenance.
- Specific consideration of human and organizational factors.
- Evaluation of measurement needs.
- Consideration of tools and training needs.

The self-assessment done within the experiment was not made against any specific maturity model. After a basic knowledge of reuse issues was acquired by the work group members, the method for this self-assessment was to conduct a number of meetings, each of them focused on a specific part of the process, in order to identify and evaluate the different factors influencing the reuse practices, and to collect, discuss and select ideas for improvement. The main criteria for selecting the proposed ideas were their envisaged effectiveness and feasibility in the 'real world'. Total

effort spent on this self-assessment was around 150 hours.

The main outcomes of this stage were the following.

- A document describing the whole process was generated, considering reuse activities explicitly.
- Templates and guidelines were generated for all significant documents.
- Coding style rules were revised.
- The need for a Software Library and its basic requirements were established.
- A need for revision of requirements, design and testing documentation was identified. Specifically, a revision has to be done at the end of the development process, in order to avoid any inconsistencies.
- Considering the requirement analysis step of the life cycle, introduction of domain analysis into the process was done as a major improvement. This is explained in detail in Section 9.2.5.7.

9.2.5.3 Metrics methodology

One important activity of the project was to identify and set up metrics.

First, we considered different known methods. We selected the AMI method because of the availability of the 'AMI handbook' (ref [1]) intended to be used for introducing metrics. AMI is a method to derive metrics from a set of goals defined by the organization, and was developed under the ESPRIT programme.

One conclusion from our work is that direct measurement of benefits derived from reuse practice is not feasible, and so indirect measurements of the process attributes must be carried out. This is because, to measure the benefits, one must compare the real situation with a hypothetical situation without the application of the process improvement actions. Obviously this comparison cannot be done directly. The savings generated by improving the process are really difficult to estimate even when good historical cost data are available. Many factors affect the software costs, and an improvement in the order of 10–20% will be hidden by the effect of other factors (the specific people assigned to the project, the amount of previous experience, the errors incurred when estimating the size and complexity of the project, customer influence, etc).

Anyway, the figures obtained in the project are considered to be useful, if properly used. Quantitative data from ISORUS should be used as a reference in every project in order to decide the reuse practices to be carried out. These data give the manager a more realistic view of the economic effects of reuse.

In order to be able to evaluate the results of the experiment, specific metrics were defined to be used only during the experiment itself. Specifically, two different sets of goals were defined.

- The first set was intended to measure the results of the experiment.
- The second set was defined to measure the efficiency of the process.

In order to measure the results of the experiment, the identified goals were as follows.

- Measure the extra cost of reusable assets.
- Measure the number of uses of reusable assets.

These metrics were applied only to the baseline projects. The method of measurement was a detailed accounting of the work performed, and an analysis of these data to derive the metrics.

In order to measure the SW process efficiency, the goals, as defined by the management, were as follows.

- Reduce SW costs.
- Reduce delays.
- Increase customer satisfaction.

Metrics according to these goals were identified within the project, following the AMI method, as a part of the methodology to be introduced. After a careful selection of the more interesting candidate metrics, two specific metrics were finally selected for introduction.

- Detailed project-oriented effort accounting. Specifically, testing and customer acceptance processes are measured separately. The defined methodology establishes a periodic review of the project accounting sheets, with the participation of the development team, in order to track progress and take appropriate measures to prevent or correct deviations. This metric was tested within one specific project, and the results achieved were considered valuable by the participating people and adopted for general use after the project.
- Software problems accounting. Problems must be weighted according to how critical they are and the phase when they appear. This metric is intended to cover all detected defects in the software, starting from the internal delivery of the software. In most cases software is delivered to another department in the company which takes charge of the customer acceptance. The weighting scheme adopted is as shown in the table.

	Phase of occurrence	
Defect class	Before customer acceptance	After customer acceptance
Improvement	1	2
Non-critical	2	4
Critical	5	10

9.2.5.4 Selection and installation of tools

In order to support the experiment, a number of tools were selected, bought and evaluated. We realized that the first step to achieve reusability is to produce good quality software, and more and better tools are an important component of improvement, provided that their contribution is well understood and planned. Evaluated tools included design tools (both structured and object-oriented methods), code auditing and documentation, testing tools, complexity metrics, etc.

We identified that a specific tool needed is a Library system in order to organize the information about reusable assets, allow search and browse operations, and provide some metrics about the use of the reusable assets.

After unsuccessfully searching for a valid commercial tool, we decided to implement a Library system using standard database management software, in order to have adequate support for the experiment. Activities carried out were: implementation and testing of the Reusable Software Component Library, installation of new networking facilities to support it, presentation and training about the use of the Library to the people involved.

The Library allows for adding, deleting and modifying data about components, as well as search and retrieval facilities and printed reports.

The following types of components were considered, and selected to populate the Library: source and object code, specifications and design documents, testing procedures and testing reports. Source and object code can be introduced into the library at module level or at subsystem level (a set of modules that perform a high-level function). Normally the components are stored in the Library only as a reference to a repository which is maintained with a configuration management tool. Some components that were not under configuration management have been stored directly.

Each asset has a short identification text, reference data and a description, whose content is dependent on the type of asset. Additionally, one or more keywords, and the projects where the asset has been used, can be associated with the component in order to allow search operations. The Library has the capability to specify one or more related assets. This is useful, for instance, to define the link between a piece of code and the related documentation. Some simple metrics are also stored (for instance, lines of code for source code or number of pages for documents). The Library generates some component usage metrics (number of retrievals and modifications). It has multi-user capability, with three levels: user, administrator and superuser. Components must be reviewed and approved by an administrator. Some other operations (for instance, adding projects or keywords) are also restricted to the administrator level.

Some specific information about real-time and concurrence constraints can be introduced as part of the component description, in the case of code components. Also, the language used and the operating system are stated as part of the description. According to our analysis, most of the code that has real-time or concurrence constraints is only reusable under the same operating system and similar hardware, so this information is important to assess the reusability of an asset for a candidate application.

A user-friendly interface for the Library was identified as a major need. In fact, the first version of the tool needed some improvement in its user interface in order to attain better acceptance from users.

An interesting finding of the experiments with the Software Library was that it is very desirable to integrate the Library system with the configuration management tool. This is a key feature in order to facilitate reuse, because the direct storage of components in the Library causes problems when the components are changed. This problem was experienced but unfortunately not solved within the project. A first reason is that we did not identify this need in an early stage of the project, but the principal reason is that no suitable commercial tool was found featuring this integration. Additionally, CM is currently done with a specific tool (PVCS) which has no adequate facilities to allow it to be used as a reusable Software Library.

9.2.5.5 Training

In the first stages of the project we held some training courses on software environments. The courses were given by external experts, supported by people from the company in order to assure consistency with our current practice. The aim was to let people know the basic information about software environments used by other people in the company, and so facilitate the horizontal reuse of software assets. Later, the emphasis of the project was placed on vertical reuse, and at the end of the project this training was evaluated as

not very significant in terms of facilitating reuse, but it had good acceptance.

The more significant training activities were held at mid-term and at the end of the project. Mid-term training was devoted to the following topics.

- Explanation of ISORUS objectives and findings.
- Reuse approach adopted.
- Practical use of the Software Library.

Training held at the end of the project was devoted to:

- detailed explanation of the process improvements introduced;
- explanation of the metrics introduced;
- discussion about project conclusions.

One very important objective of the training activities was to gain acceptance for the planned improvements. To accomplish this objective, it was very important to encourage the active participation of the attendees and to allow open discussions about the topics presented.

Training activities were evaluated with a questionnaire. The results showed a good degree of interest in the topics presented. The practicability of the proposed improvements was evaluated a little lower than the interest, showing some degree of 'resistance to change' in the people involved.

9.2.5.6 Selection of reusable modules

Two different methods were used to select reusable assets.

- Assets for 'planned reuse,' according to the defined methodology, must be identified as a result of domain analysis activities. This is described in Section 9.2.5.7.
- Other assets, intended for 'unplanned reuse', must be identified from existing software. This is described in this section.

The identification and selection of reusable software from the existing assets were considered necessary in order to have the minimum amount of reusable software required to encourage people to search for reusable software with a reasonable probability of success. Several types of components were selected.

- Internally developed, general-purpose software, intended for horizontal reuse.
- Commercial general-purpose software for horizontal reuse.

- Internally developed modules and complex subsystems, for vertical reuse.
- Components other than code (documents).

The activities carried out to obtain such reusable assets included:

- evaluation of reusability, to decide the suitability of the asset for reuse;
- adaptation, involving only formal changes;
- introduction of the asset into the SW library (normally this also implies obtaining some metrics of the asset).

The evaluation of reusability considered the following aspects (ordered from higher to lower weight).

1. General quality (this includes formal compliance with applicable internal directives).
2. Usefulness (anticipated by the evaluator).
3. Maintainability.
4. Maturity.
5. Generality.

Because the criteria for selecting the components exceeded the average level of the existing components, only a relatively small number of modules were introduced into the Library and approved: 74 previously existing source code modules, with a total of 49 KLOC, and 48 documents, with 864 pages in total, and including different types of documents (specifications, design, testing programs, testing procedures and testing reports).

9.2.5.7 Domain analysis experiment

Domain analysis can be defined as the task of identifying the objects, operations and relationships between what domain experts perceive to be important about the domain.

We identified domain analysis as a key activity for planned reuse, and decided to carry out an experimental domain analysis (see Section 9.2.5.2) in the first stages of the project. Some literature about this subject was studied. This allowed the project workgroup to understand the basic ideas and techniques of domain analysis. The decision was to put these ideas and techniques into practice in a way acceptable to our culture and fitting smoothly within our current practice, in order to facilitate the integration of the new activity in our process.

A project suitable for conducting an experiment on domain analysis techniques was selected. This project was the development of a new product, the first of a new family of products. In our case, the domain is the new family of products. It is important to highlight that the domain itself was not new to ELIOP, because this new family of products is being developed to replace an old one within a very similar domain of application. This is a simpler situation than coming into a completely new domain. The selected domain is a specific class of products developed by ELIOP.

The domain analysis was conducted by a 'domain analyst' who was a senior software engineer with experience in the development of software for the old family of products, so this person had a considerable background knowledge of the domain. Other people within the company were identified, in the marketing and commercial areas, as additional sources of knowledge. Other valuable sources were information about competitor products and published or draft standards applicable to the domain. The domain analyst was in charge of capturing, selecting and organizing all the useful knowledge from these sources. The adopted approach was to generate two documents, with a structure very similar to the specifications and high-level design documents of a software product. This approach has two advantages: first, it fits better into the existing 'culture', because the structures of the documents are similar to the existing ones, and second, deriving the specification and design documents for a particular product is relatively easy from these general documents related to the complete domain.

The domain specification document contained the following information.

- A domain definition, including the following.
  1. Background information: description of the previous experience within the domain.
  2. Informal description of the domain, and definition of domain boundaries.
  3. Basic specific concepts, and a list of the identified functions and objects.
  4. Characteristics of the users.
  5. Applicable general restrictions, assumptions and dependencies.
  6. Domain glossary: definition of terms specific to the domain.
  7. List of reference documentation.
- A description of the functional requirements related to every identified object and function. The requirements were qualified, in order to distinguish between common requirements within the domain, and those that are dependent on the class of product.
- A description of the non-functional requirements, including interfacing, design restrictions, perfor-

mance, capacity, security and reliability, qualified using the same criteria explained above.

Regarding the term 'object', when referring to domain analysis activities, its meaning in this context is very similar to that used when referring to object-oriented design. The difference comes from the fact that, when analysing a domain, the level of abstraction must be higher than for a specific system.

The high-level design document produced by domain analysis was intended as a framework for the specific design of the different products of the domain, with the goal to achieve the maximum similarity between the software design of these products, and consequently to facilitate reuse. Another aim of the design document was to establish a software structure that was as simple as possible, in particular regarding the number of different concurrent tasks, in order to simplify the real-time problems that often act as barriers to software reuse.

Some problems were encountered when doing our domain analysis experiment.

- The process of knowledge acquisition was slow and time-consuming, and involved highly qualified people, who are costly resources with very limited time availability. In fact the only practical way we envisaged was the acquisition of knowledge by the domain analyst by means of a number of short, direct contacts with domain experts, discarding any direct participation of these experts in the domain analysis process.

- Sometimes the difficulty was that the company was not able to define clearly some key strategic points of its market objectives regarding the domain of application.

- The high level of abstraction required makes it difficult to express the requirements clearly and unambiguously. An additional complication comes from the need to consider the commonalities and differences between products within the domain. This sometimes makes the document very hard to read, understand and review by the domain experts.

- The domain design document could not be refined up to a level that allowed a precise definition of interfaces for the reusable modules identified. The effect of this problem is probably not very important, because of the white-box reuse approach adopted.

- Some modules, specified, designed and coded according to the domain analysis, generated some problems. These problems derived from an excess of complexity due to unnecessarily generic specifications, and showed poor real-time perfor-

mance (slow execution speed) that demanded some redesign and optimization work to be done.

As a result of the domain analysis, a number of reusable, generic source code modules were identified as reusable software within the domain, and included in the Software Library. The documents produced by the domain analysis itself were also considered reusable assets within the domain.

9.2.5.8 Development and use of selected modules

As stated earlier, two different kinds of reuse were performed and studied: planned reuse is the use of modules that have been specifically developed as reusable modules to be used for the first time in a known application; unplanned reuse was not predetermined at the time an asset was selected as reusable and included in the Library. Because of the limited time schedule of the project, only four months were available for monitoring the reuse of available assets. As a result, planned reuse was higher than unplanned (approximately 80% planned, 20% unplanned). Most reused assets were reused only once, but several were used twice.

It is expected that, outside of the context of the project, the planned vs. unplanned ratio would be much more balanced, because the experiment was more focused on planned reuse, and opportunities for unplanned reuse come with time. A 50/50 ratio seems to be reasonable in the long term, provided that the company maintains a policy of planned reuse based on domain analysis activities.

The amount of software that was selected and stored in the Software Library for unplanned reuse has been stated in Section 9.2.5.6.

For planned reuse, 27 source code modules were generated as reusable modules, with a total of 22 KLOC, and 10 documents with 318 pages in total. Regarding planned reuse, the average total amount of effort to develop a module of source code following the approach identified in the project was 60% higher than the effort needed using standard procedures.

This 60% extra cost was incurred up to the first use of the module, and is derived from two facts: (1) domain analysis activities and (2) the extra complexity of the modules including domain analysis activities. These domain analysis activities generated nearly half of the 60% extra cost. The second use often demanded some additional effort, which was around 20% on average. Effort had been accounted only for the development, including testing, but it is expected that the failure rate and maintenance effort will decrease. According to our experience, we estimate an average effort no higher than 10% for further uses.

For unplanned reuse, the effort needed to adapt the selected pieces of existing software was quite small. Considering that this adaptation involves only formal changes and the introduction of descriptive data into the Software Library, average efforts of 5 hours/KLOC for code and 0.2 hours/page for documents were measured. These efforts are a small fraction of those needed to produce the first tested or revised version of a code or document. Additionally, these efforts will decrease if better quality procedures are introduced. The effort of selecting reusable assets is included in the effort involved in adapting the selected modules. This effort does not include the effort devoted to discarding non-selected candidate assets. Unfortunately this effort was not accounted for. An estimate of 2 hours on average per asset is realistic. Normally the decision takes less time, but sometimes a decision to reuse must be changed later and this increases the average effort.

At a first look at the figures above, it may appear that unplanned reuse is clearly more profitable than planned reuse, because the costs of converting to a reusable form are lower for unplanned reuse, but please note that: (1) accounted costs are only those required to incorporate formal changes and to add descriptive data to the software asset and the Software Library; (2) when such an asset is reused, the cost incurred is expected to be higher than for assets built for planned reuse, because normally they should need more internal, functional changes. A conclusion is that a key requirement for benefitting from unplanned reuse is to avoid the reuse of assets that need too many changes. If so, unplanned reuse can be cheaper than planned, but its scope will be very limited. To increase the amount of reuse, it is necessary to introduce planned reuse.

Some positive experiences have been obtained from reusing documents. An example is the reuse of specifications for software supporting communication protocols in remote stations for telecontrol systems, giving evident benefits in several aspects: the quality of the specifications, the effort required to produce them, and the better acquisition by inexperienced staff of general knowledge regarding this particular type of software.

9.2.5.9 Review, evaluation and introductory plan

At the final stages of the project, the documents describing the methodology were reviewed. The

human and organizational aspects of the methodology were also reviewed.

The evaluation of the experiment focused on productivity and quality issues, with regard to the business objectives of the organization. A permanent problem of software development activities at ELIOP (and probably at any SME) is the limitation of resources, specifically qualified staff. So, any reuse practice that is to be adopted successfully must accomplish two conditions: the extra work in the development of reusable assets must be limited, and the time to obtain the return on this investment must be short.

The results of the evaluation are explained in detail in Section 9.3.

As the main conclusion from the evaluation, a decision was taken to introduce this methodology as a regular practice in all software engineering activities at ELIOP. A plan for introduction of the methodology was produced, including the final review and approval of the methodology by the management and an internal presentation that was the starting point of its regular use. The objective of this presentation was to provide technical skills for working with the new methodology, but also to clarify the new organizational roles and to remove the identified barriers related to human and organizational aspects.

9.2.6 Internal Dissemination

By the mid-term of the project, we held a presentation of the progress of the project to all software engineers and management, emphasizing process improvement proposals and specific reuse issues.

After the end of the project we held a detailed presentation and training on the methodology to be introduced.

Some actions were taken during the project to facilitate the dissemination of results:

- participation of team heads in the work group;
- wide participation of other people in experimental tasks.

9.3 RESULTS AND ANALYSIS

9.3.1 Technical

In the first stages of the project, as a result of the general approach study conducted by the work group, we reached some important conclusions that were very valuable in focusing all further work to be done within the project. A summary of these conclusions was given in Section 9.2.5.1.

Some important results were derived from the internal assessment and analysis of the process, in order to introduce systematic reuse practices.

- The process itself must be well defined and properly documented. In our experiment, we generated a document globally describing the process.
- Reuse activities should be considered explicitly in the process description.
- Domain analysis should be introduced as the first stage in the development of new product families.
- Templates are important elements of the methodology, and should be produced for all types of relevant documents.
- Coding rules should be used.
- Reviewing of all generated documents should be enforced.
- A Software Library is needed to organize information concerning reusable assets.

Some problems associated with the domain analysis activities were explained in Section 9.2.5.7. Nevertheless, it is important to highlight the benefits that we identified from our experience with domain analysis within the project.

- Domain analysis created a foundation for planned reuse within the domain. The identified objects and operations were translated into reusable software managing those objects and performing those operations, in most cases satisfactorily.
- Documents obtained from the domain analysis contained valuable accumulated knowledge about the domain and facilitated its acquisition by new staff. Specifically, this helped us to add a new developer to the project in order to speed up the development.
- Domain analysis helped us to improve the quality of the specifications for new products within the domain.
- We estimate that domain analysis will help us to make better estimates of the effort needed for new developments within the domain. This is because we can identify the new functions and the existing ones more easily.

Regarding metrics, two main findings should be emphasized.

- Direct measurement of costs and benefits derived from reuse practice is not feasible. Only costs can be directly measured. Regarding benefits, we cannot compare the real practice with a fictitious situation, so indirect measurements of the process attributes must be carried out.
- The AMI method can be applied in a practical manner following the AMI Handbook [1]. The method demands considerable effort. Also, the cost of implementing metrics must be considered. We recommend selecting metrics following a goal-oriented approach (as in the case of AMI), but trying to implement only a few, simple metrics.

The main results regarding tools are the following.

- Strong configuration management practices are very important for reuse. We realized that a prerequisite for starting a process improvement focused on reuse is to have well-established and tool-supported configuration management procedures. These practises are very important to guarantee the consistency of the reused assets and, consequently, to obtain good results and acceptance of reuse practices.
- It is also important, in order to facilitate reuse, to standardize on tools.
- Tools intended to improve the quality, documentation and standardization of the software assets are also important for reuse. Specifically, this is the case for design tools (both structured and object-oriented methods), code auditing and documentation, testing tools, complexity metrics, etc.
- The only tool identified as completely specific to reuse is a 'Reusable Software Library'. Details of our Library implementation were given in Section 9.2.5.4. The most important requirements identified for this tool were the following.

  1. Search and browse capabilities (search by keywords or other attributes of the assets).
  2. Capability to identify related assets.
  3. User-friendly interface.
  4. Multi-user capability.
  5. Integration with configuration management tool (if possible).

- Object-oriented techniques were evaluated. The conclusion was that they have some advantages but are not essential in our approach to reuse.
- From the quality point of view, it was clear in the evaluation of the experiment that reuse methodology promotes better quality. Unfortunately, we did not find out how to perform comparative measurements of the quality attributes of the assets designed to be reused, within the time limits of the project. ELIOP is committed to improving the quality of its software as a general management direction, and this positive assessment of

quality issues has been very important in deciding on the introduction of the methodology.

Additionally, a clear conclusion of our experiment is that quality is a prerequisite for reuse. Only good quality software produced by a good quality process can be successfully reused in a systematic way. We strongly recommend the introduction of reuse as part of a quality improvement programme. At the very beginning of the experiment, we were very focused on productivity goals, but as the project progressed, quality was identified as a major condition for reuse practices, and became a principal concern.

This finding reveals that a positive feedback loop exists between quality and reuse. First, an organization must improve quality (and specifically some aspects of quality), because the more important barriers to reuse are closely related to bad quality software and bad practices. Once these barriers are removed by quality improvements, reuse is not so difficult to do and this gives a payoff in terms of productivity, but also of quality (because good quality reused software is better than new software), and this is the point at which positive feedback appears.

As the main conclusion from the evaluation, a decision was taken to introduce the methodology experimented with in ISORUS as regular practice in all software engineering activities at ELIOP. Another important conclusion is the need for continuous improvement in software practices. A decision was taken to continue the improvement effort, establishing software process improvement as a regular activity, with yearly objectives and budgeting.

Some decisions taken in the project derive from the fact that an SME requires a low-risk approach to software reuse, because the organization cannot devote many resources to developing software components without the certainty that they will be used. The following low-risk approaches were identified and adopted during the experiment.

- Do improvements based on an evolutionary, step-by-step approach, rather than a 'revolutionary' approach.
- Use of domain analysis to identify and specify reusable components in the development of new products.
- 'White-box' reuse: components can be modified when reused, if necessary. This decreases the cost of development of reusable components.
- Good management of reuse issues. Careful revision of the specification of reusable software components, in order to avoid too complex or unnecessarily generic specifications.

9.3.2 Business

The key business objective of the project was the reduction of software costs. Other objectives were to reduce delays and increase customer satisfaction.

An evaluation of the economic impact of reuse was made according to the quantitative results shown in Section 9.2.5.8. The following table gives these results in a clearer way, by reference to a 'standard cost' of 100. The data refer to planned reuse of newly developed reusable software.

	First use	Second use	Third use	Fourth use
Accumulated cost	160	180	190	200
Average cost per use	160	90	63	50

According to this table, savings appear from the second use, and reach 50% at the fourth use of a module. However, these results should be interpreted carefully, for several reasons.

- The estimated savings are computed according to a simplified model, in which we suppose that the alternative to the planned reuse is 'no reuse'. If the alternative strategy is 'unplanned reuse', the relative benefits will decrease, because we must suppose that this 'unplanned reuse' should give some benefit over the 'no reuse' approach.
- Probably some portion of the extra cost should be compensated by the lower maintenance effort that is expected.
- Part of the extra cost is due to the immaturity of a newly introduced method.
- Additionally, we identified the trend to issue unnecessarily complex specifications for reusable assets as a major cause of the extra cost. This complexity is responsible to some extent for the extra cost of the reusable modules, and for some efficiency problems, such as low execution speed. It should be corrected by means of a correct management review and control of the specifications.

This last consideration is important: if complexity generates software efficiency problems that must be corrected when the software is reused, it can appear an unacceptable extra cost and reuse becomes a costly practice.

In order to interpret the results from the above table in a realistic manner, one must compare the approach tested in our project with a 'standard' practice with no regard to reuse. Even in this standard practice, reuse is performed when the opportunity arises, even if such reuse may be not optimized.

Let us call this 'opportunistic' reuse. In practice, cost reductions should be accounted by comparing them with this opportunistic practice, not comparing them with an 'absolutely no reuse' practice. Considering this fact, cost reductions are small. For instance, if an asset is reused four times, normally some kind of reuse will also be done under a standard practice.

A conclusion from the above is the critical need for good management of reuse: software managers must be aware of these issues. Correct evaluation of reusability, and control and review of specifications are needed.

Regarding the adaptation of existing assets into reusable ones, the required efforts are only a fraction of the initial production cost of the asset (of the order of 10%), and should decrease as higher quality procedures are introduced. However, actual cost reduction for unplanned reuse of these assets should be estimated considering: (1) the modifications to be done to the assets in order to allow its reuse, and (2) the average probability of reuse of the assets. In our experiment, the time devoted to using the assets was not enough to extract reliable quantitative results regarding probability of reuse. A low probability of reuse will increase the costs, so only assets showing good reusability should be included in the library. Again, the need for a correct evaluation of reusability appears.

Analysing the above information, the conclusion is that the introduction of the methodology will provide a small reduction in software costs. To reach this conclusion, it has been necessary to estimate in a realistic manner the impact of all factors influencing the results.

The benefits in quality, and in better estimating and control of software projects, are clearer to us. These are important issues, directly related to customer satisfaction, whose improvement was one of the project goals.

9.3.3 Organization

The organization of the project, as described in Section 9.2.1, has proved to be adequate. The main advantages are as follows.

- The involvement of experienced people in the higher-level technical work needed for this project.
- Participation of team heads and wide participation of other people in order to facilitate the internal dissemination of results and introduction of the new practices.

However, this organization has the disadvantage that no one was devoted full-time to the process improvement project.

Organizational issues were also considered in our assessment. One important finding is the need for long-term management support. Process improvement focused on reuse is an investment that gives its benefits in the mid and long term, with the following consequences.

- There is a need for a business strategy looking beyond current projects.
- This strategy must anticipate needs and define product lines in order to facilitate reuse. Some problems were experienced in our domain analysis activities because of insufficient definition of product strategy.

With the approach that we selected for the introduction of reuse, there are no requirements for major changes in the organization of the software process. Only minor changes are required.

- A specific role appears: Administrator of the Software Library. The project and team heads take specific responsibilities in promoting reuse.
- Managers and software engineers must be aware of specific reuse issues.

9.3.4 Culture

Our project took special consideration of human issues related to reuse. A first conclusion is that the key for reusability is the understanding of the software to be reused. Only a piece of software whose function, interface and restrictions are well understood can be successfully reused. Many failures to reuse come from a misunderstanding of the reused software.

We also realized that there are negative attitudes towards reuse among software engineers, and also among software managers. The main causes that we identified were as follows.

- Resistance to change. This is a 'natural', psychological and sociological fact in any individual or organization.
- Bad reuse experiences. In the specific case of reuse, this is a very important source of negative attitudes. Often this has been motivated by the attempt to reuse bad quality software, or because there are no systematic procedures for reuse (that is, reuse is done in an 'opportunistic way').

The solutions we identified were as follows.

- Information and training, including open discussions in the context of project and methodology presentations. The presentations held within the experiment proved to be efficient ways to gain acceptance for the new practices.

- Correct management of reuse practice, in order to prevent bad experiences.
- Application of systematic methods.

In general terms, the degree of acceptance of the new practices during the experiment was good. The main problem encountered derives from the use of the Software Library, which is considered slow and less friendly than expected.

9.3.5 Skills

The skills that the new methodology demands from software engineers are easy to learn. The most evident skill required is the use of the Software Library. Additionally, with the new methodology, some engineers must produce new types of documents, and they need some training and practice to acquire the needed skills.

More important than specific skills is the need for better quality and discipline that the methodology requires. When coding, software engineers should strictly respect the approved coding rules, and produce easy-to-understand codes. Similar considerations should apply to other software documents.

9.4 KEY LESSONS

The following subsections briefly state the key lessons that ELIOP has learnt from undertaking the experiment. These lessons are directly related to the issues that have been described in detail in Sections 9.2 and 9.3 above.

9.4.1 Technological Point of View

- Reuse of other assets apart from code has proved to give real benefits: better quality documents with less effort have been generated from good quality reusable documents. This practice helped inexperienced people to acquire the needed knowledge more quickly.
- Reuse of software within a specific domain of application has demonstrated higher potential than horizontal reuse. This 'vertical reuse' within a domain offers more opportunities and can be better planned than horizontal reuse, because most software in a system is application-dependent, and so it is difficult to reuse it horizontally.

Domain analysis is the foundation for this kind of reuse, but it needs a considerable effort from experienced people and domain experts. Our approach gave good results in general terms. This approach is to learn the basic ideas and objectives of domain analysis and introduce it with some activities according to our process and culture. See Section 9.2.5.7 for details.

- It is necessary to have strong configuration management practices in place for all software assets, not just code, in order to carry out reuse successfully.
- The 'white-box' reuse paradigm, which allows the software assets to be modified when reused, was a good choice in order to reduce risks, because it decreases the development cost of of reusable components and has lower organizational impact. 'Black-box' opportunities can arise, of course, but our approach considers this case a special one, because of the reasons stated in Section 9.2.5.1 (fourth paragraph).

9.4.2 Business Point of View

- During the experiment, we realized that an appropriate level of process and product quality is a prerequisite to starting software process improvement focused on reuse. It is very dangerous to start a reuse programme without sufficient regard to quality, because of the high possibility of bad experiences. We strongly recommend the introduction of reuse as part of a quality improvement programme.
- The experiment has shown that human and organizational barriers must be considered when introducing reuse-based improvement. To overcome them, we have clearly seen the usefulness of defining explicitly the process and all organizational roles, and keeping managers and developers informed as closely as possible. Correct management of reuse practice has been identified as essential to achieve the objectives of a reuse process improvement.
- In order to facilitate reuse, the organization must define a business strategy looking beyond the current projects, anticipate needs and define product lines. Some problems encountered in the experiment derived from deficiencies in this field.
- To reduce risks and better overcome organizational and people barriers, our experiment shows that it is better to do improvements based on an evolutionary, step-by-step approach, rather than a 'revolutionary' approach.

9.4.3 Strengths and Weaknesses of the Experiment

After the final evaluation of the experiment, the following main weaknesses were identified.

- The unavailability of adequate commercial tool support for the Software Library created the need to adapt standard database management software to implement this tool. This has some disadvantages: the tool is slow and less friendly than expected, and is not integrated with any configuration management tool. On the positive side, the data managed by the tool was selected according to our needs.

- Because no formal process assessment has been done in the context of the experiment, it is difficult to describe precisely the level of maturity needed to successfully implement a reuse improvement programme. This could be helpful for those organizations interested in such an improvement.

- A direct measurement of costs and benefits derived from reuse practice has proved not to be feasible. Only costs can be directly measured. This makes it difficult to justify the return on investment gained by the introduction of the improvements.

On the other side, these are the identified strengths.

- The experiment has made clear to us that quality is the key that allows the application of systematic reuse practices, refuting the ideas that show quality as a cause of decreasing productivity.

- Because the experiment was not restricted to a very specific phase of the software process, it has allowed us to identify practical improvements in many aspects of software practice in our company.

- From the work done within the experiment, it is not a difficult task to disseminate its results internally and to put them into practice.

- The experiment has familiarized ELIOP with all the problems associated with software process improvement. This will facilitate future actions in this area.

9.5 CONCLUSIONS AND FUTURE ACTIONS

Although the focus of this experiment was reuse, we discovered that we could only support reuse by improving all the steps of the process. Only a few improvements can be identified as very specific for reuse purposes. This raises the expectations of benefits for the organization, because they are not critically depending upon the degree of reuse achieved. In any case, the introduction of some domain analysis practices and the existence of a software assets library will certainly encourage reuse, and this is expected to produce clear advantages for ELIOP in the mid-term. These considerations, together with the company's long-term commitment to quality, have led to the decision to adopt the methods as a regular practice in all ELIOP software engineering activities.

Another important conclusion is the identification of new fields for software process improvement, and the decision to establish software process improvement as a regular activity, with yearly objectives and budgeting.

GLOSSARY

Following is a list of acronyms and very specific terms used in this chapter.

KLOC:	1000 lines of source code
SME:	Small or Medium Enterprise
Software asset:	A result of any of the steps of the software production process. Usually it refers to a source code module or a document.
Domain of application:	A set of similar systems that exhibit some relevant common characteristics.
Domain analysis:	The task of identifying the objects, operations and relationships that domain experts perceive to be important about a domain of application.
Horizontal reuse:	The reuse of general-purpose portable software assets over different domains of application.
Vertical reuse:	The reuse of application-dependent software assets over different systems of the same domain of application.
Black-box reuse:	The reuse of existing software assets without any modification.
White-box reuse:	The reuse of existing software assets by modification and adaptation.

REFERENCES AND BIBLIOGRAPHY

Books:

[1] The AMI Consortium. *AMI Handbook*. ISBN 0-9522-2620-0

[2] Prieto-Díaz, R. and Arango, G. (1991) *Domain analysis and software systems modelling* (IEEE Computer Society Press). ISBN 0-8186-8996-X.

[3] Software Productivity Consortium (1993) *Reuse Adoption Guidebook*.

Articles/papers:

[4] Prieto-Díaz, R. (1993) Status report: software reusability. *IEEE Software*, May.

[5] Maiden, N. (1991) Human issues in software reuse. Paper presented at the Seminar on Integrating Software Engineering with Reuse. UNICOM Seminars.

[6] Kruzela, I. and Brorsson, M. (1990) Human aspects and organizational issues of software reuse. Paper presented at the Seminar on Software Reuse and Reverse Engineering in Practice. UNICOM Seminars.

[7] O'Connor, J. *et al.* (1994) Reuse in command and control systems. *IEEE Software*, September.

[8] Frakes, W. and Isoda, S. (1994) Success factors of systematic reuse. *IEEE Software*, September.

10

Some Final Reflections

Colin Tully

Colin Tully Associates, UK

10.1 COMMON FEATURES OF THE CASE HISTORIES

In Chapter 1 we looked at ESSI as a whole, and at general factors influencing success or failure in software process improvement (SPI). Chapters 2 to 9 then presented, in the words of those who took part in them, the stories of eight specific application experiments (AEs) from the pilot phase of ESSI.

In this final chapter we reflect on the experiences of those eight AEs. First, in this section, we identify a number of features that are common to all the case histories. Then, in the second and concluding section, we will suggest a tentative way of characterizing the approach to SPI adopted in ESSI, and compare it to the American CMM-driven approach.

We will not attempt to summarize the eight AEs. That would be presumptuous – they each know best how to tell their story, and how to place the emphases in it. Nor will we refer in what follows to individual AEs by name – that might appear to attribute particular praise or otherwise; that would be inappropriate, since each AE in its distinctive way has done a great job, and none can expect to be perfect. All we wish to do in this concluding chapter is to discuss a number of themes that recur persistently throughout their stories.

10.1.1 Clear Recognition of Improvement Priority

In each case, the companies concerned were clear about the focus for improvement. In five cases, the focus was to introduce or improve specific technical practices – testing, reuse, formal specification, or quality engineering. In two cases, the focus was to reengineer the overall technical development process to allow it to handle the additional requirements of usability engineering or multimedia product development. Only the final case had a non-technical focus, on project management. There was a frequent recognition of the benefit of shifting effort toward the upstream parts of the process – sometimes referred to as 'left shift'.

What the companies did not do was to carry out an overall assessment, covering the whole of the software process or a major proportion of it, produce a profile of strengths and weaknesses, and then derive a prioritized improvement plan. While we have not been told explicitly what the decision process was, it seems probable and plausible that a natural consensus existed (at least among senior practitioners), based on their experience, about the area of practice where the greatest problems and/or opportunities lay.

10.1.2 Initial Evaluation

All projects carried out some kind of initial evaluation of the practice they had selected for improvement, though perhaps with varying degrees of thoroughness. Broadly the purpose of these evaluations was to assess the nature and extent of the problem encountered with the selected practice, and the nature and extent of the improvement opportunity it presented. Projects thus followed the principle quoted by Watts Humphrey (the originator of the CMM): 'If you don't know where you are, a map won't help.'

This is one of the aspects of ESSI projects where the European Commission was instrumental in encouraging good practice, through the project guidelines and recommendations which it set out as funding preconditions. In many cases, of course, projects will only have gone through the superficial motions of adhering to the guidelines; but the case histories in this book are evidence of the benefit gained when the guidelines are followed with at least a reasonable degree of commitment, and of the positive effect that a public initiative such as ESSI can have when it is well designed and implemented.

Note that none of the projects used external public-domain generic assessment methods. They used evaluation methods that fitted their circumstances and the specific improvement which they were setting out to achieve. CMM and ISO 9001, for instance, are at most mentioned in passing.

10.1.3 Improvement Goals Related to Initial Evaluation and to Business Goals

The improvement goals defined by the case history projects were derived from the initial evaluations, and clearly were also consistent with the wider business goals of the companies involved. That comprises in effect a two-stage decision process.

- Given the evaluation results, what is a feasible improvement goal?
- Will achieving that goal have a sufficient impact on business performance to justify the cost and risk which the change will incur?

10.1.4 Improvement Effort Planned and Managed as a Project

Since the ESSI programme is structured as a set of projects, it is unavoidable that AEs should all exhibit at least minimal characteristics of project organization. But (as those with experience of programmes of this kind know!) that is not at all the same thing as really applying sound project management in practice. All of the companies involved in the case histories, however, applied their normal in-house project management practices to the AEs, as though they were normal development projects. As we saw in Chapter 1, treating improvement actions in this way is recognized as an essential success factor.

One project explicitly (and one or two others implicitly) went further, took on board the implications of the term 'application experiment', and added some of the practices of scientific experimental design to those of project management. One AE explicitly went as far as adopting a systematic method (DESMET) for doing so.

10.1.5 Incremental and Evolutionary Approach

One or two of the case histories explicitly draw attention to the need for improvement initiatives, while being organized as projects, also to be relatively small in scale. This arises from the interaction of two factors. First, improvement projects are rarely full-time for all those taking part (often, indeed, no individual is full-time), and therefore the rate of progress may be slower than for a full-time project. Second, if the dynamic for change is to be sustained, it is undesirable for improvement projects to have a long elapsed time: they should aim to deliver usable and observable results quickly. One project went as far as to state that an 18-month duration for AEs could be undesirable if it encouraged projects to pursue single large goals rather than a series of smaller ones.

There is, however, a degree of complexity underlying this issue. None of the projects undertook what would be regarded as more than a relatively small incremental improvement step. At the same time, none of the projects complained that 18 months was an unnecessarily long time. Two points may help to deal with that apparent paradox.

- First, it may be useful to see improvement projects as dividing naturally into two phases, which could be called the *change design* phase and the *change implementation* (or 'roll-out') phase. In those terms, we may recast the discussion above as follows. Improvements should, desirably, be packaged into fairly small increments, corresponding to short change design phases. In each case, however, the subsequent change implementation phase may be much longer. Improvement projects may be thought of as being rather like comets, with a compact nucleus followed by a less dense tail streaming out behind.

- Second, if the dynamic for improvement is to be sustained, there should be a regular flow of short change designs, each generating a longer change implementation, of which several will overlap in time. That has interesting implications for the management of process improvement, which may be handled differently in different companies. For example, projects may be defined in such a way as to combine design and implementation phases; or projects may include only the design phase, leaving subsequent implementation or roll-out to be handled concurrently on a non-project basis by a central process management group.

10.1.6 Process Model Documentation

There was a recognized need, reported in all the case histories, to define and document the specific processes affected by the improvement actions, before and/or after improvement. This was seen to be necessary both as a modelling activity for those who designed and implemented the process changes, and as a learning and reference source for the wider groups who subsequently had to use the changed processes. No standard means of representation was used or necessary: AEs used whatever means would be effective and matched their existing documentation practice.

10.1.7 Evaluation, Selection and Adaptation of Methods and Tools

All the improvement actions needed supporting methods and/or tools. In many cases, indeed, it was the desire to introduce a new method/tool that triggered the process improvement; but in those cases introducing the method/tool was not seen as an end in itself or as an isolated change. In the remaining cases that were not method/tool-driven, it was nevertheless recognized that method/tool support was a prerequisite for effective improvement. In all cases, a degree of care (albeit a varying degree) was exercised in the evaluation and selection of methods and tools.

There was a consistent recognition that tools are subordinate to the methods they support, and that methods are similarly subordinate to the processes they support. At the same time, methods are impacted by their supporting tools, and processes are impacted by their supporting methods and tools. Those who plan and implement process improvement must anticipate and deal with those impacts, which are not always predictable. Methods/tools were rarely found to provide a good fit to initial requirements or the practical needs of users, and thus had to undergo adaptation; in at least one case that was a cause of major delay.

Note that, where external public-domain generic methods were adopted, in no cases were they to support the *improvement process* itself. In all cases they were to support the *target process* being improved. So far as the improvement process itself was concerned, companies used their own *ad hoc* improvement method. It would be interesting to discover whether they have since refined and standardized those methods, to the point where they have achieved a degree of repeatability and maturity.

10.1.8 Measurement of Results

All AEs attempted to put in place metrics which would enable them to measure the effectiveness of their improvement initiatives. This again was a basic precondition of ESSI funding, and therefore a credit to the European Commission. Again, however, projects could probably have got away with more half-hearted measurement schemes than are reported in the case histories. In all cases serious efforts were made, based on an apparently genuine belief that measurement is an essential part of improvement: if you haven't measured it, you can't say that improvement has happened. The distinction between base metrics, and the fundamental (often business-oriented) indicators that are derived from them, was well understood.

There was a common recognition that measurement is costly in terms of effort and money, is not to be embarked upon lightly, and should be kept as simple as possible. Set against that was the discovery by several AEs that it is a far from simple matter to design and implement the metrics that are necessary to give meaningful measurements of success. Measurement of the objective benefits of reuse posed particularly severe problems – while the projects concerned were subjectively in little doubt that real benefit was achievable.

One or two projects recognized that, however good your measurements, it is usually very hard to be sure how much a measured amount of improvement effort has contributed to a measured amount of actual improvement. Reasons for this include the length of time over which improvements take effect, and the difficulty of being certain about cause–effect relationships given that multiple causal factors are at work concurrently.

One project laudably exposed a causal loop (positive feedback, reflexive dynamics, virtuous circle – call it what you will), by which reuse and quality were self-reinforcing. Such loops are of critical importance: once discovered, they should be harnessed and exploited to the full, because they are powerful engines of rapid and continuing change.

10.1.9 Human Factors

AEs were united in attaching great importance to the influence of human factors in achieving successful outcomes. That was manifested in at least three main ways.

- All AEs invested in training, and recognized the dynamics of the learning curve and its effect on the rate of achieving benefits. Training was always developed within the company or consortium, to fit the specific improvement needs, and for delivery 'just in time' (i.e. when it was needed for immediate use). There were suggestions about the value of establishing competence centres to maintain and develop specific skills on a continuing basis beyond formal training (often called 'mentoring').

- All AEs were convinced of the need to communicate with, and to involve, the widest possible number of staff, and to gain their acceptance of change and their active participation in it.

- Typically the 'best' staff had a leading participation in change. That is important motivationally, to avoid the impression that process improvement is of secondary or background importance, and that being assigned to it is a backward or sideways career step.

10.1.10 Improvement Is Not One-off

All the case histories are regarded as successes by their participating companies, and readers will no doubt agree. Of course there are variations in the extent to which all the objectives were or were not fully met. The significant thing, though, is that all AEs talk about future change. If there are unfulfilled objectives, they want to go on until they are achieved. If they are satisfied with their results, they see further avenues of change.

Perhaps overall that is the most significant result. Process improvement, once embarked upon, should become a continuing way of life, built into the structures, processes and culture of an organization. There seems to be a strong likelihood that, for these eight projects at least, ESSI has achieved that very important outcome.

10.2 ALTERNATIVE IMPROVEMENT PARADIGMS?

In Chapter 1 we made some references to the CMM as the engine of change in the USA, and to the SEI's rôle as sponsor of that change. This final section considers whether the early experience in ESSI may offer the outline of an alternative paradigm to the CMM-driven improvement approach dominant in America.

To assist in discussing those alternative paradigms, let us give them labels. Although it may be a little provocative, we will call the SEI–CMM paradigm the *theory-driven approach*, and the ESSI–AE paradigm

the *practice-driven approach*. What then are some of the characteristics of those two approaches?

10.2.1 Theory-driven approach

- *Model-based.* The SEI CMM for Software is central to software process improvement in the USA. The CMM provides a model of three things:
  - the software process,
  - process maturity, and
  - a recommended improvement path to achieve high maturity levels.

The model constitutes a theory of process, maturity and improvement, and it is in that sense that the US paradigm can fairly be called a theory-driven approach. The term 'theory-driven' should not be regarded as offensive; as someone once rightly said, 'There is nothing as practical as a good theory.' A good theory encapsulates knowledge and practical experience, making it available for reuse and exploitation by others. It is essentially a form of investment – in concepts – and the return on investment depends on the quality and applicability of the theory.

It is worth adding that the quality of a theory is strongly dependent on the degree to which it is subjected to criticism ('peer review'), to determined attempts to refute it, and to being tested in practice (to destruction if possible). Theories should not be protected like new-born babies, however strong the parental urge of their originators, but should be cast out into the evolutionary real world to suffer the dangers of the survival of the fittest. It is true that the CMM has been widely used in practice, and widely reviewed when undergoing change. On the other hand there has been a tendency to treat it very protectively in the face of any fundamental critique. It is possible that it would be a stronger theory if counter-arguments and counter-evidence had been encouraged to flow more freely. There is possibly a conflict of interest between CMM-as-theory and CMM-as-commercial-product, which may result from the SEI's position in the no man's land between academe and industry.

There is, however, another saying, much loved at the SEI: 'All models are wrong, some are useful.' There can be no doubt that the CMM has been an immensely useful model, irrespective of its qualities as a theory.

- *Central authority.* For over a decade the SEI has exercised central authority over the CMM, its development and deployment. Its rôle with respect to the CMM is

– to be the development authority,
– to promote, and to exercise quality control over, its application,
– to maintain a data repository of results, and
– to publish and disseminate information.

The development authority rôle is exercised through collaborative mechanisms such as working groups, reviewer groups and correspondence groups; that degree of collaboration lessens the extent of centralization, although the SEI remains the ultimate authority. Quality control extends to such things as the licensing of training courses and the registration of lead assessors. Dissemination includes organizing an annual conference of process groups, and supporting the large number of SPIN (software process improvement network) groups nationwide.

● *Strong marketplace.* There is a flourishing marketplace for CMM-based services in the USA, in which specialist vendors offer assessment, training and consultancy to many hundreds of clients. The SEI uses its central authority to exercise effective regulation of the marketplace. Any appraisal may only be termed an SEI appraisal if it is led by an SEI-authorized lead assessor. The requirements for becoming a lead assessor are the completion of a lead assessor course and approved assessment experience. Lead assessor courses are run only by the SEI, and approved assessment experience can be gained only under the leadership of a lead assessor. The SEI itself has a special position in the marketplace, offering a wide range of courses, events and publications.

● *Public-sector support.* The US government (specifically the Department of Defense) supported CMM in two main ways.

– Through its funding of the SEI, the DoD effectively subsidized the development of the CMM itself.
– Through mandating specific maturity levels for software suppliers, it used its procurement power to foster the first (critical) phase of industrial takeup.

10.2.2 Practice-driven Approach

● *Framework-based.* European SPI, whether inside ESSI or outside it, is not characterized by the existence of a dominant model or theory. CMM is used in Europe, but its use is relatively

rare – and it was even rarer at the time of the ESSI pilot phase on which this book reports.

There are also other models of assessment and improvement, developed and used in Europe, and more or less derived from CMM. Perhaps the leading example is Bootstrap, itself developed with European Commission funding as an ESPRIT R&D project in the early 1990s. More recently, Europe has played the lead rôle in the SPICE project, an attempt to produce an international standard for assessment and improvement, and a number of organizations have participated in trials of the SPICE model as a basis for assessments.

That diversity of available models has not led to their widespread adoption. It could indeed be argued that their diversity has been one factor militating against their use.

Instead of the CMM as a dominant model, Europe has the ESSI programme. ESSI offers not a model but a loose framework for improvement. This framework is manifested through the broad requirements set out in successive calls for proposals. Proposals have to demonstrate sufficient compliance with those requirements in order to have a chance of being selected for funding. As we have seen in Section 10.1 above, such requirements encourage:

– assessment (but without mandating a specific model, or indeed the use of any external public-domain model at all),
– measurement (but without mandating specific metrics),
– organization and management of improvement effort as a project (intrinsic to the nature of ESSI as a project-funding programme).

Such a framework is designed to identify a minimal set of broad success factors, but to leave the maximum discretion to individual organizations, and thus to encourage the maximum diversity of approach. That is consistent with the general industrial philosophy of the European Commission (and of many European national governments), that it may be desirable to persuade free market forces in certain directions, while keeping unacceptable constraints on freedom to a minimum.

● *Central authority.* Just as the SEI exercises central authority over the CMM, so the European Commission (through the ESSI office in Directorate General III) exercises central authority over the ESSI framework. Its authority is exercised in two main ways:

– definition of the framework, as expressed in the calls for proposals,

– quality control over selected projects, achieved chiefly through contract negotiations and through review of key deliverables.

The nature of ESSI's central authority is to permit the widest diversity of approach to SPI. In contrast, the nature of the SEI's authority is to promote the widest use of a single approach.

It should be noted that the European Software Institute in Bilbao, in which the European Commission is (also through its ESSI office) a major stakeholder, has never chosen to try to replicate SEI's rôle.

- *Weak marketplace.* No marketplace in SPI services, of equivalent strength to that in the USA, has yet developed in Europe. The reasons for that may lie both on the demand side and the supply side.

  – Fewer companies are involved in SPI in Europe. The potential demand for support services is therefore smaller.

  – Possibly a smaller proportion of European companies involved in SPI are prepared to consider the procurement of external services, perhaps for a combination of economic and cultural reasons. Thus the actual demand falls short of the potential demand.

  – The diversity of approaches in Europe, and the lack of a central model, means that any demand for support services is more fragmented. If a supplier attempts to cover all approaches, he has to have a wider product range; if he focuses on supporting a single approach, he can only address a part of the market. Thus the market is not only small but fragmented, acting as a discouragement on the supply side.

  – A significant part of the 'product development' activity for the US marketplace has been carried out by the SEI. In defining the model, and defining supporting methods and training material, it has effectively provided the generic material which can be rapidly adapted into specialized market offerings by individual vendors.

- *Public-sector support.* The European Commission has supported SPI in Europe in two main ways.

  – The ESPRIT programme funded a number of R&D projects focused on SPI issues. These included (but were not confined to) Bootstrap and **ami**. Their results have been productively applied by European companies, but (because they were R&D projects with limited durations) they have not benefited from the long-term development and maintenance effort that the SEI has provided for the CMM.

  – The ESSI part of the ESPRIT programme has funded specific SPI projects in industry.

In summary, comparing the USA and Europe, the direct funding has been of a different nature in the two cases, and there has so far been no equivalent in Europe of the strong procurement incentive provided by the DoD.

10.2.3 Discussion

Readers may have formed their views on some of the strengths and weaknesses of the two approaches. It is not within the purpose or scope of this final chapter, however, to try to evaluate them; and certainly no one would suggest that either paradigm is clearly superior to the other. Instead, three observations are offered in conclusion.

- If Europe lags behind the USA in its take-up of SPI, the difference in the two paradigms may or not be a significant cause. The lag is likely to have much more to do with the deep differences in industrial cultures between the two sides of the Atlantic. The paradigms themselves, of course, are manifestations of those underlying cultures.

- The CMM provides a standardized set of success factors for the software process, and users of the model are recommended to work their way through them in a standardized sequence. No equivalent standardization is provided for ESSI projects, who exercise their technical and business judgement about process improvement priorities. What is striking about the experience of ESSI projects, as reported and discussed in this book, is that many of the success factors prescribed within the CMM have characterized at least the more successful ESSI projects, independently of their chief focus. That may be interpreted both as a pragmatic endorsement of the CMM model, and as evidence that pragmatic autonomous projects can adopt good practice without resort to external generic models.

- Those companies that deploy SPI with the greatest success, for outstanding business benefit, combine the two approaches. Whether in the USA or in Europe, the SPI strategy for those companies is derived from the problems and opportunities facing the individual business. Whether in the USA or in Europe, a model for assessment and improvement (which may or may not be the CMM) is used as one weapon in the SPI armoury, but never as an end in itself.

Index